SCENES

AND

ADVENTURES IN THE ARMY:

OR

Romance of Military Life.

BY

P. ST. G. COOKE,

LIEUTENANT-COLONEL SECOND DRAGOONS, U.S.A.

PHILADELPHIA:

LINDSAY & BLAKISTON.

1857.

Entered, according to Act of Congress in the year 1856

BY LINDSAY AND BLAKISTON,

In the Clerk's Office of the District Court for the Eastern District of Pennsylvania.

C. SHERMAN & SON, PRINTERS

19 St. James Street.

"I ADDRESS not, then, the shallow or hurried worldling; but the friendly one, who, in the calm intervals from worldly cares, grants me the aid of a quiet and thoughtful, and, if it may be, a poetic mood."

CONTENTS.

PART I.

CHAPTER I.

CHAPTER II.

CHAPTER III.

CHAPTER IV.

CHAPTER V.

CHAPTER VI.

CHAPTER XV.

CHAPTER XVI.

CHAPTER XVII.

CHAPTER XVIII.

CHAPTER XIX.

CHAPTER XX.

CHAPTER XXI.

CHAPTER XXII.

CHAPTER XXX.

CHAPTER XXXI.

PART II.

CHAPTER I.

CHAPTER II.

CHAPTER III.

CHAPTER IV.

CHAPTER V.

CHAPTER VI.

CHAPTER VII.

CHAPTER VIII.

CHAPTER IX.

CHAPTER X.

CHAPTER XI.

CHAPTER XII.

CHAPTER XIII.

CHAPTER XIV.

CHAPTER XV.

CHAPTER XVI.

CHAPTER XVII.

CHAPTER XVIII.

CHAPTER XIX.

CHAPTER XX.

CHAPTER XXI.

SCENES AND ADVENTURES IN THE ARMY.

PART I.

CHAPTER I.

My furlough was past! What varied emotions did that reflection excite! Strong were the regrets at parting for an indefinite period from devoted relations; and the young heart yearning with romantic hope, might well shudder on the threshold of the real life.

The stage-coach was at the door.

Those sorrowful partings over, with happy elasticity, I was soon enjoying the rapid motion of the coach—always exhilarating—but then severing me from the safe haven of home affections, and hearts which trembled painfully as I was thus launched on life's perilous voyage.

For at careless eighteen, impressions are fleeting; and the world, aye, the western world, was all before me, and bright with the anticipations of novelty and enjoyment: and the freshness and adventure of travel, were to be shared by the warm friends of my academical youth.

With a number of these, who, like myself, obeying the calls of duty and inclination, were to make a long journey westward, I had planned a meeting at a village in

Maryland. And never was appointment better kept, than by my before widely-separated comrades; and eager and warm were the greetings of that midnight hour! But we were hurried, by an unsympathizing driver, to resume, together, our night-ride; we had the coach, fortunately, all to ourselves; but right soon, in darkness, came the reaction of our exuberant spirits, and we began to drop off into wonderfully confused and uneasy postures, and the sleep of careless youth.

And thus we journeyed on; joking and joyous by day, —at night, snarling from unceremonious slumbers.

At Wheeling we made a halt for some days: we had been jolted and jumbled enough for lovers of variety, and "*la belle rivière*" tempted us to embark our fortunes, or rather persons, on its shining currents; but, in truth, its beauties were too superficial; and we were assured that the lightest bark would make but a tedious progress through its deceitful shallows. So we were fain content, with our ranks further swelled to a most lively number, again to take stage, and thus pursue our journey to Cincinnati. I remember the numberless black squirrels which we saw the first morning, sharing the rich fruits of those many corn-crowned hills; and the number which we found in a tree in front of our breakfasting house; and how, after being routed out of its topmost branches, the poor fellows were forced to make beautiful leaps to the ground.

From Cincinnati we went by steamboat to Louisville. There we mustered twenty strong; and remained eight rainy days, waiting for the river to rise. Our time passed pleasantly enough in that hospitable city, which would seem to be a favorite with the army, for many of its officers have formed the tenderest of ties there. During our stay, we shared in the most popular sport of the sport-loving Kentuckians,—a horse race. The course is several miles from the city; but we were all there, and beheld seven long-legged colts contend for the prize; and that Kentucky spicing to such pleasures—a fight or two—was not wanting to complete the day's experience.

In due time the river did rise, and we embarked for Jefferson Barracks, the new "School of Instruction." The boat seemed to be chartered by the military; we filled the cabin, and the deck was monopolized by a detachment of recruits. The passage was a long, but merry one; and that cards *were* played, I am too faithful a historian to deny.

Many years have elapsed, but I have now before my eyes the vivid impression of a night-scene near the mouth of the Ohio. The moon was a graceful crescent, and the glassy waters, glittering with its beams, reflected, too, many a lovely star, and caught the soft azure of their airy depths; and this beautiful reflection of a bright and starry sky, seemed to tremble at the mysterious and thorough gloom of the primeval forests. And another boat passed by, with its brilliant lights, magical motion, and solemn, echoed sounds; its bright path, too, and its long succession of regular and polished waves, each a mirror for the lovely moon. There is something startling, if not awful, by night, in those hollow but sonorous echoes to the escape pipe, which the lofty forests of the western river-bottoms give out; they seem the angry bellowings of wood demons, aroused by this intrusion of man and his wondrous works.

Right well do I remember, too, a scene different as possible, though by night: a western storm upon the waters! The boat was, fortunately, moored under the verge of one of those immense Mississippi bottoms,—in itself, by night, awful as the wastes of ocean. The rain fell as if nature was dissolved: the caverns of earth are never darker than it was then; the roar of waters and darkness were the universe. I was alone, and enjoying its sublimity, forgot that my poor body was exposed to the tempest.

The boat touched at dawn of the eighth day at Jefferson Barracks. Those who had slept at all, had risen; an adjutant, mounted on an immense black horse, and having for suite, a whole troop of dogs, received us on the bank, and proceeded with us to report to his chief, Colonel L. We were exhilarated in our walk over that delightful spot by three bands, striking up from different hill-tops and groves, the familiar, beautiful, but never so charming reveillé. The Colonel, evidently just out of bed, received us with great kindness and frankness; and readily consented to our proceeding in the boat to St. Louis; and in a few hours we were all on shore, exploring the *terra incognita* of that rising city of the West.

CHAPTER II.

THE characteristics of St. Louis, in 1827, which first struck me, were the muddiness of the streets—the badness of the hotels—the numbers of the Creole-French, speaking the French language—working on the Sabbath —a floating population of trappers, traders, boatmen, and Indians—and finally, an absence of paper currency. These were all very distinctive; and in truth, St. Louis had very little of the Anglo-American character. *Rowdyism* was the order of the day—the predominating influence of the street population of Indian traders and other northwestern adventurers. These men, in *outre* dresses, and well armed, were as characteristic in their deportment as sailors; exhibiting the independence, confidence, and recklessness of their wild and lawless way of life. All this was food for my companions on the *qui vive* for novelty; they were to be seen in all directions, on voyages of discovery through the mud, and seemed suddenly to have become a very homogeneous element in this rare compound: and parties of officers from the barracks daily galloped into the town, which they enlivened in a sort of sailor-like style. Fun and frolic then prevailed in St. Louis.

But our duties at the barracks did not permit us to remain long in this attractive city; so after a punctual call upon a certain army official, who cures that most distressing of human afflictions, a consumptive purse, and after receiving a quantum of hard dollars (not sufficient to produce a plethora), we bade adieu to the lively town until—the next time. Some of the party, like children pleased with a new toy, had already purchased Indian ponies, upon which they shuffled off, after a most unmilitary fashion, to their post.

None of the actors in those scenes can fail to recur with some pleasure, to the gayeties of 1827–8 at Jefferson Barracks. One of the regiments was in cantonment on the south side of the first hill; a quarter of a mile farther on, another, the 6th infantry, was encamped; on the crest of the next hill, were extensive stone barracks in progress; and still lower down, on its southern declivity, were encamped the 1st infantry; some staff and other officers, with their families, were in huts in various detached situations. Two of the regiments had, a few months before, arrived from a remote outpost. There, cut off from the world, and dependent on their own resources, the officers had not failed to make themselves what amends they might, and to cultivate the most friendly intimacies, on which were founded a thousand practical jokes and endless adventures; and the pleasures and incidents of this, a kind of golden age, they had in truth, the least disposition in the world to consign to oblivion.

A day or two after joining, I, with several friends, dined at the regimental mess of the 6th. It then was a mess indeed—in numbers and in spirit, a delightful mess, such as few regiments now have. Noble spirits! brave friends! How devoted, how social were you then! How modest, yet how ardent, was your *esprit de corps!* where-ever active service was to be done, on the borders of Mexico, or in the far North, *you* were there! And have you not led the "moving battery" to victory, and poured out your life-blood, like water, in Florida? You are scattered and gone, but well I "remember the regiment to which you belonged."

But the past and the present must be kept distinct. I thought them a glorious set at that first dinner. The president was Capt. ——, with his splendid whiskers and mustaches, dignified and easy in his manners, he seemed a type of the old school; and from that, the inference may be drawn, that he took wine freely when in such happy company; to the life of which, indeed, he gave a constant impulse. And the caterer was Adjutant J., a noble fellow, whose looks alone could make a friend; and R—— delighted us with his endless sallies, his jokes and merriment. I have now before me his immense whiskers, and his twinkling, deep-set eyes, lost nearly in incessant laughter—and his dance, too, upon the dinner-table, which was the finale.

Capt. ——, soon after became in low health, and being of impatient temper, his spirits sunk under it. His life was in danger; and as a last resort, Surgeon G. prescribed a singular mode of treatment—a novel kind of *excitement*—which was intrusted to Lieut. R——. He paraded daily around the Captain's tent with a long face, whistling the dead march; and it so happened that, being first on the list, the Captain's death would cause his promotion. But Capt. ——, taking this view of it, very seriously waxed wrathful, and swore he would not die for his tormentor's sake; and the cure was made.

What would thirty young officers be at? Not much time was consumed in considering such a question; in all intervals of duty we gladly resigned ourselves to the influences of chance or impulse, and sufficient to the day were the pleasures thereof; none thought of the morrow; to the many all was new, even the service itself—a new country and manners, and there were some new *Beauties*. Daily, numbers of us would be surprised by the dinner-drum at the camp of the hospitable 6th or 1st, and then it was useless to attempt an excuse; go you must to the mess. Many and delightful were those dinners at mess! Right joyous was it to mingle with those officers, whose minds and manners had received a fresh mould from their life in the generous, the open-hearted, daring and adventurous—the frank and hospitable *far* West; and what stores of anecdote and right marvellous adventure had been laid up in seven years' service at the famous Council Bluffs! Wine flowed freely, our spirits overflowed.

What other could be more delightful than this favored spot, with its gently-rolling hills crowned with lofty forest trees, without undergrowth, save grass and wild flowers; and a river, the noblest in the world, running by? Such is Jefferson Barracks. On a level space just upon the bank of the river, shaded and adorned by clumps of venerable but vigorous trees, oaks and sycamores, was the grand guard parade, generally enlivened by the music of a full band—a delightful resort! Ay, and other attractions were wont to fill the measure of its popularity; beauty added its spell to the charming scene; the young and lovely came often there at an early hour of rosy morning, when nature is in her happiest mood.

But how can garrison life be dwelt on? It cannot, unless, indeed, we descend to all those trifles that fill the precious hours and steal away the days. A soldier is all his country's; his irregular though numerous duties divide his time, distract his attention, and defeat his plans. How difficult, then, to avoid the fate of becoming the *mere soldier*. A knowledge of the world, a graceful carriage, easy manners, general but *superficial* information, with lofty aspirations, bitter repinings, and habits of idleness—these are his inheritance; the light and easy garment that he receives in exchange for the mantle of eminence. But why *now* question the seal of fate?

The middle of December found the 6th still in camp. Our log-fires in front of tents had become centres of attraction; but the smoke was a great enemy to our comfort. It was amusing to observe a gathering round a fire; the little circle seated on stools, boxes, or logs; some one was continually attacked, and would run for his breath, and forming his circuit, his enemy, less quick, though airy, seeming to follow at first, would leave him for another, who, in his turn, uttering broken maledictions, would make his circular retreat, seeking another or the same seat, ere long again to be routed.

The sporting tribe might be seen here and there examining a horse, or physicking a dog, or restraining vociferously the vagaries of a whole pack of them. A few sly ones would find their way to old Capt. ——'s tent, which had a brick chimney, together with the luxury of a mantel-piece; and this mantel-piece had notoriously a remarkable capacity for holding sugar dishes, whole battalions of mint phials, not to omit a great julep pitcher, which was commonly well filled. Oh camps! with your exposures and privations, how you encourage and excuse the solid comfort of a julep!

Before Christmas, the 6th were in the stone barracks, half finished and uncomfortable, and were crowded several in a room; and it was our lot, after turning into bunk, in the "small hours" of the night, to be saluted at day-dawn with the din of hammers overhead, an occasional shower of dust and mortar, with a sprinkling of brickbats, which fairly bade us, at the peril of our heads, "sleep no more."

On new-year's morn many were they who found themselves at that log temple of hospitality, the mess-house of the 1st, and paid their devoirs to a half whiskey barrel in the middle of an immense table, foaming to the top with egg-nog. The 6th regiment that day entertained all at the post at a dinner, and midnight found us still at the table.

On the 8th of January, the 1st gave a splendid ball in an unfinished barrack; a noble display of flags was above and around us, with hundreds of bright muskets with a candle in the muzzle of each. Many from St. Louis were there; and Louisville, too, had several beautiful representatives.

Thus flew by six months on the wings of pleasure. But the time came when the 1st and 6th, long associated as a band of brothers, were to part; the former being ordered to the Upper Mississippi. Their furniture being packed up, the whole of them for several days messed with the 6th. Our last dinner I shall never forget; we sought to drown the bitter regrets of parting in the extravagant enjoyment of the last fleeting minutes. At the winding up, Capt. G. delivered from a table, in an Indian language, a characteristic farewell speech, which, as interpreted, began—"Our great Father has long smiled upon our fellowship; his councils now are bad, a cloud is before his face," &c.

The summer came, and was passed pleasantly enough. At its close I was well pleased to be ordered on my first active service.

CHAPTER III.

On the 27th of September, 1828, I left Jefferson Barracks, to conduct a detachment of about forty recruits to Fort Crawford, at Prairie du Chien. There was no officer with me. I embarked in two "Mackinaw" boats, as they are called; they are of about three tons burden, without deck or box, sharp fore and aft. Mine were old and leaky. I found it tedious and laborious for eight oarsmen to force them against the current in many parts of the Mississippi; and, according to the custom of the country, took advantage of bare sand-bars and open banks to use the "cordel;" that is, to send ashore ten or fifteen men to tow the boat by means of a long rope attached to the head of a small mast. In doubling the points of bars, and in other shallow places, these men would wade along with the cordel on their shoulders, sometimes for a mile, perhaps half-leg deep; it was "working a passage" with a vengeance at that season. I made my first camp on Bloody Island, near St. Louis. While I was in the city next morning, getting a barrel or two of hard bread, my sergeant, who was an old hand of the 6th, made, with no other tool than an axe, a very good rudder, from a standing tree.

The morning after, I passed the mouth of the Missouri. This river, after draining the valleys of the Rocky Mountains, and receiving tributaries throughout a course of three thousand miles, precipitates its turbid currents right across the placid bosom of the Mississippi, to which, losing its name, it imparts its character.

A few miles above the junction is the mouth of the Illinois, itself a great river, navigable for steamboats some four hundred miles; but little known to fame, eclipsed, as it were, by the grandeur of the West. I encamped at Portage de Sioux; it was a moonlit night; on the opposite verge of a noble sheet of water—the river, placid and calm, but giving to the ear the solemn, distant music of its currents—stood lofty and fantastical rocks, of the height and a little resembling the Palisades of the Hudson; but these were cavernous, and there were arches, pilasters, and isolated turrets. They appeared the ruins of a castellated city; the soft light of the moon helping out the imagination, with a most perfect clear-obscure.

Some dozen miles below Clarksville, in company with my sergeant, I went on shore, as I frequently had done, to hunt. We had moved leisurely along an hour or two, when we began to find ourselves a little out of our bearings, or rather had become entangled with the sloughs of the river; after much fatigue we found ourselves in the edge of an immense level prairie bottom, where the grass was seven or eight feet high. A high bluff rose beyond, and I confess that, left to myself, I should have made for it, firmly believing that it was the opposite bank of the river; but my companion, an excellent woodsman, knew better, and saved me a seven or eight miles' trudge through this prairie sea. But the best *he* could do was to strike the main river at night; opposite, as it happened, to Clarksville. We crossed in a crazy canoe; and I found the boats had not passed or arrived! What a predicament for a young commander! I was much annoyed, but made out to take a good night's rest in *bed*, with philosophical resignation.

My men arrived next morning, to my joy and surprise, with nothing amiss, save numerous red eyes, and a broken demijohn, which it was plain had been well hugged before being subjected to such ill-treatment.

Some fifty miles below the Des Moines rapids, when weary of our slow progress, and with our store of pork very low, it was reported to me early one morning that some of the men were in pursuit of wild hogs. They soon after brought in two immensely large black ones, which they assured me were selected as the smallest of the herd, which had rushed at the men and forced them to take refuge in trees. A settler or hunter of the vicinity had joined in the sport. They were a seasonable supply, and were forthwith skinned and salted. While thus employed, a steamboat hove in sight below. On its arrival I had my boats taken in tow. My recruits soon gave me a spice of their quality; they were enlisted at Natchez, and were as precious a set of scoundrels as were perhaps ever there collected; they were drunken and mutinous from this time until after we quit the steamer at the rapids. One of them, whom I had tied up with a half-inch rope, repeatedly gnawed himself loose!

At the foot of these rapids was a passenger barge in tow of a steam keel-boat, with about twenty passengers, who had already waited some two weeks with Turkish resignation, for fate, or higher water, to forward them on their journey. Genius of railroads! spirit of a travelling age! Think, ye eastern locomotive bipeds, who, spirited over the earth at the rate of 600 miles a day, snarl at the grievous detention of a minute—think of this, and learn moderation. These said *travellers* spent their nights, I discovered, playing at cards; how they got through with their days passes my comprehension.

On the rocks of these rapids I abandoned one of my boats, having a second time overhauled and attempted to caulk it. I left it bottom upwards, giving it at parting, out of pure malice, several gashes with an axe. It was soon afterwards seized by a wrecker as a lawful prize, sold for five dollars, and again for ten; and the last purchaser, by sawing it in two and planking up the stern, had a very good make-shift craft for *down* stream work.

I had now to leave a party on shore, with orders to march as much in sight of my boat as they could. Night came on, and nothing was to be heard or seen of the detachment. Until 10 o'clock we kept on, firing signals, but to no purpose. We encamped on a miserable island; and in the middle of the next day we found them at a hut near the shore. All this was occasioned by the immense number of islands; the main shore had not been visible for thirty miles on either side.

I was now about three weeks out, and this point was fifty miles below Fort Armstrong, at Rock Island. Our provisions were exhausted; nothing but a few potatoes could be had at the house. I heard that there was a trail to Fort Armstrong, which cut off much of the distance; so I immediately ordered my adventurous land detachment to take it, while my naval affairs went on as usual, save "that our faces had become longer, and our belts contracted." My rifle was sole commissary, and a deer and a few birds were all it supplied. We reached the vicinity of Rock Island next mid-day, in a heavy gale. I had previously ripped a wall-tent, and converted it into a sail. It was exceedingly cold, the wind almost ahead, and the waves very high; but I did not feel like standing on trifles, under the circumstances, and so near to port. A flaw struck and would have swamped us, but for the frailness of our tackle; in an instant a great hole was blown through the sail, then every rope snapped, and the old tent stood straight out from the mast-head. My men from numbness, fear, or ignorance, gave me no assistance, so that necessity suddenly made me a tolerable fresh-water sailor. All arrived safe; but my land party spent another night out, as the ferrymen at the fort were afraid, or so pretended, to bring them across to the island, although they had such a boat as mine.

The next day but one, having taken in supplies, and been treated with true hospitality by the officers, I proceeded on my voyage.

About this point in ascending is observed a change in the river scenery; the solemn and drear "bottoms," and the falling in banks of the lower Mississippi, are scarce observable above the mouth of the Missouri, where the river assumes very much the appearances of the Ohio. At this point again (marked by the passage of a great rocky chain, developed in dangerous rapids, and in this, the *first*, rocky island above the Gulf—and a beautiful one it is) the shore scenery becomes, like that of many *smaller* clear streams, variegated with rock and hill, pretty valleys, grassy slopes, and gravel beaches.

I arrived at Fort Crawford, 180 miles above Rock Island, and about 600 above St. Louis, on the 23d of October, and having marched my party into the fort, "Where is your order?" quoth the officer in command.

"In my trunk, sir."

"Get your orders, sir, and I will then receive your party," was his answer.

After this was complied with, no point of ceremony was wanting; but I was ordered to proceed with the detachment to Fort Snelling. My orders had been to return from this point "forthwith;" a steamboat was in "port," a rare chance, and the gaieties and other attractions of my post, and St. Louis, arose on my youthful imagination, only to embitter my real prospect of winter quarters in the frozen region of the St. Peter's; but,

"I am a soldier, and my craft demands,
That whereso duty calls, within earth's
Compass * * * I do forthwith obey."

CHAPTER IV.

THE commander of Fort Crawford fitted me out liberally; gave me two more boats, one of which had been made as comfortable as possible for a lady; and luckily there were ten disciplined soldiers to go up. To crown all, I was intrusted with a monthly mail-bag, *tied* up, the papers and periodicals of which I was recommended to read. I dare say I felt, the first day, as pleased and comfortable as a new-made commodore.

The scenery grows still more interesting as we ascend beyond the mouth of the Wisconsin; the bluffs, or small mountains, always rising from the water on one side or the other, assume a thousand picturesque shapes; some are clothed with forests, others with grass—are now rocky, and again are perfectly smooth. Perfect cones are to be seen, and then two such, connected by grassy plains. Frequently the interior structure of rock is exposed by the action of rains, and art could scarcely fashion more regular walls than you see; at places they are vertical and lofty; again, they recede in steps, like the terrace-walls of a falling garden.

It seemed that all the millions of migrating water-fowls passed me in review; they appeared to follow the course of the river, and I ascertained, I thought, that they stopped regularly at nightfall. How many posts of refreshment a squadron of them would make from the Lake of the Woods to the Balize, was not so easily settled; but our repose was frequently disturbed by the deafening clatter of their myriads, that happened to anchor for the night in some neighboring bay.

I encamped one evening in a narrow but lovely valley between a towering massive bluff, covered with oaks, and a lofty prairie hill. After night, I walked to its grassy top; the moon was just full, and a long path of smooth water glittered with its reflected light. Very far, on either hand, the river was seen amidst the hills, which it reflected like a polished mirror. The little valley, softened by the mellow light, wound its graceful curves, until lost to the eye in the dim primeval wastes. My camp was out of sight and forgotten; and after a long view, full of admiration, a sense of utter loneliness crept over me, and added to the excitement of many rushing thoughts. I felt as a wandering being, cast upon a new world, that beheld from its summits lifeless but strange beauty. A light air rustling, made me aware how awful a silence had reigned, thus gently stirred as by a spirit voice, uneasy at the first intrusion of a mortal. I could hear the beating of my heart; the spell which bound me became painful, and I ran at speed along the narrow summit; I stopped, and would have uttered a cry, but in very truth my voice refused to obey me; at last it came forth, but so unnatural and shrill that it seemed a mockery. I rushed down from this hill, where white man had never trod before, and was soon in the midst of those beings plainly insensible to the stamp of quiet beauty on all around—the rugged pioneers in these new regions of a race who would willingly mar it all, and plant here, too, the seeds of care, of strife, and of misery.

Nature, like the character of man, is full of contrasts; the elements are often stilled, as here, in the calm repose of beauty, to soothe and soften our earthly passions; and anon are stirred up to fearful conflict, and seeming to threaten the world with wreck, inspire man with the dignity of strong emotion and lofty thought.

The next evening I was tempted by a favorable wind to ease the labor of much rowing, and sail long after night. As I advanced, I found the prairies of all the surrounding country to be on fire. It was a dark and cloudy night; the winds at length blew boisterously—the world seemed on fire, and there was a lurid reflection of flames from water and cloud, and tossed columns of smoke: it was awful. We sailed on in spell-bound silence, we scarce knew whither; the other boats of my little fleet, now seen and now disappearing, like phantoms in the horrible obscurity. How many objects of sublimity! the storm contending with the waters, and darkness with the dreary light of a general conflagration!

At one point we saw a long mountain bluff, which was partially separated from a lofty prairie hill, shaped like a sugar loaf, by a narrow and precipitous ravine. The bluffs had been charred black as a coal, but so lately that spots of fire still shone, brighter and scarce larger than stars; the ravine, its steep sides densely timbered, was like a blazing furnace; the grass of the conical hill adjoining was just on fire, and the flames ascended in graceful spiral curves to the top!

This is an accurate description of the most singular contrasts and beautiful sight I ever beheld. I had never imagined mountains in masquerade; but here was one by which NIGHT was accurately typified.

It came on to rain very hard; it was midnight, and utterly dark. I steered, I knew not whither, but to touch land. We did not strike the shore, but an island; it was covered with rushes, those vegetable files, which I can hardly think of without having my teeth set on edge.

My recruits spent some hours in kindling a fire; but, wrapt in my cloak, I resigned myself to sleep in the bottom of a boat.

We lay a day, wind-bound, at the foot of Lake Pepin. This is an enlargement of the river, about twenty-seven miles long, and from two to four broad; it is very deep, and is bounded by mountains and rocky shores; it is subject to high winds; and lofty waves and sunken rocks render it dangerous. While staying here, I witnessed (and was exposed to some danger from) the burning of a "prairie bottom," the grass of which was very tall and luxuriant. I have read a description (I believe in "The Prairie") which is very accurate, of its wonderful rapidity —the flame *leaping* forward with almost the wind's velocity, the stems of great weeds exploding like pistol shots. Only under these circumstances, very rarely upon the rolling prairies, are these fires dangerous.

The wind lulled at sunset, and the lake being notorious for boisterous weather, I determined to row through in the night. So, hoisting a light in my boat, in which I had a Creole pilot, we took our departure. A long and dreary night it was, and very cold; the water froze upon the oars. We arrived in the river above soon after sunrise, landed and took breakfast.

When my men flagged, and the progress was slow and weary, it was my custom, on this voyage, to make long races, offering for prize an extra gill of whiskey to the crew of the successful boat. To judge from their extraordinary exertions, a greater prize could not have been offered; it was a double stimulant.

On the 2d of November I arrived, all well, at Fort Snelling.

CHAPTER V.

At Fort Snelling I found old friends and officers with whom I had served at Jefferson Barracks: but independent of the most hearty hospitality—which I have ever met with on these occasions—an arrival, a new face, at such an outpost of civilization as this, is a bright link in that nearly severed chain which connects it with the world, gives an exciting impulse to its small society, which reacts upon the visitor, and is the source of unwonted pleasure to all.

The defences of this fort are high stone walls; it stands on an elevated point, the confluence of the Mississippi and St. Peter's rivers. In the rear is a prairie, nearly level, and many miles in extent: an agreeable circumstance, when it is considered that chasing wolves and racing are almost the only resource for amusement and exercise. I rode over it nine miles, to the Falls of St. Anthony. The Mississippi here falls twenty-two feet perpendicularly; in places, immense masses of rock, disjointed and fallen from immemorial abrasion, add to the scene a sublime confusion and roar of waters. I heard that evening at the fort the sound of the falls very plainly. They are said to mark the 45th parallel of north latitude.

During my stay of two days, one of the Mackinaw boats in which I had gone up was condemned, and sold at auction (for $5!) to an officer of the fort, an old friend, who decided to accompany me on my return. We took our departure in the afternoon, having for crew my pilot and a discharged soldier, with a negro lad for "cabin boy;" one of us was always at the helm. Some eight or nine miles down, my friend discovered that he had unluckily left a well-stored liquor case. We landed in consequence, near an Indian camp, and despatched two Indians with a note for it; they went in a canoe. We encamped, and were somewhat annoyed by the intrusion of our red friends.

While waiting for the messengers, let me give an account of our messing. There was abundant store of cold boiled ham, of the true Virginia flavor—of corned beef, and of chickens: and the buffalo tongue should not be forgotten. Our coffee—not used with the stinting hand of a frugal *housekeeper*—was made after the most approved method, and with extreme care and attention; it was drawn with boiling water, like tea, and not suffered to boil afterwards. But who shall do justice to the venison, roasted in bits on a stick, with alternate pieces of salt pork? First, the pleasing toil of the hunt, and the triumph of success; then the labor-inspired appetite, after the long fast which excitement forgot; then the lively fire at night, under majestic forest trees; and oh (climax), the pieces of venison, bitten with nature's weapons—not profaned with cold dull knife—and reeking hot from the wooden spit! "O, let me die eating ortolans, to the sound of soft music!" Bah!

About midnight I was awoke from a sound sleep; a candle was just expiring in the tent; I looked up and saw two dark forms almost over me, uttering with violent gesticulation the loudest and most uncouth sounds. I had instinctively grasped my rifle, and was very near putting it to its natural use, but it was our messengers, with the liquor case, who were half drunk, and making an ill-timed speech to my companion: seeking, I suppose, to raise the means of *completing* their happiness.

The next morning early, while steering, wrapped in a pea-jacket, the currrent "took a sheer" on the rudder, and quick as thought precipitated me backwards into the river. I got out without much difficulty, but it was a rather rough adventure, when the freezing weather is considered.

True to its character, we passed Lake Pepin with a tempestuous wind; we had a large sail up, but so deficient in tackle, that any sudden flaw of wind would have sunk us. The waves were very high, and I steered with a man holding my leg, to prevent my being thrown overboard. But the wind was steady, and we went through safely and right speedily.

The next day, while sailing with a high wind, we beheld another Mackinaw boat, making its way to meet us, rowed by six or eight lively Frenchmen, dressed *cap-a-pie* in red. We boarded her in the middle of the river; in doing which, I unluckily snapped in two our best oar, in endeavoring to lessen the concussion. We beheld a friend, Mr. T., an Indian agent; and, surmounting a vast pile of furniture, &c. &c., his newly-married wife—a rough introduction to the Northwest, she thought, no doubt. I had passed this party at the Des Moines rapids.

We sailed late, seeking a fit spot to encamp. The red light of burning prairies reflected in the troubled clouds, and again from the waters beneath—the sombre forests of shore and islands—the winds, now rushing in fearful gusts through the mountain passes, now heard in the moaning of distant forests—presented a wild, dreary, and fearful scene. The boat, scarcely manageable, was tossed and driven, stern foremost, on a mud-bank, where in shoving off, I further reduced our scanty stock of oars, by leaving one firmly imbedded. My companion lost his temper; we made a landing, kindled a small fire, and wrapped in our cloaks, sought repose in moody silence, each upon his blanket.

We arrived at Prairie du Chien, early on a cold and frosty morning, and found the troops drilling. That drilling, before breakfast, is not a fine thing in practice, if it be so in theory, either in cold or warm weather. I well remember at the Military Academy, mere lads as we were, that fasting and exhausted, with feet thoroughly soaked with dew, we found such drills almost intolerable. They no doubt looked very interesting to the Board of Visitors, or others, strolling out for a few moments for fresh air, on gravelled walks, between rising and breakfast.

We luckily found a steamboat at the Prairie, and the next day took passage for Galena. We arrived off the mouth of Fever River at the same time with another boat from below, and a spirited contest took place for precedence, as the river is too narrow to admit of two passing at the same time; several skilful manœuvres were executed by both vessels, and all hands became much excited. We plainly saw them loading a swivel, which they loudly threatened to fire into us. We gave them the go-by, however, without loss of life or limb. They had loaded with potatoes, it afterwards appeared, and I believe we were well contented with escaping the test of their efficacy.

Galena (so appropriately named) is eight miles from the mouth of Fever River, narrow, deep, and sluggish to this point; above, it is a shallow and insignificant stream. This is the depot for the mining district; and though destined to importance and wealth, it was then merely a place of business, and as rough and lawless as new. Our stay there was rendered particularly disagreeable by constant rain; and it seemed that no other mud in the world possessed so nearly the tenacity of glue: so that the town was rendered nearly inaccessible from the boat by the high bank.

The Galenians, jealous of the reputation of their town for health, or discontented with an ominous name, contend that "Fever" is a corruption of the French name *Feve*, or Bean River. (Prairie du Chien, or Dog Prairie, is said too, to be properly P. de Chene, Oak Prairie.)

I was politely invited to breakfast with a young merchant, with whom I had formed a slight acquaintance above. So the morning after my arrival, at a seasonable hour, I abandoned, with some misgivings, the scene of very comfortable arrangements for that meal in the cabin; effected an escalade of the bank (of mud), and after much difficulty in ascertaining the whereabout of my intended host, arrived at a retail store in a log hut, and was shown *over the counter*, into a cuddy of a counting room. Here I was allowed ample time to make a survey of the dirty void around me, and to wonder at an alarming delay of any sensible sign of preparation, or any mention of the meal, which the damp air and the late hour constantly conjured to the imagination, before my considerate host chose to find time to offer me his salutations. A new period of anxious doubts was then passed in the most commonplace remarks, which an effort of politeness seemed to extract from us. At length my kind friend seemed posed, and seized the desperate expedient of offering me a glass of—heaven knows what!—gin—or whiskey.

Of the three meals, commend me to my breakfast; 'tis the one I love, and linger over, with silent and grave complacency; but now, all desperate in prospect, the matter could no longer remain in suspense. A conviction of the unaccountable folly of having put my trust in a bachelor establishment, in the new and dismal depot of the mining district of Northwestern Illinois, or the *savoir-faire* of its Yahoo head, flashed over me:—an explanation was demanded; and I *believe* Mr. M. took the trouble to intimate that he boarded at a certain eating-house, distant a quarter of a mile of chaotic mud, where he had satisfied the cravings of nature, as well as he could, at some indefinite antecedent period of that gloomy and ill-fated morning! No apology being offered—I believe the fellow had forgotten his ridiculous invitation—I made him my politest bow, and escaped from his den, vowing never again to accept an invitation to breakfast; a vow I have seldom broken, and never, I believe, without regretting it.

That evening, for the sake of a nearer view of men and things at this Ultima Thule of civilization, I accompanied an acquaintance to a tavern; and I had in my mind, I confess, a distinct conviction of the basis of the developments of character which were expected in these miners, adventurers, and outlaws. I was ushered into a large barn-like room, the common scene of eating, drinking, smoking, lounging, and sleeping; and it now presented strong evidences, as I expected, of still another appropriation, to wit, gambling. With little delay, and less of ceremony, I found myself one of seven (I had reason to believe, the most respectable citizens of the town), around a table in a corner, and the "papers" in motion; every man "bragging" according to his "pile;" and I emphatically, on my "own hook;" for I was a stranger in a strange place. I was more intent upon my observations, than the matter before me, and it was not long before I could count eight or ten different tables, each surrounded by players, say fifty men, all swearing or talking loudly; many intoxicated, disputing, and quarrelling.

My interest in this characteristic display might be thought a little exciting, when it is borne in mind that of this large and turbulent assemblage, very few were above my suspicions of any particular accomplishment, from the slipping of a card to the cutting of a throat.

Being careless, fortune seemed to favor me; and as my "pile" grew, so the force of circumstances seemed in a strange manner to increase the visible protrusion of the handle of a trusty dirk-pistol from the left breast pocket of my overcoat. Perhaps it was an instinctive action upon the maxim, "do at Rome as the Romans do." My apprehensions, however, on the score of the silver, were premature and groundless; I was spared the dangerous responsibility of guarding home any extra amount of treasure; and in fact, trying to persuade myself of a *quid pro quo*, I very philosophically congratulated myself on a specific gravity lessened by a few pounds avoirdupois, as I made my soundings through the street, on the dark errand to my steamboat berth. The next morning—a stranger may be allowed to remark it—a man was found at the river edge, quite dead, from a wound of his carotid artery.

Mining, or rather the search for veins or "leads" is, in itself, a pursuit dictated by a restless, unsettled spirit of adventure, of the same character as that which finds vent in gambling; and in a new pioneer settlement of adventurers thus attracted, and of lawless, licentious workmen, a decided prevalence of this and its kindred vices might be calculated on with certainty. But the same, in a less degree, is the character and spirit of the inhabitants of all new States; and accordingly, gambling is found openly to prevail in the West. That indolence, satiety, and a natural thirst for excitement, debarred from more honorable outlets in old established and formal societies, lead to the clandestine indulgence of this vice, and to excess, in the old States, is very well known; but it is concealed carefully beneath the smoother surface of affairs. In the West it was almost universal, and is open and unimpeached. It was not uncommon for traders or farmers on the way to a market, to adventure their produce at the gaming-table, then, but happily not now, so universal on the steamboats.

We were fortunate, so late in the season (the end of November), to obtain a passage in a steamboat to St. Louis; so, after a stay of some days at Galena, we gladly embarked for more congenial scenes. Cards were the order of the day, and of the night; it was nothing strange that the captain and other officers of the boat should be thus almost constantly engaged; but it *was* remarkable that the former personage should be rather more than suspected of cheating, a circumstance that was very publicly and plainly insinuated by my companion, Lieut. H.

We arrived in St. Louis, December 2d.

CHAPTER VI.

Another winter was passed at Jefferson Barracks. It has left little impression on my memory; and I lament, that I may say, less on my mind. It is a confession that many might make, under the unfavorable circumstances of the service. I had determined to throw up my commission, and to seek a more stirring and exciting profession. At the very crisis, Fate—it is a favorite word with your soldier, or your Turk—decided differently, inasmuch as I was ordered on active service, which I did not consider it honorable to decline. Four companies of the 6th infantry were ordered to be filled up—officers and men by selection—and to march as the first escort of the annual "caravan" of traders going, and returning, between Western Missouri and Santa Fe.

May 4, 1829.—We were embarked; the steamer was aground. I stood on the gunwale of a flat-boat lighter, filled with men; the scabbard of my sword (fastened to the belt by a ring) unaccountably became detached, and fell into the river and disappeared, leaving the blade still more strangely suspended: it was an omen. Thenceforth I was devoted to the service of the Republic.

It was remarkable how large the proportion of married men was among those selected to fill our companies (but not strange—for your bachelor, when a little "old," is good for nothing but to take care of himself). The boat swarmed with their wives and children; the deck was barricaded with beds and bedding; infants squalled, and chickens cackled; the captain was at a nonplus; the quartermaster was in a fever of contention and official opposition, and voted all contraband; our commander was wroth, and stuck for the "free bottom" principle, where the Government and its servants were concerned. General A. had to interpose to restore peace; and in the guise of the founders of a colony, we *set forth* for our adventures in the western deserts, where we were destined to see no woman for near half a year.

In ten days we landed at Cantonment Leavenworth

(then *abandoned* by the 3d infantry for unhealthiness). It was the quickest passage that had then been made. We were not to march for a week or two; a day for meeting the traders at the "Round Grove," some fifty miles west, having been agreed upon.

Probably in consequence of most of the oxen having been bought and conducted to the river opposite Fort L., it was determined to commence the march on that side, and cross back to the right bank above Independence (thus avoiding the Kansas, where there was no ferry). We had twenty wagons, laden heavily with provisions, and four ox-carts for camp equipage.

The battalion marched on the 5th of June. I had breakfasted and mounted guard at 4 A.M., and at a much later hour brought up the rear; and it was dark night when, having marched *seven miles*, I found myself in the miry and dreary bottom of the Little Platte River, where half the baggage train were fast stuck for the night. I passed on with my men to the ford; the companies (and my mess chest) were somewhere beyond. So, hoping that my next breakfast would be as early as my last, I lay down in my cloak and went to sleep.

Next morning, one of my guard, "an old soldier," brought me a nice broil. "*Left'nt*," said he, touching his cap, with a suppressed grin, "will the Left'nt have a piece of *cub?*" But, verily, if I had been a Jew, I was hungry enough to have eaten it.

After a laborious march of five days, averaging some seven miles a day, through the Missouri and its creek bottoms, we had again crossed, and encamped on the verge of the "Grand Prairie." After delving so long in lofty but sombre forests, we felt highly exhilarated to view from a light and airy grove its green and flowery expanse, which seemed to return the smiles of this sweet month of June.

Here was delightfully situated on the edge of the grove, with the advantage of the seldom-failing breezes from the prairies, like those from the sea, the house (and the last we were to pass) of the sub-agent of the Delawares—the hospitable old Major C., who, with ready joke and julep, did his best to make our long farewell to the settlements, a lively one.

The next morning we struck out boldly into the great prairies—a constant succession of rolling hills—here, and for more than a hundred miles beyond, variegated and beautified by wooded streams, running first to the right into the Kansas, then to the left into the Neosho; or, like that, into the Arkansas River. This first day's march was twenty-six miles, and after 11 o'clock we met with no water; I was scarcely able to raise a foot from the ground when we arrived in the evening at the Round Grove, the rendezvous, where we found the "Caravan."

The traders were about seventy in number, and had about half that number of wagons, with mule and a few horse teams. They organized themselves into a company and elected Mr. B. of St. Louis, their "captain," an office that experience had pronounced indispensable, but was nevertheless little honored; for danger itself, uncredited, because unseen, could not overcome the self-willed notions and vagrant propensities of the most of these border inhabitants—self-willed and presumptuous, because ignorant.

I expected to be so sore as to be scarce able to march next morning, but was most agreeably surprised to find myself as supple and fresh as ever. After marching fifteen or twenty miles a day, for five or six days, crossing two or three timbered creeks daily, we arrived at the Council Grove: it is a beautiful piece of timber, through which runs the Neosho River, though here, indeed, merely a fine broad creek, about forty feet wide. Here again, we were delighted with a change from hot prairies to a cool and beautiful retreat; where we wandered about under a lofty dome of verdure, breathing the fragrance of the luxuriant grape vine, and listening to the songs of birds; there was nothing to remind us of the ocean of prairie around, save the pleasures of a delightful contrast.

After leaving the Grove, the vast sameness of the prairies was seldom relieved by a fringe of trees, even on the creeks. Cow Creek, though much further on, is an exception, a fine stream, skirted with pleasant forest glades; it abounded with fish, which, of several pounds weight, were caught as fast as the line could be handled. And near here—the era of the expedition—was first heard the exciting cry of "Buffalo!" Many pleaded for permission to pursue; our few horses, about a dozen, were in great demand, and several went on foot. We dashed over the hills, and beheld with a thrill of pleasure, the first stragglers of these much-talked-of animals; pell-mell we charged the huge monsters, and poured in a brisk fire, which sounded like an opening battle; our horses were wild with excitement and fright;—the balls flew at random—the flying animals, frantic with pain and rage, seemed endued with many lives. One was brought to bay by whole volleys of shots; his eyeballs glared; he bore his tufted tail aloft like a black flag; then shaking his vast head and shaggy mane in impotent defiance, he sank majestically to the earth, under twenty bleeding wounds.

The "Cottonwood Fork" (of the Arkansas) is a pretty

stream, and relieves the eye, wearied with resting on nought but prairies: its banks are high and rocky. At the crossing there is a lofty bluff, near the Arkansas River, which we had now first approached; but making, as we ascend, a great southern bend, the trail taken in wet seasons strikes it again eighty miles beyond; in this distance, we several times approached it for water. We encamped the night after leaving the Cottonwood on Raccoon Creek, which is the last that we saw; not a tree or shrub was on its banks, though abounding with the animals which give it its name: they live on fish. We were thus, and often after, dependent upon buffalo ordure for fuel.

Next day we passed (we had seen it from afar) an isolated, abrupt, and rocky hill or mound, perhaps 100 feet high; an extraordinary feature in this region of country; one that might suggest the idea of Bush's elevated camp in the "Prairie;" a novel, as remarkable for its absurd plot, as for the fidelity of its description of scenery and scenes, which the author had never visited or witnessed.

Prairies are much alike in their main characteristics; though in the region which we now approached, their immense extent made them, compared to those of the Western States, as the broad expanse of ocean, to the land-locked bays of its margin; and losing the fertility and the variety of hill and dale, of murmuring streams and pretty groves, which adorn those lake-like prairies, these further resemble the ocean in its dreary and unvarying aspect.

We marched about 130 miles, always in view of the Arkansas (or its adjoining scenery), and in all this distance saw only here and there a tree, immediately on its banks, and a few others on the frequent flat and grassy islands, which present to the eye of the hot and weary traveller, a most delightful and inviting appearance; not so deceptive as the *mirage*, which here, as in Asia, is frequently observed, but as unavailing and tantalizing. The valley of this *upper* Arkansas is about a mile wide; the river flowing generally at the foot of a lofty bluff, winding its course from one to the other side of low, flat, luxuriant savannas.

More than once, from the tops of these high sandy hills, we saw far away, in almost every direction, mile after mile of prairie, blackened by buffaloes. One morning, when our march was along the natural meadows by the river, we passed through them for miles; they opening in front and closing continually in the rear, preserving a distance scarcely over three hundred paces. It is known that when enraged, or when there is the slightest appearance of being cornered, the buffalo rushes blindly forward at any opposition, as furious as a Malay "running a muck." On one occasion, a bull had approached within two hundred yards without seeing us, until he ascended the river bank; he stood a moment shaking his head, and then made a charge at the column. Several officers stepped out and fired on him, and two or three dogs rushed to meet him; but right onward he came, snorting blood from mouth and nostril at every leap, and with the speed of a horse and the momentum of a locomotive, dashed between two wagons, which the frightened oxen nearly upset; the dogs were at his heels, and soon he came to bay, and with tail erect, kicked violently for a moment, and then sank in instant death,—the muscles retaining the dying rigidity of tension.

About the middle of July, from high hill-tops—the Pisgah of our pilgrimage—we descried the promised rest from our far wanderings—the limit of our march—Chouteau's Island, on the Mexican border. Weary and athirst, on the sandy hills, under a scorching sun, we beheld, amid the waves of the broad river, this beautiful island; its green carpet of grass and umbrageous groves, inviting us to the cool shade and pleasant breezes.

CHAPTER VII.

The Arkansas River is here the boundary of the United States and Mexico; it is above 23 degrees west of Washington City. Our orders were to march no farther; and as a protection to the trade, it was like the establishment of a ferry to the mid-channel of a river.

Traders had always used mules or horses. Our oxen were an experiment, and it succeeded admirably; they even did better when water was very scarce, which is an important consideration; and it may be mentioned here, that a pair were sent on some 400 miles further, to Santa Fe, and maintained their superiority, and that they have been generally used since.

A few hours after the departure of the trading company, as we enjoyed a quiet rest on a hot afternoon, we saw beyond the river a number of horsemen riding furiously toward our camp. We all flocked out of the tents, to see, and hear the news, for they were soon recognized as traders. They stated that the caravan had been attacked, about six miles off, in the sand-hills, by an innumerable host of Indians; that some of their companions had been killed, and—they had run, of course, for help. Major R. hesitated not a moment; the word was given, and the tents vanished as if by magic. The oxen, which were grazing near by, were speedily yoked to the wagons, and into the river we marched. Then I deemed myself the most unlucky of men; a day or two before, while eating my breakfast, with my coffee in a tin cup—notorious among chemists and campaigners for keeping it hot—it was upset into my shoe, and on pulling off the stocking, it so happened that the skin came with it. Being thus *hors du combat*, I sought to enter the combat on a horse, which was allowed; but I was put in command of the rear guard, to bring up the baggage train. It grew late, and the wagons were slowly crossed, for the river unluckily took that particular time to rise fast, and before all were over, we had to swim it, and by moonlight. By doubling the teams in succession, some of the animals could touch and pull, whilst others swam. I was thus two hours in the river, mounted on a horse, with my lame foot across his neck. When safely over, I found that three companies had marched on, and we slowly followed. Awkwardly mounted as I was, I was seized with an invincible propensity to sleep; and once having mistaken a sand-hillock for the rearmost wagon, and halted, I took quite a nap before my men discovered the state of the case. We reached the encampment at 1 o'clock at night. All was quiet, and remained so until dawn, when, at the sound of our bugles, the pickets reported they saw a number of Indians moving off. On looking around us, we perceived ourselves and the caravan in the most unfavorable defenceless situation possible—in the area of a natural amphitheatre of sand-hills, about fifty feet high, and within gun-shot all around. There was the narrowest practicable entrance and outlet.

We ascertained that some mounted traders, in spite of

all remonstrance or command, had ridden on in advance, and when in the narrow pass beyond this spot, had been suddenly beset by about fifty mounted Indians; all fled and escaped, save one, who, mounted on a mule, was *abandoned* by his companions, overtaken, and slain. He was a Mr. Lamb, the largest capitalist, and owner of the company. The Indians perhaps equalled the traders in number; but notwithstanding their extraordinary advantage of ground, dared not attack them when they made a stand among the wagons; and the latter, all well armed, were afraid to make a single charge, which would have scattered their enemies like sheep.

Having buried the poor fellow's body, and killed an ox for breakfast, we left this sand-hollow, which would soon have been roasting hot, and advanced through the defile—of which we took care to occupy the commanding ground—and proceeded to escort the traders at least one day's march further.

These "sand-hills" compose a strip of country found occasionally a few miles off, on the Mexican side of the river, and where its valley has no abrupt boundary; they are irregular hillocks of the loosest sand, seemingly formed by the sport of the wind. There is scarce a sign of vegetation, and they present an aspect as wild and desolate, and as little *American*, as possible.

Emerging from the hills, we found ourselves on the verge of a vast plain, nearly level, where it seemed nature had ineffectually struggled to convert a sandy desert into a prairie. There was a scanty and dwarfish growth of wiry grass, brown and withered, amid the white sand. On we marched, under a fiery sun, facing a burning wind. Not a tree, not a shrub, nor the slightest indication of water, could be seen in a view apparently illimitable in every direction. Thus we struggled on until noon, when the panting oxen, with lolling tongues, seemed incapable of proceeding. A halt was made, and they were taken from the wagons, but stood motionless. The wind blew a gale, a true sirocco. We sought every cover to avoid it. A messmate—one of those unfortunates who prefer the dark side of a picture, and croak when a cheerful word of encouragement is needed—gave vent to his despondency, and sought to engender discontent and fearful apprehensions; he predicted we would lose our baggage train, if not our lives, in the desert. Indignant, and without a better answer, perhaps, *I* undertook to prophesy, and actually foretold the exact event, viz.: that, pushing on, within ten miles we would find water and grass in some hollow, and buffalo too. After marching about that distance, we came to the sandy bed of a dry creek, and found in it, not distant from our course, a pool of water, and an acre or two of fine grass. On the surface of the water floated thick the dead bodies of small fish, which the heat of the sun had that day destroyed. After encamping we saw a few buffalo, attracted doubtless by the water; and several were killed. Beyond our hopes, all our necessaries were thus ministered to; it seemed a special providence.

Next morning Major R. determined to march no further into the Mexican territory. The traders held a council, and nearly half of them at first determined to remain likewise, and spend the summer with us. To combat this pusillanimous resolution we took the utmost pains; it seemed that *we* were about to lose our time and property, and be disgraced, and not themselves. They were finally talked and shamed out of it.

The sirocco still continuing, by enveloping a tin bucket

5

with cotton cloths kept well wetted, we converted a hot and disgusting fluid into "ice-water;" and with the further comforts of a buffalo hump and marrow bone, we passed a pleasant day in the little oasis, and the sufferings of yesterday were forgotten. Fortunate constitution of the mind—happy life, where pain but gives a greater zest to the fleeting pleasure!

At the first light next day, we were in motion to return to the river and the American line, and no further adventure befell us, save a night alarm, occasioned by a sentinel firing at a noble setter dog, which luckily he did not hit; the men turned out and took their places with the quiet precision of veterans, as they were.

The vicinity of Chouteau's Island is further remarkable for a timbered bottom, which stands opposite its foot on the American side. We had seen none other after leaving Council Grove, 300 miles back, although now and then we had passed pleasant open groves on the river bank. The battalion encamped immediately on the river opposite the island, a few hundred yards above the timber.

While here, the terms of service of four men expired, and they were discharged; and, contrary to all advice, determined to return to Missouri. After marching several hundred miles over a prairie country, and often on high hills, commanding a vast prospect, without seeing a human being, or a sign of one, and, save the trail we followed, not the slightest indication that the country had ever been visited by man, it was exceedingly difficult to credit that lurking foes were generally around us, and spying our motions. It was so with these men; and being armed, they set out, on the first of August, on foot, for the settlements. That same night, three of the four returned. They reported that, after walking about fifteen miles, they were surrounded by thirty mounted Indians. A wary old soldier of their number succeeded in extricating them before any hostile act had been committed; but one of them, perhaps highly elated and pleased at their forbearance, or led by some blind fatality, insisted on returning among them to give them tobacco and shake hands. In this friendly act he was shot down. The Indians stripped him in an incredibly short time, and as quickly dispersed to avoid a shot; and the old soldier, after cautioning the others to reserve their fire, did fire among them, and probably with some effect. Had the others done the same, the Indians would have rushed upon them before they could have reloaded. They managed to make good their retreat in safety to our camp.

On the 2d, Captain W., myself, and fifty men, were ordered to take a guide and proceed to search for and bury the body. We marched about fifteen miles; our guide became bewildered, led us several miles from the river, and could not find the body. We were then suffering much for water, Dr. N. particularly, who vomited frequently, and seemed to think he could neither stand, walk, nor ride. Our course was then directed to the river. So great was the suffering, and the eagerness to reach water, that the party became strung out, according to their strength, in quite a *sauve qui peut* style. The river water was very muddy and very warm; the Doctor could not drink—his stomach would not bear it; but he threw himself in, and lay a long while, to relieve nature by absorption. We got to camp from our unsuccessful expedition about ten o'clock at night, as weary a set of fellows as ever marched.

August 3, 1829. This morning a large party were sent out, with the same object, under Lieutenant I., who took other guides. The battalion was encamped in the order of the Regulations, with the rear on the river opposite Chouteau's Island; the prairie hills skirted the river for miles, at a distance of about 500 yards; along its banks, above, were trees enough nearly to conceal the prairies beyond. I was officer of the guard of forty men, stationed about 150 paces in front. About 2 o'clock, when all the cattle and our few horses were grazing about a mile off above, under a charge of five men, an alarm of great uproar and yelling was suddenly heard. I and my guard sprang into ranks, and looking to the left, saw the cattle rushing towards the camp, followed by between 400 and 500 mounted Indians, who, decked in paint and feathers, uttering horrid yells, brandishing spears, and firing guns, and riding at full speed, seemed about to make an intrepid charge. At the first instant I conceived I was entering into a very doubtful battle, and reviewed in thought all the actions of my life; in the next, seeing that the "light" company (armed with a kind of rifle, unloaded) was ordered to advance, to oppose the first onset of the enemy, I reflected that they might easily be cut to pieces, and that the cattle-guard, too, were exposed to instant destruction, and I asked for permission to advance with my command, with loaded muskets; it was granted, and I set off in double quick time to meet the Indians, and endeavor to avert these calamities. As we were about to meet the foremost, they branched off, firing on us as they ran, which, in view of the main body, I scarcely noticed, but kept steadily on, until I found they were all playing the same game; and the whole opened out at a respectful distance, like buffalo, and fled, or charged far clear of my flanks, except a body of them which seemed stationary, more than a half mile in advance. The company to my left had met the cattle-guard, and they were saved, with the exception of one man, who had received eleven wounds. I looked back, and saw the camp surrounded, at a respectful distance, by the Indians, all in rapid motion, a part still in pursuit of a body of cattle, rushing along the sand-bars and island, and heard two companies, formed in rear of the camp, firing at them regularly by platoon. I then marched round towards the front of the camp, which was wholly exposed; the 6-pounder, as we passed, threw a round shot over our heads, and I saw it strike just in the midst of the body of the enemy which remained above, perhaps a mile from the piece; it made a great commotion amongst them. The piece was then directed against the enemy galloping four or five hundred yards off, along the hill-side in front; the grape-shot struck like hail among them, but seemed to hit but one. I then saw a company advancing in pursuit far beyond the right flank, and a bugle-signal, "double-quick," was sounded from the camp; but of course they could not overtake a mounted enemy, but entered the woods to their right. The Indians were now beyond fire, though to be seen in every direction over the country; but they gradually drew off, assembled on the hills beyond the river, fired a volley, gave a general yell, and disappeared. They carried off their dead, afterwards ascertained to be nine in number. Our loss was one man mortally wounded, and fifty oxen and twelve horses killed or driven off.

On my first advance I saw an Indian handsomely mounted on a gray horse, gaudily ornamented with feathers, conspicuous for his rapid action and loud commands. A corporal on the right of my detachment was so much struck with him, that, unobserved, he came to a halt, and took a deliberate shot, but, I believe, came much nearer hitting myself. The Indians who dashed by the rear—their left flank exposed to a sharp fire—extended themselves along the right sides of their horses, hanging by the left foot and arm; this last, with a bull's-hide shield attached, passed around the horse's neck, from beneath which they rapidly discharged their arrows—the shield covering arm, horse's neck, the head, and right arm below! Excited as they were, they seemed the best of horsemen; and rushed up and down places which few persons in cool blood would think of attempting. A number of horses and cattle were killed. An Indian horse was at one time in our possession; but a gun, bow, quiver, and shield remained the only trophies of a doubtful victory.

We now felt some little uneasiness for our detachment, though well commanded. It soon returned, having heard the cannonading; they were hastened on, but unluckily could not arrive in time to meet the Indians retreating from the right flank.

These Indians, who thus, from education and on principle, avoided our bold opposition, had we wavered or fled, would have proved the fiercest and most formidable pursuing enemy perhaps in the world. Their plan seemed to have been to cut off the cattle and their guard by a combined movement of two divisions; the one moving over the hills on our side of the river, the other hidden by trees, from beyond the river, to meet the first. It was in a great measure disconcerted by the first party making its appearance too soon; but it was still a *surprise.*

Late that night, I received a report from the rear that the Indians were gathered close by for a rush upon the camp; a sergeant was ready to swear to it, as he had distinctly heard hundreds of horses crossing the river to the island, which was near by, and the water very shallow.

I instantly proceeded to the spot with a platoon: whilst patrolling up and down through the high, rank grass, leading the men, with a pistol in one hand and my sword in the other, I felt conscious of a want of prudence in being clothed in white, while all the men had greatcoats, and expected at each moment to receive an arrow or a shot; but no discoveries could be made in a quarter of a mile along the bank. I then heard myself what I thought must certainly be the noise of horsemen fording the river, and the battalion was quietly put under arms; but nothing happened, and it was afterwards ascertained to be wolves, which were crossing to the carcasses of horses and cattle which had been killed. I am certain I could not now distinguish their motion in shallow water from that of horses.

CHAPTER VIII.

After the attack of August 3d, our camps were formed in an order more suitable to our circumstances: in a square, open at the corners, a company in a single row of tents on each side, and across the angles, slightly masking the flanks of each company, were rows of wagons, the whole forming a kind of octagon. The cattle, always yoked, were grazed at a more cautious distance, and at night were tied to the wagon wheels.

We were instructed to wait here for the return of the caravan, expected early in October. Our provisions consisted of salt, and half rations of flour (besides a reserve of fifteen days' full rations), and as to the rest we were dependent upon hunting. When buffalo became scarce, or grass bad, we marched to other ground, thus roving up and down the river for eighty miles. The first thing after encamping, we dug and constructed, with flour barrels, a well in front of each company; water was always found at the depth of from two to four feet, varying with the corresponding height of the river, but clear and cool. Next, we would build sod fireplaces; these, with network platforms of buffalo-hide, for the purpose of smoking and drying meat, formed a tolerable additional defence, at least against mounted men.

Hunting was a military duty, done by detail, parties of fifteen or twenty going out with a wagon. They threw out three or four hunters, and remained under arms for the purpose of protecting them, &c. Completely isolated, and beyond support, or even communication—self-dependent in any emergency that might arise, and in the midst of many thousands of Indians, whose concentration our long stay seemed to invite, the utmost vigilance was maintained. Officer of the guard every fourth night, I was always awake, and generally in motion the whole night. Night alarms were frequent; when, all sleeping in their clothes, we were accustomed to assemble instantly, and with scarcely a word spoken, take our places in the grass in front of each face of the camp, where, however wet, we sometimes lay for hours. I never failed for months to sleep in pantaloons and moccasins, with pistols, and a loose woollen coat for pillow; my sword stuck in the ground in the mouth of the tent, with my cap upon the hilt; and although I have often slept undisturbed at the firing of a cannon thirty paces off, here, always after the firing of a musket, if 500 yards off, in less than ten seconds I was out and prepared to perform my duty.

August 11th. We were encamped in our new order, a few miles below Chouteau's Island. An alarm was given, and we were under arms for an hour until daylight.

During the morning, Indians were to be seen a mile or two off, leading their horses through the hollows. Captain P., however, with eighteen men, a wagon and team, was sent across the river after buffalo, which we saw half a mile distant. In his absence, a large body of Indians came galloping down the river, as if to charge the camp; the cattle were secured in good time. Captain W., with his company, of which I was Lieutenant, was ordered to cross the river and support Captain P. We waded in some disorder through the quicksands and currents, and just as we neared a dry sandbar in the middle, a volley was fired at us by a squad of Indians, who that moment rode to the water's edge. The balls whistled very near, but without damage; I felt an involuntary twitch of the neck, and cried out with a great laugh, "Did you see that Wick? I dodged, by ——." Wishing to return the compliment instantly before they fled, I stooped down, and the company fired over my head; with what execution was not perceived, as the Indians immediately retired out of our view. This had passed in half a minute, and we were then astonished to see, a little above, among some bushes on the same bar, the party we had been sent to support; and we heard they had abandoned one of the hunters, who had been killed. We then saw above, on the bank we had left, a formidable-looking body of the enemy in close order; and hoping to surprise them, we ascended the bed of the river: in crossing the channel we were up to the arm-pits, but when we emerged on the bank, we found that the Indians had detected the movement, and retreated. We then rested on our arms, and observed the fire of cannister from a six-pounder nearer camp, upon Indians who were galloping by, beyond musket range; one was shot down,—when instantly, two others stopped, remounted him, and rode off, sustaining him on either side. Casting our eyes beyond the river, I saw a number of the Indians riding on both sides of the wagon and team, which Capt. P. had deserted, urging the animals rapidly towards the hills. I counted the Indians on that side, and there were but eighteen. At this time Captain W. received an order, through the Adjutant, to cross and recover the body of the slain hunter. On reaching the ground, we found it within the distance, as we were told, from whence the party, by order of Captain P., had made their precipitate retreat, although the cries of the poor fellow had been repeatedly heard, that they should not desert him. He was an old soldier, and a favorite,—bugler K. He was brought in, with an arrow still transfixing his huge chest; the scalp was gone.

We were then surprised to see the wagon and team at a distance, and no enemy near; and on approaching, were astonished at finding the oxen unwounded. I then begged, but was refused, the independent command of a platoon, with which I wished to try some experiments with the Indians, who were still in sight above, and near a cover which might have concealed my approach. I was stung by the contempt which these well-mounted savages showed for our powerlessness, on foot, to avenge the disgrace which they had inflicted on us; and to descend too, at such a moment, to the guard of butchers and a meat wagon,—for a buffalo had been unluckily killed there,—was a bitter pill.

And now a storm approached; and angry clouds settled heavily amid the shades of evening, while portentous columns of smoke rolled up, far and near—the answered signals to unseen foes; and on the high hills, motionless horsemen were revealed like spectres against the sky, by the glare of lightning; a stricken corpse lay in our midst. Nature's gloom, with all its wildness, was infused into the spirits of our little band; for fearful whispers of a sacrifice passed like a panic to men in groups; a voice for the vengeance of blood seemed moaning in the winds.

And then, with darkness so dense as seemed to hush the very winds to silence, came a falling flood, the roar of whose approach appalled our shaken hearts.

August 12th. The brilliant sun of a serene morning, followed this awful night, and cheered somewhat our wretched plight in a flooded camp. More calm at noon, all fell in the silent ranks for the solemn duty of consigning, with all honor, our fallen brother soldier to his last wilderness home; a week before, the beautiful but mournful notes of the dead march, had—first in all time—pealed on this desert air; and now again, but far more gloomily, was heard this martial requiem.

It was a humiliating condition to be surrounded by these rascally Indians, who, by means of their horses, could tantalize us with the hopes of battle, and elude our efforts; who could annoy us by preventing all individual excursions for hunting, &c., and who could insult us with impunity. Much did we regret that we were not mounted too; and I believe nearly all prayed that the enemy would become bolder, and enliven us with frequent attacks; but this was their last, though they were frequently seen hovering around; and the running of buffalo was a sign of their vicinity, frequently observed on our hunts. It is known that they crawl to the tops of commanding hills, and using the head and skin of a wolf as a mask, spy out the motions of an enemy, with little or no risk of discovery; but despising us—wholly on the defensive—they now took not this trouble, but appeared openly on the hills.

We learned afterwards, through Mexican traders, that our motions had been watched the whole route from Council Grove; whilst we, concluding from appearances, scarcely conceived that a human being could be within hundreds of miles of us. The spies who had watched us reported our coming in great force, and *with white buffalo.* It would seem that these Indians had never seen the ox before. We saw a singular proof of the ignorant interest with which they regarded this animal, a few days after the action of Chouteau's Island. One of the oxen that had fallen into their hands somehow escaped, and appeared on the river bank, opposite to our camp, making its way to water. It was secured, and I was sent across to search for others in the country around. After going some miles, we found carcasses among the sand-hills, with all the white spots carefully cut out from the rest of the hide. These pieces of white were doubtless taken away by the Indians as trophies.

Unfortunately, but few books had been provided—Shakspeare, a copy of the old Regulations, and but one or two others; all of which I read regularly through, and the first-named more than once. Hunting, except by detachment, was dangerous, and forbidden; but occasionally an antelope or a deer was killed. Of that singular animal—the antelope—we saw great numbers; and in the fall, once or twice, many hundreds in a gang, which, all of one accord, would dash hither and thither with wonderful swiftness, looking at a distance, like the shadow of a moving cloud. There was a remarkable species of hare, near twice the size of the Eastern; the fleetest of the prairie animals, though in very tall grass they were easily caught. I had a nearly tame one, which fed on rushes, which would disappear in its mouth as if pushed through a hole. Badgers were common; and prairie foxes of light and elegant proportions. We met with many prairie dog "villages;" whole acres of their burrows, with entrances in a small mound; the animal more resembles a ground-squirrel than a dog; being of the same color, and not more than thrice the size. They are very shy, and quick as light in their motions; they come to the mouths of their holes, and bark at intruders; it is a bark, in manner of utterance, but of a treble intonation, more resembling that of a bird than of a dog. Of wolves, there were thousands, of all kinds and sizes, except the large black wood wolf; never an hour of a night passed without the accompaniment of their howls, even by day they were to be seen around. One dark night, being officer of the guard, I advanced some two hundred paces to a spot where there was an excavation and a small mound of earth, and where garbage had been thrown; from the mound, I saw perhaps a dozen snarling over their unclean food; sword in hand, I sprang down among them; they scattered, but I did not stay long to see how far. Rattlesnakes were very numerous, and dangerous; we lost several horses by their bites. Wild horses we saw frequently, but not many. A horse which we lost August 3d, was recovered from a gang a month or two afterwards. We only saw elk once, about two hundred together. Buffalo, wolves, rattlesnakes, and grasshoppers, seemed to fill up the country.

But to return to our occupations. We fished a little, hunted, and read a very little; and the only alternative seemed the manufacture of buffalo powder-horns. Hundreds were made in the camp, and some very beautiful; the horn is quite black, and receives a fine polish, and being exceedingly thick, admits of much carving; with the laborious and patient care of Chinese, some were carved and inlaid with bone; but many other articles were made—spoons, combs, cups, buttons, wine-*glasses*, &c.; some very pretty pocket-combs, with white handles, were made by one of the men.

CHAPTER IX.

But little occupied,—so limited in books and amusements,—the time passed heavily enough; but happily our little society,—there were just a dozen of us,—was harmonious and cheerful. We were accustomed, in the fine summer nights, to form a little circle,—lying in easy attitudes upon the grass,—and thus to hold communion of thoughts and speculations upon the past and future. Gazing like Chaldeans, on the stars, our imaginings and discourses were ever of the distant and unseen. The telling of stories was, of course, a favorite resource. Here is one which I wrote out with some of the reporter's accustomed license; although from a youthful source, its accurate descriptions of Rocky Mountain scenery, as well as some Indian traits, induce me to record it.

Sha-wah-now.

Late in the afternoon of a spring day, and many years ago, a solitary Indian might have been seen toiling at the dangerous ascent of one of the Rocky Mountains. He followed the deep-worn chasm of the mountain torrent, where often the flood of waters bore in awful confusion, earth, rocks, and trees. Now, with the nerve of a chamois hunter, he cleared a fearful space: a moment's contemplation of the void below, bounded by the naked jutting rocks, must have disturbed the brain of the most hardy. And now, he traces the projecting ledge of the mountain precipice ('twas never meant for a path); below him is death; a look must cost his life; above him vertical granite; not a vine nor twig to help him to life; his fingers grow to the rocks! his eagle gaze, if a moment averted, were dimmed; that step may save him! it is made; he is safe!

Sha-wah-now was safe; the last difficulty was behind him, and he stood upon the mountain's brow. Brave was he, and distinguished for success in war; his person bore about it the ægis of dignity, which commanded the respect of the men, and the fond attachment of the women, of his tribe. He was dressed in skins of the purest white; his bust was bare, but for a furred robe which was folded beneath his shoulder, leaving his right arm freed for action. He wore at his back a bow and well-stored quiver, and in his belt was a tomahawk.

He leaned his lofty form against a rock, and contemplated the dangers he had passed—the valley below and the mountains beyond, with mingled feelings of simple devotion to the Great Spirit, and admiration at a view where beauty and sublimity were mingled in the happiest proportions. The sun in mid-heaven is but a tame spectacle; his effect, though dazzling, is simple; there he is something alike beyond our ken and thoughts, merely *useful.* But when he approaches, as it were, our earth in setting—is surrounded by the horizon's mist—it is then that he is the glorious father of a thousand beauties; a hemisphere blushes red as roses; a mountain structure of calm and motionless clouds, seems a palace of fancy adorned with every heaven-born hue. It was such a sun that shed its divine influence over that valley. The ground swelled into slight undulations; a stream wound its way in the midst; its banks were dotted with trees; all was rejoicing in the influence of spring; all was covered with the most delicate hues of green. The soft light of the sun's lingering rays fell upon some spots only to contrast the richer shade, and the surface of that valley appeared as fair, as soft, as a maiden's cheek; and its contemplation filled, for a moment, as large and tender a spot in the heart of the Indian, as did the thoughts of his beloved, his beautiful—the lost Ayeta.

And Sha-wah-now mused on, and to his excited mind came swelling tumultuous thoughts. Untaught by man and his vain books, he had drank deep of the inspiration of Nature in her majestic solitudes. Amid mountain storms he had ever rioted with wild joy. Amid the warring elements his spirit had ever sought fellowship of its own creations; and then the pent-up broodings of his heart had fierce and loud utterance. His aspirations were wild, and turned on a nation's wrongs and their revenge: "Oh! that I could clothe myself with the wings of the northern blast, and sweep with desolation the oppressor's race."

And Sha-wah-now mused on, and perhaps grasped with intuitive perception the dim future of ages. He saw in mountain and valley, fresh from the hand of the Creator, the rise of a pastoral race, and beheld its glad youth delighting in the health and innocence of athletic games, whilst afar the generous earth smiled, o'er all the boundless plains, with the green promise, or the golden fruit of the husbandman's noble toil—the "Father of

Waters"—master of old, turbid and fearful—was now the humble slave of man, subdued by a kindred power, his *offspring*, kindled by the fire genius' spark set on. His ever-heaving bosom now seemed whelmed by a world's supply, commanding the undreamt perfections of slavish art. His Mentor, the genius of the valleys, pointed to this fair picture with a smile of godlike youth.

His aspect changed, and lo! there stood a graybeard stern! He waved his arm—another hundred years rolled by.

Sha-wah-now saw now a new world grown old. Simplicity and innocence had shrunk, or fled, or changed. No poet now invoked the forgotten goddesses of his art, nor lover in green solitudes could mingle his sighs with nature's soothing music. The granary of nations had become a smoky workshop of myriads of coal-begrimed men. He saw numberless dusky clouds that ceiled the dens of vast hosts, called cities—hotbeds of seething vice and crime, like foul insect swarms, in burnt earth and iron cells; promiscuous they lived, but under slavish rule, finding in crowd-created and encouraged pleasures, sensual and oblivious, sole refuge from despair.

Sha-wah-now long and intensely gazed. *He saw no red man's face.* But ere the simple question which his look betrayed, the demon mocked him, and was seen no more.

The chief aroused him from this horrid dream, and sought the calm of communion with nature.

The sun was now gone; but oh! how far on every side were mountains, some of majestic naked rock, some softly clothed with evergreens, clearly revealed in a flood of yellow light, or sharply outlined, to the earth's very border, it seemed, against a sky of purest air.

The solemn twilight was settling fast in the deep valleys; the last rays of the sun were reflected from some distant snows, which, like hope to the dying, rose over the deathlike gloom below, pointing toward heaven.

The universe, it seemed, was a solitude, where silence profound awaited a new creative voice.

And now, to those faded snows, the new moon and evening star began to beam, like an answering sign; and now, too, a sound of praise was heard in a gentle breeze, which stirred the mountain firs, as with a spirit anthem. Sha-wah-now was softened into prayer.

Yes, the Indian prays!—prays in these sublime solitudes, where he feels the Great Spirit very near!

Sha-wah-now thanked aloud the great Wah-con-dah, that he was there, firm in soul, and strong in arm, and asked but guidance in his desperate purpose.

But what was the motive of Sha-wah-now's perilous journey?

Though fierce and inexorable in war, eloquent and profound in council, he, like some of the greatest men, had reluctantly at first, and then with enthusiasm, yielded to the heart's ascendency.

Ayeta was the daughter of a brother chief. Early had she been marked as an extraordinary child; one of retiring modesty, and fond of pensive solitude. Her eye was remarkable, as different from almost all her race; it was blue, whilst the long lash and brow were of glossy black. Owing to youth and little exposure (she was the favorite and pride of her father), her complexion might have been envied as a clear brunette. Her mind was well fitted to so superior a mould. Sha-wah-now had marked her with a tender interest as early as her twelfth year. Before her sixteenth, he had wooed and won her heart. She admired him for those qualities which made him the pride of his nation, and which seemed to mark him as alone worthy to win so great a prize; but more from hidden sources had sprung that holy sympathy of love which bound their hearts.

But "the course of true love never did run smooth." War, relentless war, at once the scourge of love and pride of lovers, had fallen upon the tribe with unusual severity. Some of its governless, ambitious, and ever-restless youth had been unequal to a temptation to steal horses from their vagrant neighbors, the Chians; reprisals were made; at length a scalp was taken; the tribe was aroused to revenge; the warrior put on his red and black paint, and struck his battle-axe into the war-post. Cupid was frightened from his summer bower; the maidens trembled for their lovers; but each brave rejoiced in the confusion —in the storm which each aimed to direct.

But, for Indians, this war had been conducted with extraordinary severity. In the absence of a very large party, conducted by Sha-wah-now, the Chians made a daring irruption, and took many women and children—and, what was unusual, some warriors—prisoners, with whom they were now on their retreat. Returning, and unsuccessful, he learned the unhappy truth. The nation had suffered severely; his reputation was at stake; but his inmost soul confessed, that worse than all, was his Ayeta a prisoner! Great within him was the conflict of rage and despair; he retired from all witnesses that might discover his weakness. He deemed that a curse was on him; and, entirely alone, spent the night in fasting, and rude chants and prayers. He then made a vow to the great Wah-con-dah that he would not again enter a lodge, nor commune with his people, until he had avenged their honor, and rescued his betrothed from the hands of the foe; this he would do, or offer himself a sacrifice to the offended Deity.

Such was Sha-wah-now's desperate errand. He that night allowed himself but little rest, for as he approached the probable vicinity of his enemies, caution and concealment were necessary to that safety through which alone he could succeed. The next day in the trailed grass he discovered the fresh sign of a large party, the one, he was induced to believe, which he sought; ere dusk he had gained, by untiring exertions, a high point, from which to make a close survey of the surounding country. After a long and anxious examination he thought he had detected a slight appearance of smoke rising from a spot not very distant. But then it was most improbable that his enemies would thus betray their night-camp. He watched the spot until, to his strained eyes, the "sign" became wholly uncertain, and when nearly in despair of making so soon the much wished discovery, his keen and practised ear detected the sound of horses. He no longer doubted. He was prepared, mind and body, for every risk, and commenced his noiseless approach.

Hours were thus spent, but at length the whole truth was before him. He beheld, in a deep ravine below him, the camp of his foes, with the bound captives in the midst. The war-party, elated with success, and tired by the long and rapid excursion, had ventured, in their partial concealment, to light fires for better refreshment. Their dusky forms were extended in sleep around the dying embers. The horses were picketed almost in contact. Though eager for action, he made a deliberate survey of his enemies, and of the ground, both near and far as the eye could penetrate, by bright starlight. His plans were formed; but an obstacle to probable success was presented in the wakefulness of an Indian who sat near the captives, gnawing at a bone. What must he do? Wait till he should sleep? It was absolutely necessary. It seemed an age. And would not another take his place and watch? He knew that although they keep no sentinels, with all Indians in such camps, some one or a few are nearly always awake, generally eating. But at length his feverish anxiety was relieved; the unconsciously tantalizing Indian sank apparently into deep sleep. Now was his time or never. He commenced his stealthy approach, crawling flat on the earth, and was soon in the midst of those whose highest ambition was his scalp. He discovered his Ayeta; she was sunk in deathlike sleep. Sha-wah-now touched her form; she uttered a low murmur; he whispered in her ear, "Be silent or die." She opened her eyes, and beheld the warning face of her lover; his finger was on his lips, enjoining silence. By an effort of a well-disciplined mind, she suppressed any audible emotion. He cut the thong which bound her, and those of the other prisoners, but with the utmost caution not to arouse them. He then slowly extricated himself from among his sleeping foes; she as cautiously followed. He had cut loose a horse; he clasped the maiden to his heart, and sprung upon its back.

The first sounds of its motion, and the alarm was given. The Chians sprung to their feet. A moment for astonishment, a moment for discovery, and the next, an astounding yell of rage burst from the lips of all.

Some rushed forward on foot with uplifted tomahawks, others hastily strung their bows, whilst the first cares of the many were to secure and mount their horses. Favored by the obscurity, the arrows flew harmlessly by the fugitives. They could only be arrested by horsemen; and Sha-wah-now had chosen one of the best. Doubtful was the pursuit. Shame and rage stimulated the pursuers to desperate efforts. Darkness and the winding valleys favored the flight; but the enemy were widely dispersed, and all could not mistake the direction, though many were at fault. Encouraging shouts occasionally marked the point that all aimed at. But it would not do; the pursuers dropt off, until, at last, one, who had outstripped all the rest, was left to his efforts. This Sha-wah-now soon discovered; and right glad was he that it was no worse, for his jaded horse had begun to fail under its double burden. He was fast losing ground, and something must be done.

Sha-wah-now was one of those whose faculties seem inspired to the mastery of great emergencies where the multitude are confounded; and such men are known only in times of great or general calamity. Thus calm, he was prepared to meet the danger to which he considered his precious charge, rather than himself, was exposed. Practised in strategy as he was, a happy thought was soon suggested by the circumstances, which he hastened to execute. He spoke encouragingly to the half senseless girl; explained his intention; told her to sit firmly, and to continue to fly; and then easily slipping from the horse, suffered himself to fall flat upon the ground. As expected, the change was not noticed by his pursuer, who rapidly approached straight to the spot. The bow was strung, the arrow was notched, and when he was within a few paces, it whizzed through the air. By the time the horse had reached the chief, who stood tomahawk in hand, his reeling foe fell headlong to the earth. He gave a signal yell of triumph, hastily took the scalp, and having mounted the horse, was soon by the side of Ayeta.

Sha-wah-now now slackened his speed; but continuing steadily on, corrected his course as landmarks were recognized, with the view of reaching his village by the nearest route.

Soon after the sun had risen, they suddenly found themselves in full view of a large and mounted body of men. The chief was much alarmed at the new jeopardy in which he saw placed his beloved Ayeta, now well-nigh exhausted with such unwonted efforts. His first impulse was a new retreat, the chances of which he endeavored to scan, by rapid glances at the country around. But he soon perceived that such was impossible; that he had been discovered on the instant, and now about a score of them approached at full speed. But Sha-wah-now's practised eye had not failed ere they reached him, to penetrate their true character. They were friends, and of his own peculiar band. The delighted chief, exulting in his fortune, uttered the loud and swelling cry of triumph, in that well-known voice which now electrified this band of eighty devoted braves.

The first greetings over, the chief recounted to his brave friends, in the loud and rapid tones of eloquence, the incidents recorded; and announced to them his readiness instantly to lead them to pursuit and certain victory. His address was received with peals of applause, tinctured with that enthusiasm, with which master-spirits can never fail on occasion to inspire the multitude. Ayeta was intrusted to the care and guidance of a friend; and the chief, without further delay, set forth at a rapid pace, in the direction whence he came, at the head of the war party. The swift motion of fresh horses, and by daylight, carried them in a short time over the ground which he passed very slowly, after the pursuit had ceased. Within two or three miles of the enemy's camp, the troop came so suddenly upon a footman as to endanger his life in their bloodthirsty excitement; but he was instantly recognized. He was one of the captives whom Sha-wah-now had so thoughtfully released from the restraint of his bonds, and who, in the subsequent confusion, by large drafts upon that store of cunning, agility, and presence of mind, which Indians generally possess, had made good his escape, so far as to reach a neighboring place of concealment; and there he lay perdu, until the enemy had taken their departure, which they did at daylight, with some indications of haste, if not confusion. This was a fortunate rencontre in two respects: for it so happened, the fugitive was one of the best guides of the nation, who, in the spirit of that habit of observation, which was the foundation of his skill, had watched critically the course which they took, and remarked those general features of the country which must necessarily modify it. He was mounted by direction of Sha-wah-now, behind one of his followers, and undertook to lead the party by a near route, which would intercept the retreat of the Chians.

His judgment was verified by the result; for the sun had not passed in his course to the meridian, through many more than that number of degrees which we designate an hour, when, on issuing from the defile of two abrupt hills, upon one of those high level "table land" prairies, the enemy were exposed to view. The leader, by a powerful effort, suppressed a yell which was incipient in so many open throats, and led them at a sweeping, but little noisy gait, a good space—which was all gained—ere, owing to these precautions, they were discovered.

The instant that was ascertained, he ordered a charge, and set them a powerful example in one of those shrill outbursts of sound, of which the object, intimidation or panic, is often attained. It has an awkward effect upon the nerves, the sudden salute of fierce and quavering yells, especially when you see its accompaniment of extravagant and threatening action; the flourishing of arms, the brandishing of spears, and the glaring colors of paint and feathers.

But the Chians made efforts at organized resistance, honorable under the circumstances—of surprise, and the furious onset of rather superior numbers; and their leaders too, were absent. Its only result was the loss, upon the spot, of some of their bravest men. A superstitious anticipation of misfortune (to which Indians are subject), seemed to have taken hold upon their minds from the moment of their disaster in the night. The natural result was a panic, which soon led to a flight of desperate disorder. The scene which ensued, the East can never witness; and its stirring interest, the *regular* shock of embattled thousands can scarcely equal. A race, a fox chase, an ordinary battle, are but in comparative progression toward the intensity of excitement, which the sight and sounds of that flight and pursuit inspired! And it *was* witnessed by two spectators, under peculiarly painful circumstances. The Chians had been led by two "partisans," who, at the moment of the surprise, were separated from their command, together on a hill, for the purpose of reconnoitring. For a few of those moments, big with results, they seemed paralyzed by their misfortune; but quickly recovering, their minds were intensely wrought upon to decide upon the alternatives—death or dishonor. They decided differently. The one, with a devotion unsurpassed in ancient or modern times, rushed onward to certain death. He charged furiously into the midst of his foes, and all alone, bravely fought and fell! His enemies, full of admiration, spared his scalp!

The Chians, on the verge of the prairie, found themselves rushing down the descent of what seemed a valley, and congratulated themselves with the hopes which uneven ground inspired; but their cruel fates had decreed them unlimited misfortune. The valley soon fearfully narrowed, and finally ended in a ravine or immense gully, at the bottom of which was a stagnant pool; into this the wretched fugitives were precipitated by an impetus which was irresistible, and all found their death. Their other leader, the only survivor, returned in safety to his tribe, and was suffered, by a species of cruel mercy, to live, thenceforth, the life of a despised and miserable outcast.

Sha-wah-now entered his village in an imposing procession of triumph; in which, after the liberated prisoners, all of whom he had safely rescued, the most imposing spectacle was seventy reeking scalps, borne aloft on spears, the bearers of which chanted triumphal songs. But were not his thoughts busy with the humble Ayeta? Her safety he esteemed the happiest fortune of that eventful day. The grateful and devoted maiden thenceforth graced his lodge.

Sha-wah-now had performed deeds that day, that could add lustre to even *his* name; and long he lived, ever sustaining his reputation and unrivalled influence. But at the festival, he ever recounted the rescue of his cherished Ayeta, as his greatest action.

It is recorded, with the subsequent victory, upon a buffalo robe, in rude hieroglyphics, which were explained to me by an old chief, as a proud record of his tribe.

This romantic story did not escape some good-natured ridicule, in which the words "love-sick" and "unnatural," did not fail to be heard. After some discussion, Phil. assured the critics that all the circumstances of the battle and massacre were *true* and *accurate:* and this advantage gained, he began a serious argument to prove the high-toned, intelligent, and even romantic character often exhibited by the better Indian,—when suddenly he bethought him, rather to demand of one of the critics, a story of his own; when D., a little to his surprise, promised to comply, so far as to give us, some other time, an account of some incidents which had really happened to a Punca woman.

CHAPTER X.

THE next evening, accordingly, we were all assembled on the grass in expectation of the story, when D., after a little rallying, delivered himself as follows:

MAH-ZA-PA-MEE.

The Punca Indians are a reduced band; their warriors amount to no more than one hundred and fifty. They are invariably friendly to whites; and are noted for bravery and swiftness of foot. Their village is at the mouth of the L'eau-qui-court, on the Missouri, a thousand miles from the spot where that river mingles with the Mississippi. In the spring of '14, a calumet party of about twenty Grand Pawnees paid them a visit in their villages; the two tribes being on as good terms as Indians ever are. These are called by us, begging parties; but with a desire always to make the best of human nature, I would ascribe to them less degrading motives; for though custom decrees that presents be made on such occasions, all in turn give and receive. The visitors were "smoked" as usual; feasted on fat dogs; and then they sang, danced, and "counted their coups." What a simple but powerful incentive to virtue (Indian virtue), is this custom! and how innocently is ambition thus sated! The time is night; brilliant fires burn around; the stately chiefs are seated with all the cross-legged dignity of Turkish Pachas; the animating music of the song peals forth; the exhilarated braves dance with emulous ardor and activity;—for a moment they cease;—one of them recounts a *coup*, deposits some article of small value, and tells the actor in a greater feat, to take it as his own. The dance is renewed with increased animation, till at length another relates his superior adventure;—his form seems to swell, his eye glistens with delight, as he removes the prize and lays it at the feet of the chief. Long they continue, but with endless variety; until finally the chief distributes the simple honors, and thus adds his sanction to the merit of the prizes. *Fashion* decides that modesty is not wanting in this self-praise; but it also requires and has the most powerful means to enforce, that the recital be the strictest truth. Thus does the red man of our forests closely imitate the noblest customs of Greece, in the day of her virtue and renown!

Thus were the visitors treated; but a faithless return was made for open-handed hospitality. A young brave of their number, being very *unceremoniously* entertained by the principal chief, Shu-da-gah-ha, and his family, easily discovered an unfortunate difference; a jealousy between his two wives; and, struck with the appearance of the favorite, Mah-za-pa-mee—for she was a pretty woman—he determined to improve a temporary advantage, and engage in an intrigue. His affections, and ambition too, became engaged in the suit, and he warmly urged it. His good looks and eloquence combined to persuade her that nothing could equal the Pawnees, and the delightful life they led: he told her that they killed more buffaloes, planted more corn and pumpkins, and had more scalp dances than any other nation; and above all, they stole more horses too, and their squaws never walked. How could she resist so happy a picture! She did not: she consented to fly with him to the promised paradise. His arrangements were easily made; and the next night, like Paris, the beau *ideal* of beaux, he escaped triumphantly with this modern Helena. Mah-za-pa-mee took with her an infant son; and, guided by her lover, in due time arrived at the village of the Grand Pawnees, on the Rio-do-la-plata, *Anglice*, the Big Platte.

On discovering the flight, the chief was quite outrageous: it was too late for pursuit: they had taken the best horses; but the sacrifice of the remaining Pawnees, until then perfectly ignorant of the proceeding, could well appease his ire; and, though innocent, they had paid with their lives the forfeit of the indiscretion, but for the active influence of Manuel Lisa. They were dismissed without presents, and with dishonor. But Shu-da-gah-ha had more pride or policy than Menelaus, and war did not immediately result.

Not long after this affair, a small party of Dahcotahs, probably to prove the truth of Hobbes' theory of our nature, by carrying on a war, "whereof the memory of man runneth not to the contrary," directed their footsteps to the village of the Grand Pawnees; and there prowled about undiscovered, until at length they killed and scalped a son-in-law of that very distinguished chief Car-ra-ra-ka-wah-wah-ho, whom the whites called Long Hair. This was done in darkness, and very near the village. A trail cannot be followed at night; but very early the next morning, eighty braves were in pursuit as fast as their chargers would carry them. During the night, the Sioux had not been idle. An Indian afoot can travel as far perhaps in twenty-four hours, as another on horseback. The next morning, the sun arose upon them near fifty miles from the Pawnee village; the Pawnees perceived from their trail, that their enemies were but five or six in number, which induced them to continue in untiring pursuit for three days. The Sioux, in their flight, passed by the Punca village, simply because it was in their nearest direction home. The conscience-stricken Pawnees had, from the first, suspected them to be Puncas; but on perceiving that the trail led directly to their village, doubt yielded to certainty in their minds, and they continued the pursuit—not to attack the Puncas, but in the hope, if failing to overtake the party, to cut off some straggler at a respectful distance from the village. Accordingly, when arrived within two miles of it on the fourth day, they were delighted to discover two young Punca hunters; they instantly engaged in hot pursuit. But the ground was much broken, and the young Puncas were determined that the reputation of their tribe for swiftness of foot, should not suffer on this occasion; so they ran like heroes, for their lives were at stake. The Pawnees did not dream of their escaping; nor did they, which was more important, perceive how near they were approaching the village, so warmly were their imaginations engaged with the idea of the two scalps that were careering before them. But the Puncas did escape, and soon did they make it known; for never, till then, was heaven's conclave saluted with such horrid discord. The braves all yelled like devils; each squaw howled for *ten*, and wolf-dogs were ten to their one, and gave distinguished proof of the power of their lungs. The luckless urchin that disturbs a nest of hornets, is not more warmly assailed, or sooner put to his heels, than were the panic-struck Pawnees by this nest of fiery Puncas. Those that could not lay hands on horses, sallied forth scarce the less swiftly on foot. Away! away, they went! with what a sublime confusion of sound and motion! a mighty chase, with life and death upon the issue! On! on they go! now they dash into that bushy ravine, and how the awful din is mellowed. But the hill is gained, and they burst pell-mell into view with that astounding shout! Away! away! Now, Pawnee, do thy best! Hear that cutting sound, that shrill war cry! sweet music to the Punca; to the Pawnee, the jarring signal of his doom. Six times was heard that well-known yell of Shu-da-gah-ha. He was avenged. Noble feats of horsemanship were that day performed by the best of riders; feats which made one shudder to examine in cold blood. But most of the horses were run down and abandoned, and Punca and Pawnee ran on foot. The latter threw away their guns, and strewed the prairie with cumbrous finery; and to this, many were indebted for their safety. The Puncas ceased to pursue at night, more than twenty miles from their village; they had taken eight scalps, and captured many horses and guns.

Thus we see two tribes fairly in a war, originating in

the indiscretion of Mah-za-pa-mee, which led to the mistake which caused the war.

But, to return to our heroine and the Pawnee village. In due time, the foremost of the scattered messengers of misfortune arrived: it was in the night. Fortunately, Mah-za-pa-mee had made a warm friend of an old squaw, who hastened with the first news of the disaster, to warn her of her impending danger; for then no one could doubt the fate that was in store for her; she and her son would be sacrificed to Pawnee revenge. The old woman furnished her with moccasins and smoked meat, and she immediately escaped from the village, alone and on foot; and she took with her her son.

This was late in June; and she determined "to strike" for the nearest waters of the L'eau-qui-court, hoping to meet her band, who usually followed up that river on the summer buffalo hunt. Her meat was soon gone, and roots were her sole resource; and she was without any means of kindling a fire. Thus she journeyed, carrying on her back her child, now two years old, enduring the scorching heat of the shadeless prairie by day, and chilled by its cold dews at night. Thus simply are the facts narrated. But who shall paint to the senses the full horror of her sufferings of mind and body!

She reached the L'eau-qui-court, and found that her entire tribe had passed many days before. Mah-za-pa-mee did not despair. She could not hope to overtake them; but for days, she searched their trail and camps, endeavoring to find something left or "cached" that would serve for food: but all failed. She then resolved to follow down the river, and, if able, to reach the village; she would find there green corn and pumpkins, always planted before the annual hunting migration. More than a hundred miles were before her, starved and burdened as she was, wasted by the extremes of the weather, and ever assailed by that maddening pest, the musquito. But her life was prolonged by the small fish which she caught in shallow streams and pools, and they of course were eaten raw!

Late in August, Mah-za-pa-mee reached the vicinity of her village on the Missouri: and she found it—oh! last stroke of unrelenting fate!—occupied by hostile Indians, before whom the last vestiges of vegetation were fast disappearing. She hid herself, but yielded to despair.

Mah-za-pa-mee and her son were discovered the next day by a white man of Mr. Lisa's company. He was of a small party that had been left in charge of a storehouse, some distance below: provisions having become scarce, they had ascended the river to see if the Puncas had returned with a supply of meat. Their appearance when found, was described as emaciated, wretched, and even horrible. And, indeed, if there were room for it, who would not doubt the possibility of their surviving?

Under no other circumstances does poor human nature show so much its weakness, become so much degraded, as when assailed by starvation. Famine! nought but thou canst reduce proud, gifted, noble man, to the level of the wretched beast. Thou shakest his reason from its pedestal! Thou makest him yield all to revolting appetite! But, no more.—Mah-za-pa-mee, well and hearty, would probably have terminated an existence then worth preserving, rather than meet her husband thus humbled, and a petitioner; but now, suffering worse than death—the loathsome picture of famine—true to the singular nature of her species, clinging the more closely to life—

she seeks to offer herself before her injured lord, for a mouthful of food.

Mah-za-pa-mee at length rejoined her tribe, and sought to throw herself at the feet of her husband. Pity is allied to affection; and much was she to be pitied: but chiefly was she to depend upon her child, that inseparable link of union, for forgiveness. It was that which succeeded: for surely the chief, Shu-da-gah-ha, did not believe her, that the Pawnee threw "squaw medicine" (love powder) on her; that "he bewitched her." She was forgiven, grew apace in flesh and favor, and has since been, as has her son, healthy and happy.

CHAPTER XI.

ONE day, about the end of August, to our utter astonishment, we saw the approach of a white man, on foot, and in tattered garments, and so poor he seemed scarce able to walk. He was instantly surrounded by a crowd, and recognized to be Corporal Arter, whom we had left at Fort Leavenworth. The following is the substance of his story. He had been sent with another man, about two months before, well mounted, as an express, with some order for us from General L. After striking the Arkansas in safety, they were one day suddenly surrounded by fifteen mounted Indians, armed with bow and spear; they did not offer immediate violence, and the Corporal succeeded in extricating himself and companion; when the latter, in good feeling produced by their forbearance, returned, in spite of the Corporal's remonstrance, if not orders, to give them some tobacco; and while in this act, was wounded by the thrust of a spear in his breast; the Indians instantly scattered to avoid a shot from the Corporal, one of them dropping his bull-hide shield; and the Corporal, at the expense of horses and baggage, rescued the wounded man, and judiciously reserving his fire, stood over him, keeping the Indians off for several hours, and receiving a slight arrow wound in his wrist; they seemed particularly anxious to recover the shield, which he gallantly defended. After the Indians were gone, Arter helped the wounded man to the river, and constructed a rough shelter for him. He had lost his ammunition, and was compelled to sustain life by eating a part of a diseased ox we had left, and snakes, frogs, &c. Soon after his adventure, he left the wounded man, Nation, as well provided for as possible, and followed our trail to the point of our crossing the river, and then gave it up for a time as hopeless, and returned to his charge. Afterwards he had heard, he thought, the sound of cannon, and soon after made this successful effort to find us. A command, with an ox-cart, was immediately sent after Nation; they found him twelve or fifteen miles below, and brought him to camp that night; but the poor fellow lingered some weeks, and then died.

The 10th of October had been named by the traders, and agreed to by the commanding officer, as the very last day of our stay waiting for them. The time approached—the weather was growing cold. We had frosty mornings, and the summer clothing of the men was nearly worn out. The 10th came, and no caravan; it was determined to wait *one* day longer; and accordingly, having waited during the 11th, the next morning, at sunrise, one gun was fired, and we turned our faces homewards.

About 9 o'clock horsemen were seen following us at full speed; the battalion was halted, and disposed for action, covering the baggage. As they approached in view of this preparation they drew rein, and the commanding officer and his staff advanced to parley, but soon discovered that they were white traders; the caravan was a few miles beyond the river: our cannon shot had been heard, and these men sent on to overtake us. We proceeded to the nearest fit camping ground, and established our camp. We learned that the caravan was accompanied by an escort of a company of regulars, and a body of Mexican militia, or Indians. Major R. had written to the chief of the province of Santa Fe, requesting this co-operation in the protection of a trade beneficial to both countries; and Colonel Viscarro, Inspector-General of the Mexican army, happening to be there, had volunteered to conduct a command accordingly.

A day or two before, they had been visited by several hundreds of Ar-ra-pa-hoes and Camanches (our old friends), who were on foot, and seemed to be on a horse-stealing expedition. They pretended friendship, as the best way, doubtless, of effecting their purposes. A guarded intercourse took place, and Col. V. was warned by some of his Indians, and the traders, not to trust them: at last, as Col. V. was talking to their chief, the latter, being a few feet off, presented his gun and fired. One of the Colonel's Indians, who had been most suspicious, and stood by watching, with heroic devotion, sprang between, just in time to receive the ball through his own heart. He had a brother near by, who, as the Indian chief turned to fly, sprang upon him like a tiger, and buried his knife to the hilt in his back. Almost at the same instant another chief fell, by a shot from a trader, who had marked him in anticipation of the result. The Indians fled, and many of the Mexican militia and the traders pursued them on horseback. The ammunition of the Indians soon gave out, and their pursuers would overtake them in succession, dismount, fire, take the scalp—without being particular whether the man was dead or not—reload, and pursue again; several of the traders were mentioned as having killed three or four in this manner—like turkey shooting—and perhaps nothing but nightfall saved the whole party from destruction. It was not ascertained that the Mexican regulars shed any blood on the occasion; but on the other hand, we were assured that the cruelty and barbarity of some of the Americans disgusted even the Mexicans and Spaniards; that they scalped one Indian at least, who had life enough left to contend against it, though without arms; and they undoubtedly took the skin from some of the bodies, and stretched it on their wagons. I, myself, saw several scalps dangling as ornaments to the bridle of a trader.

Several of our officers returned with a trader to conduct the caravan to our camp; they arrived in the course of the day, and encamped near by. That evening Captain W. invited Colonel Viscarro, Captain Obrazo, and another gentleman, secretary, and since Governor of Sante Fe, with whom he became acquainted before they arrived, to sup at our tent. I distinctly remember the feast we gave them. Seated cross-legged around a green blanket in the bottom of the tent; we partook of bread, buffalo meat, and, as an extraordinary rarity, some salt pork; but to crown all, were several large raw onions, for which we were indebted to the arrival of our guests;

a tin cup of whiskey, which, like the pork, had been reserved for an unusual occasion, was passed round, *followed* by another of water.

Col. V. was a man of fine appearance, and of perfectly dignified and gentlemanly manners. His horsemanship —extraordinary for a Spaniard—had been witnessed that day by Captain W.: an immense drove of horses, &c., which they brought, was frightened, and disposed to run; he rode at full speed to prevent it, and seemed in many places at once; stopping his horse, with the aid of the unmerciful Spanish bit, in full career, more suddenly than if shot, and throwing him on his haunches, he would whirl him around, and cause him to plant the fore foot, with equal speed, in an opposite direction. On the march he had pursued a noble wild horse, which baffled all others, and both being at utmost speed, had thrown his lazo, for a fore foot, and caught it! Unfortunately the shock broke the poor animal's leg, when the Colonel drew an arrow, and shot him through the heart.

The next day we had time to look about us, and admire the strangest collection of men and animals that had perhaps ever met on a frontier of the United States. There were a few Creoles—polished gentlemen, magnificently clothed in Spanish costume; a large number of grave Spaniards, exiled from Mexico, and on their way to the United States, with much property in stock and gold—their whole equipage Spanish; there was a company of Mexican Regulars, as they were called, in uniform,—mere apologies for soldiers, or even men; several tribes of Indians, or Mexicans, much more formidable as warriors, were grouped about with their horses, and spears planted in the ground; Frenchmen were there *of course;* and our 180 hardy veterans in rags, but well armed and equipped for any service: four or five languages were spoken; but to complete the picture, must be mentioned the 2000 horses, mules, jacks, which kept up an incessant braying. The Spaniards and their attendants were in motion, throwing the lazo, catching wild mules; and others dashed off after buffalo, which seemed disposed to send representatives to this Congress of the men and animals of two nations. I remember, too, that some Camanche dogs came over the hills into camp, from a direction opposite to that of the march of the Mexicans; but this strange circumstance was hardly noticed, though I did hear some one ask, "Where the d—l did those wild geese come from?" as a pair of them were seen dodging about.

The battalion was reviewed and drilled for the edification of the Mexican officers; and then a company of light infantry at the old tactics (which being admirably suitable, and truly American, has been dropped). Afterwards we visited the Mexican camp, when their motley force was drawn up: to judge from the appearance of their arms, &c., a volley from the regular company, at fifty paces, would have proved of small consideration. After their dismissal, we fell in with a group who were singing, and introduced, in some way to their conclusion, the name of GEORGE WASHINGTON; whereupon one of them advanced, hat in hand, for a collection. Their officers were much mortified, and kicked him off; while we considered it laughable to be thus called upon, in consideration that a single piece of money was unknown in our camp, where the very existence of "a circulating medium" had been so long useless as to be almost forgotten.

I saw a characteristic exploit of one of the southern

mongrels—a camp follower. He rode a blindfolded, unbridled donkey in pursuit of a buffalo, at which he continued to snap an antique firepiece, until it was almost out of sight.

We all dined, by invitation, with Colonel V. and his officers; his tent was very large and comfortable, oval in shape, and quite roomy. We sat down, about sixteen, to a low table, all the furniture of which was silver; which, however, we scarcely noticed, in view of their inviting contents, among which was fried ham. This course was followed by another of various kinds of cakes, and delightful chocolate; and there were several kinds of Mexican wines. All had been brought, no doubt, for the occasion, direct from Santa Fe.

In the dusk of evening, a large group of the Mexican Indians came into camp, bearing aloft on spears the scalps which they had lately taken, and singing Indian songs; dark figures, with matted hair streaming over their shoulders, uttering the wild notes of their deep-toned choruses, they resembled demons rather than men. Suddenly one would enter the circle, and indulge in an extravagant display of grief, beating his forehead and breast, and howling like a famished wolf; and then dashing the scalps to the ground, stamp on them, and fire his gun at them. After this propitiatory lament to the manes of a departed friend, or relation, he would burst forth, with the others, into the wildest and most unearthly song of triumph and exultation.

The Indian who had lost, and avenged his brother, as related, had been in camp in the day; he was a fine fellow, and seemed inconsolable. He made us speeches, unintelligible of course; but expanding his bare chest, and striking it forcibly with his palm, he would end them by exclaiming, "Me die for the Americans."

CHAPTER XII.

On the 14th of October, having relieved the Mexicans of their charge, we took a very friendly parting, and again marched early on our return. Soon after, we saw smokes arise over the distant hills; evidently signals, indicating to different parties of Indians our separation and march. Of what purport, whether preparatory to an attack upon the Mexicans, or ourselves, or rather our immense drove of animals, we could only guess.

The passage over prairies with horses or cattle, while it is free from all money expense for forage, is attended with the trouble, risk, and delays of grazing. There is always danger of horses straying off, being frightened by accident, or driven by an enemy. To provide against trouble and danger in our case, with our few cattle, a plan of camp for the return march was adopted, which *inclosed* them in a space large enough for grazing. The tents of three companies were pitched in single lines around three sides of a square, the parallel sides of which were equally extended by two rows of wagons, while the fourth company, on guard, completed the parallelogram.

For these places of camp, and many other benefits, we conceived ourselves indebted to our Adjutant, the lamented J. F. Izard, who fell gallantly in Florida. As an humble tribute to the memory of so brave, so talented, so accomplished a soldier, I can truly say, that, on this expedition, he was never known to fail in the zealous, thorough, and exemplary performance of any single point, important or minute, of any duty that could possibly be construed to be his; besides frequently volunteering to perform the arduous details of others. He is gone—but has left us the bright example of his life and his death.

Unhappy Florida! Thy soil has drunk the heart's blood of the army! Thou hast robbed her and the country of IZARD, and LANE, and BROOKE, and a host of other brave spirits, whose loss is irreparable.

Our march was constantly attended by immense collections of buffalo, which seemed to have a general muster, perhaps for migration. We found them much further eastward than we had met them. Sometimes a hundred or two—a fragment from the immense multitude—would approach within two or three hundred yards of the column, and threaten a charge, which at best would have proved disastrous to the mule-drivers and their charge. Mounted flanking parties of traders were then kept out.

The weather was very cold, and we had generally black frosts. One day it snowed a little, and seventy mules were abandoned and left, being overcome by fatigue and cold. It must not be supposed that the prairie-grass was now fit for grazing; on the contrary, so dry and rigid had it become, that it wore the feet of unshod animals until they bled; and we had to make buffalo-hide shoes, or rather moccasins, for many of the oxen; but in the river and creek bottoms, particularly where there was timber, or where they had been burned early in summer (which can always be done when they escape the previous winter), we always found green and tender grazing, sufficient for our wants.

It is surprising in what fine training our campaign had put us all (to say nothing of our fine health; and, among the men—unable to commit excesses—not a case of sickness had occurred). One day an immense gray wolf had the audacity to trot through the lines of wagons, and I set off afoot in pursuit, regardless of the laughter of my companions, who derided the idea of outrunning a wolf. I nevertheless did overtake him, and brought him to bay, when he jumped and snapped at me, with a disagreeable clatter of tusks. I was only armed with a pistol, and unluckily, owing to a very high wind, it snapped repeatedly, and I left the gentleman to take his course; but, in returning, I saw a camp-follower take my place, with a rusty sword, with which he attacked him. The wolf rushed at him, and received several blows over the head; when making a motion to turn tail, his antagonist as gladly seized the opportunity of doing likewise, and they exhibited the extraordinary and laughable spectacle of enemies running away from each other with all speed, at the same moment.

After passing 110-Mile Creek, we marched twenty-five miles without water, and then found the little branch, on which we depended, to be dry. A hole, filled with water, was however discovered six or eight hundred yards to the left; but for some unaccountable cause we were marched near two miles further, and encamped where the country was as dry as tinder; and, in fact, we were threatened with fire;—a long line of it, extending across the immense prairie, was gradually approaching. I was ordered, with some fifty men, to secure the camp, by burning round it, when a wild fellow, with a blazing brand, ran along firing so much at once that the matter was like to be made worse; it rapidly approached in a great sheet of flame to the ammunition wagon, and would have swept the camp but for the greatest exertions, to which I set the example, in the sacrifice of a cloak, and some damage to whiskers and eyebrows.

To my astonishment, my mess was that night supplied

with a keg of water, for which two of my men had gone, unasked, near two miles. But about midnight it commenced raining hard and steadily, and it continued for eighteen hours; and, but for this, it seemed impossible that the cattle could have got on; they were few in number, and had suffered much before, and, indeed, the men were required to assist in pulling the empty wagons for several days' march. The piece of artillery which had been pulled out in fine style by six mules, came back with a yoke of oxen.

The next day we marched twenty-five or thirty miles through a hard rain; and, bearing off to the left, struck a bold creek and encamped.

In our long absence from the world, and with so little occupation for the mind, it seemed that our imaginations had become disordered, and we had lost the power of forming a just estimate of the most familiar objects. I saw a group of officers examining, with seeming admiration, a brass-mounted rifle which they found in the hands of an Indian hunter; and when the friends of the traders met them with fresh horses from the settlements, I thought them, at a little distance, splendid stallions, when they were, in reality, work mares, though in fine order. Such questions as, "Is the President dead?" were asked of these men.

The day after the hard march mentioned above, I walked twelve miles in three hours, without the slightest fatigue. We returned by the Agency on the Kansas; and the log-houses there, were the first habitations of men we had seen for five months.

Under the friendly cover of the shades of evening, on the 8th of November, our tatterdemalion veterans marched into Fort Leavenworth, and took quiet possession of the miserable huts and sheds left by the 3d infantry the preceding May.

CHAPTER XIII.

FORT LEAVENWORTH was re-occupied by our battalion; a "fort" by courtesy, or rather by order; it was in reality but a straggling cantonment, but on an admirable site. The Missouri, in an abrupt bend, rushes with wondrous swiftness against a rock-bound shore; from this the ground rises with a bold sweep to a hundred feet or more, then sloping gently into a shallow vale, it rises equally again, and thus are formed a number of hills, which are to the north connected by a surface but slightly bent, to which the vale insensibly ascends; every line of every surface is curved with symmetry and beauty. On these hill-tops, shaded by forest trees, stands Fort Leavenworth. On the one hand is to be seen the mighty river, winding in the distance through majestic forests and by massive bluffs, stretching away till mellowed to aerial blue; on the other, rolling prairies, dotted with groves, and bounded on the west by a bold grassy ridge; this, inclosing in an elliptical sweep a beautiful amphitheatre, terminates five miles southward in a knob, leaving between it and the river a view of the prairie lost in a dim and vague outline. How feeble are words! how inadequate to give a general idea, much more to paint this rare scenery, where grandeur is softened by beauty, and the beautiful enhanced and dignified by a magnificent outline.

Blessed with an harmonious and congenial though small

society, the days, the months, flew by. Our duties performed, and studious improvement not neglected, the pleasures of female society gave the greater zest to diversions and exercises. Often the whole of us, in a party, would canter for miles through prairie and grove, and spend the day on the shady banks of a pretty stream; there, where the world had never made its mark—forgetful of its very existence—we gave our whole hearts to sylvan sports, to feast and merriment, to happiness. A week seldom passed without dancing parties, to which rare beauty and fine music lent their attractions. Sentinels on a distant frontier, ever ready to throw ourselves in the face of savage enemies, though severed from the world with its selfish jarring interests, its contentions and tortuous intrigues, its eternal struggle for dollars, we continued, amid our books and social pleasures, with hunting and the chase, to pass happy years. We always enjoyed the contemplation of Nature in her untamed beauty, fresh as from the hands of the Creator. The greatest danger of our situation was that lethargy and rust of mind, so naturally induced where no exciting motive, no *necessity*, urges on to the labor of exertion. It is not in human nature, in such passive circumstances, long to escape their impression. But some of us strove hard to improve those faculties which an unhappy world would not always, as then, suffer to slumber.

But we were not without our visitors from the world, who sufficiently refreshed our conceptions of its existence and nature; nor, from the regions of *our* far West, the then accomplished officers of the Indian Department, from agencies between us and the Rocky Mountains, and some members of the Fur Company, fresh from natural scenes, and full of racy anecdote of adventure; they were frequently an enlivening addition to our small society. The memories of these years come back as in moments of tranquil enjoyment some happy dream steals on our rapt senses—a past too kindly for reality—gilded by loving thought.

In the summer of 1831, wishing to extend my knowledge of the country, and weary of inactivity, I obtained leave of absence, in order to accompany an officer of the Indian Department on an official visit to the villages of the Otto and Omahaw Indians, and the Old Council Bluff in their vicinity. We took with us a French servant, or *engagé*, named Godfrey, and had a pack-horse, which carried a tent and provisions. Our route was to be by the south side of the Missouri.

The first day we rode but a few miles, our hired man being very drunk, as is usual with these fellows on such occasions, when their services are most needed. He fell from his horse on some tin-cups, and mashed them nearly flat; and I discovered with some surprise that they could not be restored to any approximation of their original shape. The pack-horse, at the camp-ground, turned his pack, and succeeded in kicking a small bag of crackers very nearly to the original state of flour. A good start is worth a day's journey.

Next day we got along more comfortably. Our course lay altogether over prairies, but in view generally of the timber of the river, and always of some small tributary. This night we encamped on one of the miry creeks, very difficult to cross, which here abound, indicating a country as rich as it is beautiful. This was about fifty-six miles above Fort Leavenworth.

Tuesday, June 14th. We got over the boggy stream by 6 o'clock; after riding about twelve miles over rolling prairie, we suddenly beheld before us the beautiful valley of the Grand Nemehaw; far below us stretched out, a mile and a half in width, the level prairie bottom, studded with numberless flowers of every brilliant color; the margin of the river was fringed and relieved by stately trees; five elks, disturbed by our approach, slowly galloped away along the hillside. But our attention was withdrawn from this beautiful scene; for, rather suddenly, half of the heavens were obscured by an immense black cloud; reaching from the horizon on either side, it culminated dark as night. All thoughts were turned to securing ourselves from the storm, and, placing the river behind us; we hastened on, and fortunately struck its bank where a large tree had been felled across. Removing our saddles and pack we carried them over; Godfrey swam his horse across, the others following. We mounted to seek drier ground, and about half a mile above encamped on a small prairie: we were near the edge of the bank; along and below it grew scattered trees, enough to conceal the course of the river, which made a bend above; the "bluff," or prairie hill opposite us, was half a mile distant. By the time the tent was pitched and the horses hobbled, the storm broke over us with an awful crash of thunder and lightning, which seemed close above and around us. It rained in showers from midday until dark—then it wonderfully increased; for hours it fell as violently as I had ever seen before in storms at the moment of greatest force.

We remained sitting up in the tent, our provisions, &c., raised on the saddles, and covered with blankets; our candle was put out by the rain about nine o'clock. Near eleven we determined to lie down, though the ground was thoroughly soaked, and we were wet to the skin. In about an hour the rain began to fall more steadily and moderately, and I fell asleep.

About three o'clock I was aroused, and found myself lying in water. A conviction that we were flooded was soon forced upon our minds, for the water rapidly increased in depth. The darkness was palpable. We were overwhelmed with astonishment that the river could in that time overflow its banks, and attached an importance to our awful situation which those who must see us alive and well can never appreciate. Various plans of escape or safety were now proposed. Godfrey thought we would have to take a tree, and "live on one of the horses." Fortunately daylight began to dawn, when we discovered our horses close by, trembling with fear. The water was now near knee deep, though not over the grass. I observed a remarkable bank of fog, I thought, along the foot of the hills. We had to fish for our bridles, &c., at arm's length in the water. The white fog sensibly approached, and we discovered it was water—the river in a new channel! Our preparations were hurried—the tent was left standing—I abandoned a blanket. Mr. B. was at length mounted, and tried the depth of water in several directions. I proposed to follow up the margin of the bank, knowing it was there the shallowest. I mounted my trembling horse, when he mired, plunged, and seemed incapable of exertion. I got off, and left him loose to follow. The water was half-thigh deep; I became much exhausted, and stopped and pulled off my woollen pantaloons, and threw them over my shoulder; my companions had stuck to their horses, and were far ahead; I feared to step over the bank and be swept off. At the bend I discovered the bluff, three hundred yards off. It was now quite light; I made for the hill through a swift current above my waist, and at length reaching the new shore, offered up my thanks.

I threw myself on the ground, and was soon pleased and surprised to see the approach of our pack-horse, which Godfrey had left to take care of himself. I stopped him, and finding a bottle of brandy had been saved, took a hearty drink.

On the hill-top we made a fire, and unpacked everything to dry. The cries of drowning fawns were heard the whole forenoon, and many deer swam out in our neighborhood. The river had risen now about twenty feet perpendicular: perhaps four of which, on an average, was over an expanse of two miles. I believe it had not rained over any part of its course earlier than at this point.

June 15th. After having dried our clothing, &c., and recovered the tent, about mid-day, we were mounted, and rode some ten miles west, endeavoring to "head" a little stream, emptying into the Nemehaw just below the camp; which, though now impassable, and three hundred yards wide, might the morning before have been almost stepped across. The country presents a uniform succession of prairie hills, jutting out from the more elevated ridges toward the larger creeks. On arriving at the top of one of them, we saw some hundred yards distant two deer. I instantly dismounted, fired my rifle, and one of them fell dead: it was a doe; its companion, a buck, stood gazing at us for some minutes, while Godfrey, slowly dismounting, aimed and fired; it then moved slowly off, untouched. I was well pleased, admiring the apparent chivalry of the poor animal, deliberately standing fire over the body of his unfortunate mate.

June 16th. A few miles took us around the fountain-head of the small stream, and after passing a very high prairie, the dividing ridge between the two Nemehaws, and two very boggy branches, at ten o'clock we struck their main creek, which presented a very formidable aspect; the bottom, a half-mile wide, was flooded, two feet deep; we rode through to its bank, and found it evidontly impassable, there being no timber—retraced our steps, went on a half mile, waded again to its bank, felled a tree across, led in a horse, which, swimming to the opposite bank, endeavored in vain to mount it. Notwithstanding our assistance, the poor animal remained in the water for hours, whilst we all, standing in the mire, worked hard to get it over, hoping to save its life; at last we tried the same side it had entered, which was apparently, that is, above water, much the most difficult, and succeeded in helping it out. We then once more returned to the hill, and encamped near by. I began to think it an exceedingly unpleasant *pleasure trip*, but consoled myself with shooting a curlew, sixty yards, off hand, with a rifle ball; its bill was more than four inches long, and of the size of a rye straw.

17th. Passed three hours in making a third and successful attempt to cross this vile stream at a new place. Went E. of N., and soon came in sight of the Little Nemehaw River, which in its scenery most strikingly resembles its "Grand" namesake, though we thought, after wading our horses for a mile through its rich bottom, that it was a "little" larger.

This is a beautiful country between the Nemehaws, about twenty-five miles over; a strip of it, ten miles wide, along the Missouri, has been appropriated as a reserve for the Otto and Omahaw half-breeds.

In two hours we had crossed this stream, in the same

manner as the other, and were in motion to the N. W. on a fine prairie ridge, and did not reach "wood and water," a suitable camping-ground, until nine o'clock at night.

CHAPTER XIV.

18TH. Proceeded early a little N. of west, crossing an endless succession of prairie hills, between which were generally *gutters* filled with clear water, with vertical sides, and so deep that the horses had to leap them. After two hours' rest at noon, we ascended the "divide" between the waters of the Nemehaws (or Missouri) and the Great Platte River. This, the highest ground between two mighty rivers, is an immense prairie of table land, impressing the senses with the idea of an elevation far greater perhaps than the reality, owing to the extraordinary circumstance of there being no higher object visible—no distant mountain, hill, or inequality, not even a tree, to restore by comparison a juster estimate. I was thus, for the first time, out of sight of woods; far away, in every direction, not even a shrub was to be seen—a green sea waving in the breeze! An American poet, gaining here a new idea, might add a line to these of Byron:

> "There is a pleasure in the pathless woods;
> There is a rapture on the lonely shore;
> There is society where none intrudes
> By the deep sea."

Verily I then felt

> "I love not man the less, but Nature more
> In *this* my interview."

A thousand unuttered thoughts filled my mind; I almost fancied I could hear the music of the spheres, of which old Spenser must have been thinking when he wrote,

> "A solemn silence first invades the ear."

It was a vast solitude; but, in my excitement, I found in truth "society" enough. Then, how easy for the mind to restore the scene so lately passed, though gone forever; and though dwelling upon the unhappy fate of the fallen race, to people it anew with those bold hunters of the plains. Amid the traces of reality—the bleached bones around me—my mind was filled with images of the Indian and his occupation: war and the chase. A short thirty years ago, and from this spot thousands of buffalo might have been seen, and the wild red man rejoicing in the pursuit, the slaughter, and the feast. The uncontrolled, the untrammelled, the *free*—free and happy, as God created them, ere they were robbed, enslaved, poisoned, withered by the pestilence. Alas! for the gift of civilization. The "long-knife" came, and brought with him the "fire-water" and the small-pox, and completed his work with paper treaties, construed and explained under the gentle auspices of the sword.

But lo! the alarm! A tribe is roused to arms! As the sun arose, a bold and bloody deed had been done. A whole tribe and their enemies! A thousand wild horsemen rush in pursuit, mile after mile—a long, a wonderful chase, all in sight, over the level prairie—thundering on, the heavens rent with yells, quavering in a thousand throats, the appalling cry for the vengeance of blood. 'Tis scarcely fancy—I have seen those who have witnessed such a sight.

But the Indian was gone—the buffalo was nowhere to be found;—there seems a sympathy between them, and the poor animal flies not from the Indian as from the white; their fates are alike: the buffalo has receded about ten miles annually for 150 years, and we find them together, lingering on the barren verge of the great valley. A short tarrying place was the Father of Waters, the dark flood of the Mississippi, fit boundary to the mighty empire, the vast, the beautiful regions to its east; a limit which an Alexander had scarce wept to cross. But our grasping, restless borderers, o'erleapt it at once, wandering ever onward through a wilderness of unappropriated riches. And I, too, a pioneer, was I not here, in this awful though beautiful plain, full 500 miles beyond, on the verge of the great American Desert, which caravans of weary pilgrims will soon penetrate, defying its thirsty poverty, and the arms of its poor nomad tribes—battling feebly to the last, for their starving inheritance—scaling the precipices and eternal snows of the Rocky Mountains, to seek new homes in that *weeping* climate of the Columbia and the Pacific, deprived of every vestige of the comforts of civilization—that civilization which understanding not, and sharing not, they will forswear, and abandon forever.

As these thoughts passed through my mind, a dark thundercloud had slowly arisen in advance of us, and approaching nearer and nearer, had assumed palpably the appearance of a vast spread eagle, perfect in shape, save the head, which seemed averted and hid behind a bank of cloud. We could but look and wonder in silence, till the imminent approach of the storm banished all thoughts of eagle, Indian, buffalo, or squatter, and making an anxious survey, I beheld far away a solitary oak, which, experience had taught me to believe, stood sentinel-like, the guardian, or rather offspring, of a fountain. Patiently we rode toward it, and our faith was rewarded, for such was found to be the case. We prepared our night camp in time to escape the worst of a drenching shower.

June 19. Pursued a W. N. W. course, and in a few hours came in sight of the Great Platte River, and made a halt at the Little Saline; it is twenty yards wide—a shallow stream, running swiftly over a rocky bottom: the water is brackish. We remounted at twelve o'clock, and following up the course of the river, passed over a low, sandy, sterile district. There were many trails leading to the Otto villages. The Indians, moving like the buffaloes, in single file, make, like them, deep paths. We passed, in succession, the "Old Village" and the "Lower Village," oppressed by heat and thirst, and somewhat sorrowful that all signs, or absence of signs, indicated that the Indians had all gone on the summer hunt. At sunset we reached the Upper Village, which, accordingly, we found utterly deserted.

Finding nothing but stagnant water, and hoping to do justice to an intolerable thirst, I seized a bucket, descended a lofty and very precipitous bluff on which the village stands, crossed the flat meadow bottom (having been deceived by appearances as to the distance of the river, which was in reality half a mile), and at last found that the water was exceedingly muddy and quite warm. It was now growing dark, and I turned back over the wild flats, in the midst of a thunderstorm. Gusts of rain and wind rendered my steps unsteady—the lightning's glare, revealing in the tall rustling grass the many pools of water, seemed actually to play around the bright bucket which I held in my hand. I found my party had selected quarters in a "lodge."

These dwellings of the Indian are more comfortable than the common houses in the frontier States. Around a circular excavation about three feet deep, and forty in diameter, a conical edifice of poles rests upon a strong framework; this is covered three or four feet thick with wattled bushes, &c., and earth—leaving at the apex about twenty-five feet from the floor, a small opening for light and the escape of smoke; in the centre of the hard dirt floor the fire is made; a stout stick is planted, with an inclination over it, to hold the kettle; around the wall are very comfortable berths, rendered more or less private by matting screens; there is but one entrance, through a rather low-pitched passage. Cool in summer, and warm in winter, they are never troubled with smoke. Many are much larger, but this is the usual size, in which several families live. The village consists of about fifty of these lodges; close by are pens of wattled canes, for the security of horses by night. There are fifty or sixty acres in corn on the flat below, with the slightest attempt at fencing, but distinctly divided, where it is not in patches.

June 20th. I was awoke last night by the thunder reverberating around my subterranean abode, and beheld the lightnings seeming to play around a hole in the sky of utter darkness; between asleep and awake, my sensations were the more strange and pleasing, as I could not realize my unwonted situation.

Finding the river too high to cross, we concluded to send Godfrey to a trading-house, thirty miles above, on the Missouri, for assistance. So we set to work to make a small raft of the logs we could find. He seated himself, paddle in hand, astraddle on one end, near waist deep in water, but with some articles dry on the "bow."

We lost sight of him near the other bank, and a mile lower down.

This is the largest tributary of the Missouri, and, like all other rivers entering it (or the Lower Mississippi) from the S.W., is turbid. All those from the other side are clear; and this extraordinary rule holds with respect to the tributaries of the Arkansas and Red Rivers. The Platte, in most of its course, has a perfectly level bottom, without timber, and from two to twelve miles broad. Rising at the base of the Rocky Mountains, near the source of the Arkansas, the waters of the two springs mingle, after flowing in a devious circuit of 4000 miles.

The scene in the village to-night is imposing. The stars shine brightly—it is a perfect calm; the crescent throws a doubtful shadow. I wander among the earth mounds, more like ancient tombs than the abodes of man; far below, the swollen and mighty river, "dark heaving," sounds a melancholy and awful monotone; the poetical whip-poor-will alone breaks the dead oppressive silence with the music of a living sound. Far in the wilderness, we feel doubly alone amid these deserted dwellings of man.

June 21. At 4 P.M. three horsemen appeared to our anxious eyes beyond the river; it was Godfrey with aid, and we were directed to the village, three miles below. He got over late and with much difficulty, bringing with him a half-breed and the old Frenchman, Barada, the semi-amphibious, universal interpreter, and father of forty children.

June 22. About sunrise, in a cold drizzle, we were on the river-bank, looking on with some curiosity at the doings of our savage friends. Two elk skins united were gathered round the edge, and distended with willow boughs; then called a *bouco,* it was ready for the launch; but that a Frenchman seems to make it a rule, if he find no holes, to punch some through and then tie them up. Dressed in woollen, and a blanket thrown around me, I shivered as I looked on, and then most reluctantly stripped myself—save a cloth vest—to take my place in this strange and dangerous aquatic experiment. In the bouco was placed all the baggage, and Mr. B. Godfrey took charge of the horses. Half swimming and half wading in quicksands, the two others, rope in mouth, took this leather tub in tow, while I steadied it behind. The river is half a mile wide in a direct line; we had chosen a point where there was an island in the midst. We reached it in safety; but I was almost convulsed with cold, and nearly speechless. I wrapped myself up on the sand in two blankets, and in twenty minutes was much recovered. The men had fashioned the butts of two green willows into the semblance of paddles, when Mr. B. and myself both entered the bouco—the stout Maugrain leading, old Barada behind. This side was worse; the water ran in great waves. We paddled with all our strength. At last Maugrain faltered, and would have sunk us, but fortunately he found himself in depth. With a brave heart he put out his utmost powers, and reached the bank, silent, but evidently much overcome. The paddling had quite restored my circulation.

After a short breathing-time, our horses being saddled, we left the banks of the Platte; crossing the level prairie bottom, without other adventure than miring a horse, we approached the Elkhorn, six miles distant. This, like the stream of the same name in Kentucky, is a beautiful one; it is about fifty feet wide, of a sandy bottom, limpid and deep waters. After taking here a cup of hot coffee, we pursued our ride, and eight miles brought us to the Papillon, a small and muddy stream mouthing in the Missouri; the Elkhorn empties into the Platte from the *left*, so here is a remarkable instance of the extraordinary rule applying to the Western waters before mentioned.

On approaching the Missouri, the country assumes appearances of more variety and interest than the prairie, distant from water-courses, where there is great uniformity; here are to be seen abrupt hills, partially covered with trees, and nearer the river on either side, conical in shape, with jutting rocks. Having ridden twenty-five miles in an E.N.E. direction, we arrived this afternoon at Cabanne's trading-house, which is a few miles below old Fort Atkinson, on "Council Bluff," and were delighted in having accomplished the last of our difficulties—which had their origin and aggravation in cold rains.

June 23. The Missouri having risen three feet last night, there is a probability of the Fur Company's steamboat, Yellow Stone, getting down from above; where, having been long detained by low water, preparations have been made for passing the year.

The Ottos had left their village ten days; they fear the small-pox, which is here reported to be at Liberty, Missouri. Four or five hundred of the Pawnees have died of the influenza, which has passed through this region as an epidemic. Winter, spring, and summer, the weather is very damp and cold.

An old acquaintance, a resident of the country, arriving to-day, we rode together to view the localities and ruins of Fort Atkinson. We found but melancholy memorials of the long occupation of the post by the gallant, the "marching 6th;" soon the luxuriant blue grass, will alone remind the wandering traveller of the former existence of this post, "renowned in *stories.*"

After remaining in this vicinity a few days, we procured a canoe—rather out of sorts—of which the rising waters had deprived some owner above; and sending back the horses by an Indian, embarked on our return, still with Godfrey for our only assistant. The only store of meat which we took for a descending voyage of about 300 miles, was five pounds of salted pork.

In a few hours we passed the spot where the Great Platte impetuously discharges itself by several channels right across the current of the Missouri, thus causing a turmoil amid the waters rather dangerous to our primitive navigation. A change is here observed in the river scenery, and a great improvement: it now resembles that of the Ohio, or Upper Mississippi; and it is remarkable that the bluffs rise from the river only on the right bank, for 200 miles below this point; they are here crowned with forests. On the north side is a wonderful bottom, perfectly level, and averaging about three miles in width; about half a mile of this, nearest the river, is almost invariably a lofty forest,—beyond, a beautiful savanna. About 400 square miles of exceedingly rich and beautiful, *level*, and well-watered ground *in a body!*—Thirty-five miles lower, we passed the mouth of the Rivière de Table, running from the south; five miles lower, there is a remarkable pass, where a bluff of vertical rock projects into the river, where it is not above 150 yards wide. We encamped near sunset, having run eighty miles (by French count, thirty-two leagues) in eleven and a half hours, with but one paddle, and stopping to kill a deer.

The next day we passed the mouth of the Little Nemehaw, just below which is apparently a fine place for building—a bluff handsomely sloped, and sufficient timber; and, it is said, a vein of stone-coal close at hand. About three miles lower is the most beautiful *spot* I have seen on the river. Not far from here, as Godfrey relates, the Ottos last winter killed forty elks in deep snow with their tomahawks.

Finding a deer in the river, this forenoon, we gave chase; it was nearly a mile below, but the poor animal, alarmed at our rapid approach, became confused, and repeatedly changed its course; all paddling our best, the canoe shot like an arrow; we got within twenty feet, when my rifle, for the first time, missed fire. I then tried a shot-gun with no better luck. Godfrey's rifle also missed; the deer was close to land, when at another trial Godfrey's gun went off, and deer too; but poor fellow, with a ball through his neck. The deer are driven to the bars by musquitoes by the score; we have only to give the canoe a good direction, partially conceal our bodies, and suffer it to float, to get within a few feet of them; in this manner we killed to-day a fat doe.

The third evening we arrived safely at Cantonment Leavenworth.

CHAPTER XV.

We were often visited by deputations and treaty-parties of the many wilder tribes of Indians, varying as much in dress and personal appearance as in character and pursuits. The celebrated Shawnee Prophet was once or twice at the post, and I have heard him speak in council; he was an old man, but little distinguished in appearance.

10

One hundred Pawnees paid us a visit, on business with their agent; Capot Bleu was at their head, a chief remarkable for dignity and suavity of manners—a born gentleman. Reared wholly in prairies, they seemed almost lost in the little woods around us. We all attended one evening at a dance among their camp fires; of their entertainments, one was very remarkable, resembling, indeed, an institution of Classic Greece. Of a sudden, a fine-looking warrior sprang into the circle, stuck an arrow into the ground, and thon, in the most animated language, recounted one of his deeds in arms; closing with a call upon any performer of a greater action to make his claim to the prize. He said, in substance, that he had ridden alone to a Spaniard's (Mexican's) house, shot down the owner, scalped him, and driven off sixty horses and mules. After a pause, another brave arose; described an action which he deemed more brave or reputable. He had, on a certain occasion, struck a man in battle: and then removing the arrow, laid it at the feet of the presiding chief. Others in like manner offered articles, some of more value, until many had, in their finest style of oratory, proclaimed their proudest deeds. These recitals are always strictly veracious; and fashion, or custom, decides that they are not immodest. At the close, the chief adds his sanction by a distribution of the prizes. Opinion has settled the comparative honor of many of these feats. The highest is, to take a warrior prisoner; the second, first to strike a dead or fallen man in battle: there are several reasons given for this singular honor; one perhaps is, that it is most likely to fall to the person who has slain the enemy. A wounded man is dangerous to approach, and will generally have friends near him; and it is a frequent stratagem to feign death to draw on an enemy—seeking this honor—to almost certain destruction. I once saw a warrior rushing too eagerly to strike a foe, who certainly was quite dead, killed by an *accidental* shot. Next to this feat is, to strike an opposing enemy in battle.

We were frequently visited by parties of Ottoes, from near the mouth of the Great Platte; they were a brave and interesting people. Their principal chief, I-e-tan, was a distinguished man, of great prowess, and profound judgment, or craft; perhaps his most remarkable quality was, a close observation and penetration of character and motives. I heard a gentleman, who knew him well, and spoke his language, say, that he had known him to form judicious if not accurate estimates of men, from a half hour's acquaintance, and without understanding a word that was spoken. But deep beneath the calm exterior of his character burned a lava of impetuous passions which, when strongly moved, burst forth with a fierce and blind violence.

I-e-tan had the advantage of a fine and commanding figure; so remarkable, indeed, that once at a dinner on a public occasion at Jefferson Barracks, his health was drank, with a complimentary application of the lines—

"A combination and a form indeed,
Where every god did seem to set his seal,
To give the world assurance of a man."

There was a passage in the life of this chief which has been so perverted by an Indian story-monger, that I cannot refrain from giving it rightly. In a deep carouse which took place one night in the village in 1822, his brother, a fine fellow, named Blue-eyes (that color being very extraordinary in an Indian), had the misfortune to bite off a small piece of I-e-tan's nose. So soon as he became fully sensible of this irreparable injury, to which, as an Indian, he was perhaps even more sensitive than a white man, I-e-tan burned with a mortal resentment. He told his brother that he would kill him ; and retired, got a rifle, and returned. Blue-eyes was found leaning with folded arms against a pillar of his lodge, and thus, with a heroic Stoicism which has been rightly attributed as a characteristic of the race, without a murmur, or a word, or the quiver of a muscle, submitted to his cruel fate. I-e-tan deliberately shot him through the heart.

Then was I-e-tan seized with a violent remorse, and exhibited the redeeming traits of repentance and inconsolable grief, and of greatness, in the very constancy of the absorbing sentiment. He retired from all intercourse with his race, abstaining wholly from drink, for which he had a propensity; as if under a vow he went naked for near two years; he meditated suicide, and was probably only prevented from committing it by the influence of a white friend; but he sought honorable death in desperate encounters with all enemies he could find, and in this period acquired his name or title, from a very destructive attack which he made upon a party of the I-e-tan tribe. He lived a year or two with the Pawnees, acquired perfectly their very difficult language, and attained a great influence over them, which he never lost. After several years of such penance I-e-tan revisited the villages of his nation; and, in 1830, on the death of La Criniere, his elder brother, succeeded him as principal chief.

I-e-tan married many of the finest girls of his own and neighboring tribes, but never had children. Latterly, one of his wives proved to be pregnant; and, while wavering between love and revenge, a male child was born with teeth. Vanity now proved the strongest passion; he feigned to believe it his son, and pronounced it a special interposition of the Great Spirit, of which this extraordinary sign was the proof. I-e-tan was the last chief who could so far resist the ruinous influence of the increasing communication of his tribe with the villanous—the worse than barbarous whites of the extreme frontier, as to keep the young men under a tolerable control; his death proved a signal for license and disorder.

Intemperance was the great fault in I-e-tan's character—the cause of his greatest misfortune and crime; it led to a violent death. The circumstances of this tragedy are worthy of record, if only that they develop some strong traits of aboriginal character; they are as follows. In April, 1837, accompanied by his two youngest wives, at a trading-house near the mouth of the Platte, he indulged in one of his most violent fits of drunkenness; and in this condition, on a dark and inclement night, drove his wives out of doors; two men of his tribe, who witnessed these circumstances, took the utmost advantage of them, and seduced the women to fly in their company. One of these men had formerly been dangerously stabbed by I-e-tan. Actuated by hatred—calculating perhaps on the chief's declining power, and the strength of their connection, which was great—the seducers becoming tired of outlying in hunting camps, &c., determined to return to the village and face it out. Such cases of elopement are not very unfrequent; but, after a much longer absence, the parties generally become silently reconciled, if necessary through the arrangement of friends. But I-e-tan said that it was not only a personal insult and injury, but an evident defiance of his power, and that he would live or die the chief of the Ottoes. His enemies had prepared their friends for resistance, and I-e-tan armed himself for the conflict. He sought and found the young men in the skirts of the village, near some trees where their supporters were concealed. I-e-tan addressed the man whom he had formerly wounded: "Stand aside! I do not wish to kill *you;* I have perhaps injured you enough." The fellow immediately fled. He then fired upon the other, and missed him; about to return the fire, he was shot down by a nephew of I-e-tan's, from a great distance. I-e-tan then drew a pistol, jumped astride his fallen enemy, and was about to blow his brains out, when the interpreter, Dorian, hoping even then to stop bloodshed, struck up his pistol, which was discharged in the air, and seized him around the body and arms: at this instant the wounded man, writhing in the agony of death, discharged his rifle at random; the ball shattered Dorian's arm, and broke both of I-e-tan's; but being then unloosed, he sprang upon and stamped the body, and called upon his sister, an old woman, who, with an axe in hand, came running like his nephews and friends from the village, to beat out his brains, which she did. At this instant (Dorian being out of the way) a volley was fired from the trees at I-e-tan, and five balls penetrated his body; then, his nephews coming too late to his support, took swift vengeance: they fired at his now flying enemies, and, although they were in motion, near two hundred yards distant, three of them fell dead.

I-e-tan was conveyed to his lodge in the village, where, being surrounded by many relations and friends, he deplored the condition of the nation, and warned them against the dangers and evils to which it was exposed. He assured them most positively that *if he willed it, he could continue to live ;* but that many of the Ottoes had become such dogs, that he was weary of governing them; and that his arms being broken, he could no longer be a great warrior. He gave some messages for his friend, the agent who was expected at the village, and then turning to a bystander, told him he had heard that day he had a bottle of whiskey, and to go and bring it; which being done, he caused it to be poured down his throat, when being drunk, he sang his death-song and died.

CHAPTER XVI.

AMID the quiet inactivity of an infantry outpost, I could scarcely fail to inquire into and learn much of the manners, customs, and traditions of the aboriginal tribes, with many of which I was much in contact.

The Indian is still misunderstood by bookwriters and readers. Lately we have begun to discover that the apathy and insensible sternness of disposition ascribed to them, are a mistaken exaggeration of their manners *before strangers.* It originated perhaps in an overwrought copy of the cold dignity and hardness of the reputed Roman character; and served—while it misled—to give a factitious interest to the red hero of a romance; but the world may rely upon it that those whose pursuits have led to intimate acquaintance with the native character of the aborigines, have not been writers.

The Indian, so reserved and dignified in council, and in his intercourse with strangers, at home with his tribe, and in domestic life is eminently social; full of merriment and laughter, and fond of a practical joke, he seeks lively company; attends feasts and amuses himself with ludicrous narratives, or listens to the marvellous stories and traditions of the olden time; he frequently passes the night in singing and dancing; or, in romantic mood, serenades with his flute, and sings praises to some red beauty who holds the vigils of love.

The Indian learns to control his passions in consequence of the absence of a protecting law; they fight only with weapons, and the taking of life leads to bloody family feuds, to factions, and sometimes to civil war.

He knows no moral restraint upon lying; and his life is spent in the study and practice of deceit, as a means of aggrandizement; and for the attainment of petty ends, he uses it with a liberality only limited by the fear of detection; this, as with the Spartan theft, is the only crime. Frequent exposure only brands him with the character of *fool.*

On the women, of course, falls the domestic drudgery, as it does on most white women, with the only difference, that it is of a harsher and more laborious kind; a consequence of their wild mode of life, which, too, of course, hardens the women and fits them for their duties. Some of these would unfit the man for hunting, in which he has his full share of the curse of labor. On his return to his lodge after days of exhausting exposure and exertions for the support of his family, his wife is happy in every care for his comfort; removes his stiff-worn clothing; hastens to cook and set before him the best food which she has; offers him a pipe; unpacks the meat which he has brought; and willingly, if her little son has not done it, takes care of the horse. The husband strives to obtain wealth in horses to relieve his family of travelling on foot and carrying burdens. The wife is contented and happy.

The men are fond of their children, and playful in their intercourse with them; parents give them lessons of prudence and good behavior; but the boys soon throw off the restraint of their mothers, who, when they become seven or eight years of age, begin to stand in dread of the bow and arrows of the young warriors; at ten or twelve, the boys begin to rebel also against their fathers, whom they are apt to strike on provocation with the first thing they lay their hands on; the father then goes off rubbing his hurt, and tells his neighbors what a brave warrior his boy will become.

The daughters, under the maternal eye, are very generally chaste, as a matter of policy: after marriage they are less so; but perhaps not less than among the civilized. Some tribes, however, hold this virtue in small esteem.

The Indian eats when he is hungry, and at no regular times; so that the members of a family seldom eat together, and the women very seldom with the men. They are almost equally irregular in their hours of sleep and rest.

They have no distinction of vulgar and polite language, and feel no indelicacy in using all expressive words in every society and presence.

The men all choose some animal, bird, or fish, as their own peculiar patron, to which they offer a kind of worship, much like that of patron-saints: it is their "totem," a sort of coat-of-arms, and from it they frequently take their name. An Indian will seldom kill or eat of the chosen animal; he deems it his guide and protector, and addresses to it speeches and prayers.

They have physicians, who administer a few simple remedies; as an emetic, for instance, they use a tea made of the leaves of the white willow; their treatment of most local disorders is scarifying, and the blister by fire; and in addition they are much in the habit of sucking the seat of pain, and even the most disgusting wounds and disorders. They commonly combine the office of physician with that of priest or prophet; and their French appellation has been anglicized into "medicine men." They endeavor to hide their ignorance, or artfully assist their remedies by inspiring confidence in their patients, by using much religious mummery, and the common resorts of quackery—a great instrument in which is their "medicine bag," which is held in much awe and respect; it contains a great variety of articles esteemed for one reason or another; among which some portion or symbol of the patron-animal always finds a place: one might imagine they have copied from the veneration and uses of saintly relics!

The remote Indians almost hourly worship the Supreme Being; but tinged with the materialism of uncultivated minds, and the absence of revelation, recognize his presence or attributes in the most striking features of nature; in the most fearful or beneficent elements of the scheme of creation.

The first puff in smoking, with an ejaculation, they direct upwards; and always sacrifice to the Great Spirit before eating; they cut off a portion of meat, offer it to the heavens, as his dwelling-place, and then to the earth, as the mother of all things; after which they burn it.

In the spring-time parents send out their sons, and men go forth to lonely places and hill-tops, with their faces and persons blackened with mud, as in mourning, where they fast and pray sometimes for days together, and sing rude chants in praise and adoration. With minds thus exalted and wrought to enthusiasm, they imagine that they hold intercourse with the Almighty. In stormy nights, and in tempests, the warriors generally go out and seek this intercourse of prayers. Prophets thus arise; fanatics who, perhaps, deceive themselves as much as others. With some notable exceptions, the women never sacrifice, or pray, or worship.

The Indians, at times of impending calamity, sometimes give away their children, as a humiliation and atonement to propitiate the Almighty.

Many of their ceremonies, beliefs, and traditions strongly resemble those of the Old Testament. They have prophets who seem to believe that they hold discourse with the Supreme Being; they prophesy, and pretend to give his very words; they make sacrifices, observe feasts, and fast and pray—not in sackcloth and ashes, but covered, as a mortification, with mud;—they inflict on themselves wounds, and have many other modes of penance; they have traditions of animals speaking, and believe that in former days men were sometimes turned into animals.

The following nations or tribes of Indians occupy the middle ground between the most savage and remote, and those who have been whelmed by the hitherto irresistible tide of migration, and debauched by their intercourse with the whites, viz.: Ioways, Ottōs, Omāhaws, Kansas, and Osages. Their fate is in suspense, but seems about to take an unfavorable turn. They have preserved this tradition of their origin.

Several hundred years ago, a branch of the great Winnebago family commenced their wanderings from the great lakes westward. The motive or cause of this division and migration is not assigned; faction, the exigencies of war or dearth, may have given the impulse.

It would be interesting, if it were possible, to trace their progress; to inquire whether their advance was peaceful; if the regions passed over were in the possession of other tribes; or, if this may be inferred, whether they resisted, were destroyed, or driven forward on the territories of others. It might afford a partial solution of the great problem of the origin and history of the savage tribes found by our ancestors in possession of this vast country. We daily discover the monuments of a more civilized, but perhaps soft and effeminate race, who were supplanted by these savage warriors—the hardy children of the North—as were the Southern Europeans in the fifth and sixth centuries by innumerable hordes of barbarians; so overwhelming in their course as to leave but a germ of Southern civilization, which in nine centuries after had scarce attained its ancient growth. Cortez found in Mexico such a race, perhaps their descendants, constituting a great monarchy.

After the arrival of the Winnebagoes on the bank of the Mississippi, the tradition assigns the cause of another division. The son of one powerful chief seduced the daughter of another, and refused, when called upon, to take her as a wife. This gross injury caused a violent feud between the rival leaders, their dependents and friends; and it became so warm as to extend to the great mass of their followers. A bloody conflict between the two factions was averted by a timely compromise; the followers of the offender's father, though much the most numerous, withdrew from the rest, crossed the Mississippi, and continued their migration. The partisans of the injured chief remained in the vicinity of the river; their descendants are the Ioways.

Other causes of division, the greatest of which was perhaps the scarcity of game, subsequently scattered the main body, or emigrating party, over extensive districts. Their descendants are known to compose the four other tribes before mentioned. Of these, the Ottos, Omahaws, and Kansas have permanent villages on the Missouri River, and two tributaries, the Great Platte and Kansas. The Osages, formerly extending far south, even beyond the Arkansas, are now confined to a small district skirting the west bank of the Neosho, or Grand River. They all speak dialects of the present Winnebago language, and bear a strong resemblance in person and customs. The men of all these nations are of extraordinary size; but the Osages are the largest, and, I think, exceed the white Americans.

Their numbers have been much reduced, principally by small-pox. They are brave, and fond of war, but have seldom shed the blood of whites. They are independent and bold in their intercouse with us, and are also lively and intelligent. They have fine heads; and their symmetry of person, activity, and powers of endurance, are remarkable.

Early in June, after planting corn, they are accustomed to move by whole tribes to the great plains frequented by buffalo; then they enjoy the chase, and feast for months, but are also provident enough to dry and smoke a stock of meat, and return with their horses loaded with it, to their villages of spacious and comfortable dirt houses. They now pull much of their corn while it is in the milk, and dry it carefully in the sun; it is then called "sweet corn," an excellent and almost universal dish with them;

11

it keeps well, and, when boiled, swells, and recovers the tenderness and sweetness of a roasting ear; it is superior to hominy. After gathering their crops, they again remove to the game country in October, and there pass the winter in skin lodges or tents.

CHAPTER XVII.

I CONFESS myself warmly interested in the fate of these four nations, and one other, the Pawnee, whose condition is much the same. Their location has been until of late sufficiently remote to have allowed them, in a great measure, to escape the degradation of the vices of civilization, which the depravity and avarice of the pioneers have always introduced among neighboring Indians. As a sample of their treaties with the government, I can state that the Osages ceded about 2,000,000 acres of arable land to cancel claims which were not to exceed $4000, made against them by meddling renegade whites, who have been the bane of their happiness.

Suffering a miserable decay from the horrible diseases which we have introduced among them without a remedy or alleviation, they do not complain; and driven nearly to despair by their contracted limits and the destruction of game, they have not lifted the bloody hatchet against the aggressors.

The buffalo must soon fail them; the restless white has wandered beyond, and is fast exterminating these animals, essential to the existence of many tribes. Every year at least one hundred thousand are slain for the skins and tongues. The American Fur Company takes the lead in this destruction.

Their near prospect is starvation, with the only alternative to follow the buffalo by a gradual desertion to the wandering robber tribes of the great prairies. Thus, if left to their fate, they will cause great disorders on the frontiers, and miserably linger until they disappear from the earth; or, losing character, language, and name, sink the last gradation to utter barbarism, and become the nomad outcasts of the great American desert.

To endeavor to avert this fate must be an object with every philanthropist. Any *American*, of but common humanity, must feel interested in such a good work; *we* have been the source of their injuries and evils, past and present. But it is evident the Government only can give an effectual impulse to the most beneficent plans of amelioration; and it could be easily shown, that, leaving out of consideration the humane policy which it professes, these tribes have matter of fact claims upon our justice, so great, that a mere pittance in comparison, if expended in an enlightened and judicious manner, would perhaps accomplish all that can be done to save them; and at the least alleviate their sufferings and soften the hardness of their sinking fortunes.

In this cause of justice and humanity, I propose to consider what may be done to reclaim them from barbarism, as the only possible way of preventing their total extinction.

All the efforts of Government and of charitable and well-meaning individuals, or societies, have hitherto failed. The Government, in bargains little better than robbery, has with a close and sparing hand sold them benefits; has paid them in promises of assistance in improvement; has told them that the introduction of cattle, mills, ploughs, &c., would be greatly to their advantage; caused them to assent; and engaged itself to furnish them. But these engagements, really advantageous if fulfilled in a faithful manner, have been sometimes neglected, and always, if performed to the bare letter, been paid in the same spirit of the bargain; without any further effort for their advantage, without care that they should be taught to reap any real and lasting benefit; in a word, the United States has by its functionaries and agents, grossly neglected its duties and moral obligations. Its "agents" have often been selected with any other motives than a careful regard to peculiar fitness, an intelligent and paternal interest in their welfare, a devotion to *duty*. Unprincipled traders have been ever allowed to reside with the tribes, and gain an unsalutary influence,* ever exerted for intensely selfish ends; they have been allowed to persuade the tribes to demand their annuities in specie, in preference to such goods and necessaries at cost and transportation prices, as they sell them at an enormous profit. On the other hand, all private efforts to reclaim and teach the savages, have been unwisely directed, and often, I grieve to say, faithlessly applied. Missionaries have often been incompetent and selfish depositaries of sacred trusts; in their establishments, the leading principle seems to have been their own substantial and permanent comfort; or their measures, founded on mistaken views, have been executed in an unwise and unconciliating spirit. Their

* This influence, founded on a gratification of their evil passions, is irresistible. Even in Washington City, deputations of chiefs and principal men, in treaty councils with the Secretary of War, after receiving his propositions and advice, delay their decisions and answers for a night—as usual—and then make those dictated or advised by some obscure trader, or trader's agent, who will always be found to accompany them.

efforts have been worse than vain ; lasting prejudices have been created; and in their most successful efforts, the cases of individual scholars, the effects of an unnatural advance in science—unaccompanied by the moral restraints of our religion, which their natures are incapable of receiving,—have but resulted in the exhibition of an increased capacity for vice. All such efforts have been radically wrong. All history proves that simple *Theism* —the conception of the idea of a superintending mind, capable of directing all the operations of nature,—has been an attainment beyond the powers of man, in the early stages of his progress. Then, he imagines a distinct controlling spirit, or deity, in every natural object of terror; or of peculiar beneficence, in every effect of which the cause is concealed from his untutored faculties. Thus, even the civilized and philosophic Greek worshipped a multitude of gods; and, to aid his conceptions, clothed them with human passions and attributes; and, like the Romans, rejected for ages our holy religion revealed to the Jews; but only after that nation, under the protection and guidance of the Almighty, *to prepare them for its reception*, had ages before been taught by Him, a religion of symbols, forms, and magnificent ceremonies, which, appealing to the *senses* of an untutored race, could engage their imagination, sway their passions, fix their attention, and ever renew their recollections of past signal and miraculous favors.

To attempt to teach savages letters and the mysteries of the Christian religion (not even intelligible to the most cultivated intellect), is evidently to contemn the experience of all nations. But taking for our guidance the gradual advances of Europeans, whose histories we possess, let them first be taught step by step the lessons of civilization; let us endeavor first to make them herdsmen, which alone will be found a difficult and most important advance; afterward direct their attention to agriculture, and the simplest mechanic arts. *The mental endowments of civilized men seem inherited like physical distinctions.* Let us not then *shock the natures* of savages, by attempting to force upon them at once the manners and customs, the acquirements and the *creed*, which the gradual progress, the recorded lessons of eighteen centuries have perfected for us, and *in our natures.*

Having condemned the systems for civilizing the aborigines hitherto attempted, in pointing out the causes of their total failure, my efforts in the same good cause would prove certainly fruitless, unless a more specific practical plan be added to the general principles which have already been suggested.

I have already stated, that the failure of the many treaty stipulations, made with some view to their improvement and permanent welfare, has been the result of their spiritless or faithless execution (even the letter of the law has not always been fulfilled); and in part to an injudicious or incomplete scheme. Mills have been built, and no millers provided; domestic animals have been furnished, but with no systematic provision for their preservation and proper uses; farmers have been appointed, but with so little attention to a good selection, and regulations for their government, that they have proved farmers for their own profit, instead of that of the Indian; but above all, the agent, on whom so much must depend, has but too often been selected without regard to peculiar fitness. If there is any office under Government, in the appointment to which it is essential to be actuated by pure and disinterested motives, and which calls for a most studious and judicious selection, it is this. The "agent" must be the soul of the system I would propose. It should be an office not to be sought for; but the search must be for a man possessing these three qualifications—experience, ability, and devotion to the welfare of the Indian. He must be selected as would be the guardian of one's children.

Assistants should be appointed, whose duties would be the preservation and management of the domestic animals furnished by Government for breeding. Honest men and good Christians must fill these stations; and they should well understand in advance, that they are put there for the benefit of the Indians, and that they are to earn a livelihood by devotion to their duties; and that therefore the proceeds of cultivation by Indians, must go solely to the Indians, *who should never be required to labor but for themselves.*

Mills and blacksmith shops should be built, and millers and blacksmiths appointed, for their immediate benefit and permanent example. Log huts should be built for the chiefs; sheds, inclosures, &c., be constructed for the protection of cattle, domestic fowls, &c., and farming tools furnished. But, in everything, a view should be had to their instruction, and encouragement to learn the use of tools, and to work and provide for themselves; and with this object, pains should be taken to discover and foster the inclinations or aptness of individuals for the arts exhibited or practised for their benefit.

Too much restraint would be injudicious; but the possessors of herds might gradually be persuaded, that the search for far distant buffalo was laborious or disadvantageous. The excitement of war and the chase should be substituted by all manly amusements, by all means possible. Let Government now prove its sincerity by a change of its policy, and as agriculture is encouraged, grant titles in fee, with restriction of alienation to whites: the advantages of property in severalty would speedily be apparent, and would turn the scale in favor of civilization.

As a substitute for their vicious traders, factors should be appointed to sell at the villages all suitable articles at cost and transportation prices. Barter for peltries should be discouraged; and on the other hand, liberal prices be given for agricultural productions: these might be advantageously used for the supply of military posts with forage and rations.

Physicians should be appointed to live with them; to be compensated in part by regulated and very moderate charges.

Individuals thus employed with the tribes should, for their confort and in part compensation, be allowed farming and grazing privileges; but *all* of them strictly limited to the production of articles for their *use.*

Unless the trade be strictly confined to factors, treaties or arrangements should be made by which the distribution of present or future annuities should be uniformly made in equivalents best adapted to the plan of civilization, and if practicable, be so varied as to offer encouragements to such courses of conduct as may be deemed conducive to this general object; and donations should be made for the purpose of rewards or prizes.

But, above all, a military force at convenient stations, should maintain by the terror of summary punishments, a complete non-intercourse with white men.

The world has seen herdsmen, agriculturalists, artisans, painters, sculptors, generals, and great monarchs, ignorant of letters; but never a literary savage, ignorant of the most simple and essential arts of civilized man.

Indian hypocrites have been heard of; but there was never a Christian savage Indian. The Almighty, with wise but inscrutable purposes, has seen fit that the religion of his Son should make a gradual and slow progress through the human race: first introduced amid the only civilized nations, and who had attained every excellence in literature, its meliorating progress seemed long of doubtful success. God has not implanted in the savage nature a capacity of receiving the lesson of Christian humility; or of conceiving of its being taught in the person of Omnipotence; He hath ever worked by means; and the first lessons of Christianity are to be taught in the humanizing influences of the most simple and laborious arts.

After three centuries, the civilization of our Indians is yet a problem. But I have confidence that the plan I have described would succeed even with the wild tribes I have mentioned, and a few others, not more distant, and in a similar condition.

Who will say, that it is not the *duty* of the American people to do all this, and more, for these helpless remnants of races which we have slaughtered, oppressed, and driven off from all the best of the land—the homes which they have loved and freely bled for? Unless *something* be done, they will soon share the fate of the many free and brave tribes, whose deeds in defence of their country have been illustrated in our choicest literature, but who are gone, and have left no other memorial.

If all should fail, we would at least be able to contemplate their "melancholy" fortunes with more equanimity, conscious of having done something to smooth their rugged decline, to alleviate the sufferings of want, and to lessen or prevent the miserable and degrading effects of the vices of our own introduction.

CHAPTER XVIII.

The most remarkable personage that has appeared among these tribes was Blackbird, chief of the Omahaws. This tribe, though now reduced to about 1200 souls, in his time numbered, perhaps, quite as many warriors.

Blackbird (Wah-shingah Sawby) was born about the year 1750, in the Omahaw village. It stands on the south bank of the Missouri River, ninety miles above Council Bluff.

The dignity of the principal chief or king—for the language rather indicates the royal title—among the Omahaws and most other Indian nations is hereditary, but subject to frequent irregularities. Blackbird was of undistinguished parentage; his earliest pursuits were those of a doctor. To this character he soon added that of religious juggler; he became a "medicine man." His ambition then began to be developed, and he sought by a habit of austerity to obtain the respect of his fellows; he rendered himself remarkable for the frequency and duration of his fasts and religious ceremonies. He next ventured to appear in the character of prophet; and whether from unusual foresight, from cunning and management, or perhaps some instances of remarkable luck, soon became a very distinguished one. Abut this time he made a fast of great duration, and sat motionless for several days and nights on a high white cliff, which was in view from the village; this over, he gave out that the Great Spirit had appeared to him face to face, and told him that he should become a very great man.

Having acquired by these means the importance and influence of a principal man, Blackbird's ambition was further excited to follow the only remaining road to honors and powers—that of arms; he became a partisan leader against the Sioux and Pawnees, with whom the nation is ever at war. He did not mistake his capacity, and, indeed, became highly distinguished as a successful warrior.

Greatly respected as a war-chief, and feared as a prophet, he was now nearly at the pinnacle of Indian ambition; but Blackbird was not contented: he could not brook a divided rule; his ambition was boundless.

An extraordinary circumstance now occurred, which moulded his further fortunes, and, infamously used, led to fame and despotic power. This was the solitary instance known of an introduction of arsenic into the Indian country; it is not known by whom, or for what purpose it was done; but certain it is that, perhaps accidentally, the poison fell into the hands of Blackbird, and with a full knowledge of its qualities and use.

Blackbird had no conscientious scruples to overcome—few of his condition would have had; he soon resolved on the most judicious and fatal application of this terrible agent. It was in his character of prophet that he determined to sate his relentless ambition, to rid himself of enemies, and to become the object of the fear, and even adoration of the nation.

He at once boldly prophesied the death of the rival chief: and took measures that it should be fully accomplished by means of the poison. The chief suddenly died, as had been predicted, and the tribe were full of terror.

It is needless to follow him in this sure and terrible course; he sacrificed a great number;—his enemies, and those who stood at all in his way. His religious mummery—by which he pretended to hold interviews with the Almighty—was frequently practised in his lodge; it was done with much noise and ostentation. The nation heard and trembled.

When he was known to be angry,—or in times of great distress and calamity, the people would fearfully enter, and seek by all means to propitiate his favor: prostrate on the ground, they gently raised his feet, and placed them upon their necks!

One of his wives eloped with a Pawnee; he shut himself up, and did not speak for several days:—the whole nation were in despair:—the parents of the most handsome girls took them to him, and humbly offered them for his acceptance.

The following instance is given of Blackbird's despotism. The nation were on their return from the summer hunt; near the heads of the Platte, they were forced to cross a sandy plain, in which no water was to be found nearer than a long day's journey. By some means—perhaps by their setting off before he gave the word—he was offended: he said nothing during the day, but rode on in advance until he came to the brow of a hill in view of water; the poor people had suffered exceedingly on the hot plain, and came straggling on; each pressing desperately forward with all his strength to quench a raging thirst. He allowed them to get in full view of the water, and then commanded a halt! The nation obeyed; and threw themselves on the earth in an agony of fear and suffering. Blackbird himself sent forward for water and drank. The whole people seemed in danger of destruction. There was a white man among them, named Barada; after some time he went to the chief and told him he was killing his people:—he could do so if he chose;—but as one of the whites, who held Blackbird in great friendship and respect, &c., requested to be allowed to go on. The tyrant then relented, or was glad of an excuse to give way: he gave his gracious permission that the nation should drink; and accordingly with shouts of joy and thanks they ran off in a great race to the stream.

Blackbird was in the habit of seizing traders' boats, taking, or distributing among the people every article of goods without any account of them;—after the next fall hunt he would generally make any or all go and throw down their furs and skins in a great pile before the trader, until he should say there was enough.

There was *one* warrior who quailed not before the terrible power of Blackbird. This was Maundahe Ghingha,—the Little Bow. He had become so distinguished that the chief was jealous, or held his character in some dread; accordingly, on an occasion of his absence on a hunt, Blackbird's influence prevailed over his wife, and she consented to poison him on his return.

Agreeably to her instructions, on Little Bow's arrival, she was particularly attentive and affectionate in her usual offices: and setting before him a tempting bowl of food, invited him to eat. I know not if in this case his death had been foretold,—but from some cause Little Bow was distrustful: he requested her to partake of the meal; and on her declining, positively commanded her to eat. His wife then threw herself at his feet, and with many

12

tears confessed her crime and revealed the secret of Blackbird's power.

The Little Bow dashed his tomahawk into her brain. He then threw on his war-dress,—seized his arms, and mounted his best horse. He galloped through all parts of the village, proclaimed the villany of the murderous chief, and endeavored to stir up the people by violent harangues; he paraded in front of Blackbird's lodge; accused him of his crimes, uttered every abuse, and defied him to manly combat.

But Blackbird's power, founded on the ignorance and superstitious fears of the people, was scarcely to be shaken; the result was that Little Bow raised a party of about three hundred—including families—with which he seceded, and built a village about thirty miles above. Here they lived many years, until they were nearly all exterminated by small-pox. Little Bow himself survived his great enemy.

Blackbird, or Tow-wan-gā-hi—Town-builder as he was also called,—died in 1803, about a year after this event, of the small-pox. He was buried on the point of a high bluff, immediately on the river, at the head of Blackbird Bend. He was placed sitting on his horse; and over him was erected a lofty mound; it can be seen for more than twenty miles on the river. He chose this spot, that he might see the white people—he told his tribe—as they passed on the river.

Blackbird's memory is still held in reverence and fear; Indians as they pass, are still in the habit of stopping to smoke, and make offerings at his tomb.

I would give in connection with the subject of Indian character some account of a class of self-exiled wanderers and hunters, whose restless or savage natures, lead them to sever every tie of kindred and country, and to prefer the privations and dangers of barbarism, among even hostile Indians, to the comforts and most exciting pursuits of their kind. A sketch of one may answer for the class.

CHAPTER XIX.

SOME INCIDENTS IN THE LIFE OF HUGH GLASS, A HUNTER OF THE MISSOURI RIVER.

THOSE pioneers, who, sixty years ago, as an advanced guard, fought the battles of civilization, for the very love of fighting, may be now recognized in the class of the hero of my sketch, who 1000 miles beyond the last wave of the troublous tide of migration, seek their pleasures in the hunt of a Blackfoot of the Rocky Mountains, a grizzly bear, or a buffalo. It must be difficult to give even a faint idea of the toils and risks of a set of men, so constituted as to love a mode of life only for these attendants; who exist but in the excitement of narrow escapes,—of dangers avoided or overcome; who often, such is their passionate devotion to roving, choose it in preference to comfortable circumstances within the pale of civilization. Little has been reaped from this field, so fertile in novel incident that its real life throws romance into the shade.

The class of people above mentioned, excluded by choice from all intercourse with the world of white men, are at different periods very differently occupied:—at times, as trappers; at others, they live with Indians, conforming in every respect to their mode of life; and often they are found entirely alone, depending upon a rifle, knife, and a few traps, for defence, subsistence, and employment.

A trapping expedition arrived on the hunting grounds is divided into parties of four or five men, which separate for long periods of time; and as the beaver is mostly in the country of hostile Indians, in and beyond the Rocky Mountains, it is an employment of much hazard, and the parties are under great pains for concealment. Trappers, and others who remain in these regions, subsist for years wholly upon game. They never taste bread, nor can they even procure salt, indispensable as it may be considered in civilized life.

To take the beaver requires practice and skill. The trap is set, and then sunk in the stream to a certain depth (when the water is too deep for it to rest upon the bottom) by means of floats attached, and a chain confines it to something fixed or very heavy at the bottom. This depth must be such, that the animal in swimming over it, is caught by the leg. The "*bait*" consists of some strong *scent*, proceeding from a substance placed directly opposite upon the shore; an oil taken from the body of the animal is generally used. The greatest care is necessary to destroy all trace of the presence of the trapper when making his arrangements, which, if discovered by the most sensitive instinct of the animal, it carefully avoids the place; they therefore wade, or use a canoe in setting the trap.

The solitary hunter is found occasionally thus employed, for the sake of the trade with those who visit the country solely for that purpose; getting for his skins the few necessaries of his situation,—blankets, powder, lead, &c.

The white, or more properly, the gray or grizzly bear

is, next to the Indian, the greatest enemy the hunter meets with in this region; it is the lion of our forests; the strongest and most formidable of all its animals. It is about 400 pounds in weight; its claws more than three inches long; the buffalo bull, perhaps stronger and more active than the domestic, is a certain victim to its strength. If a grizzly bear is reported to be in the vicinity of an Indian camp or village, fifty or a hundred warriors turn out (as in the East for a lion or tiger) to hunt to its death so dangerous and dreaded a neighbor.

The grizzly bear never avoids, very often attacks a man; while on the other hand, the hunter, but under the most favorable circumstances, carefully avoids him.

In the summer of 1823, immediately after the desertion and conflagration of the Arickara village, consequent upon its attack by the 6th Regiment United States Infantry, a party of eighty men, under the direction of Major Henry (that had volunteered in that engagement), left this point of the Missouri River, intending to gain the head waters of the Yellow Stone to make a fall hunt for beaver. The party had journeyed four days in the prairie; on the fifth we would introduce our hero (who has been rather backward) to the attention of the reader—if, indeed, it has not been already lost in the rugged field prepared for his reception.

On the fifth day, Glass (who was an *engagé* in the expedition) left the main body accompanied by two others, to make one of the usual hunts, by which, while subsistence is acquired the party is not detained. Having near night succeeded in killing buffalo, they were directing their common course to a point, near which they knew must be the position of the camp for the night; it was on a small stream, and as they passed near one of its curves,

Glass became somewhat detached from the others, intending to drink of its waters; at this moment his progress was arrested by the sight of a grizzly bear issuing from beneath the bank opposite to him. His companions, overcome by their fears, which no obligation to share with him his unavoidable danger could resist, profited by their more favorable situation to attempt escape by flight, leaving him to his destiny.

A contest with a grizzly bear, more tenacious of life than a buffalo, is always dangerous; to insure a probability of success and safety, all the energies must arise in proportion to the magnitude of the danger; and they must be shown in perfect coolness; the slightest falter, which with the many would result from a loss of this presence of mind, would render the case hopeless and insure destruction.

Glass would gladly have retreated, but he knew all attempts would be useless. This desperate situation only nerved him to the combat. All depended upon the success of his first and only shot;—with an aim, cool and deliberate, but quick, lest greater rapidity in the animal should render it more uncertain, he fired his rifle. The shot was a good one; eventually mortal; but its immediate effect was only to raise to its utmost degree, the ferocity of the animal, already greatly excited by the sight and opposition of its intended prey; it bounded forward with a rapidity that could not be eluded, in pursuit of its flying adversary, whom danger, with means of defence, had inspired with deliberate action, but now only gave wings for his flight. But it was unavailing, and he knew it;—an appalling roar of pain and rage, which alone could render pallid a cheek of firmness, chilled him to the soul; he was overtaken, crushed to the earth, and rendered insensible but to thoughts of instant death. The act of contact had been two blows, inflicting ghastly wounds; the claws literally baring of flesh the bones of the shoulder and thigh. Not sated with this work of an instant, the bear continued to pursue, with unabated speed, the flight of the two other hunters:—the chase was to them awfully doubtful:—every muscle of a hunter's frame strained to its utmost tension—the fear of a horrid death—the excitement of exertion—together producing a velocity seldom equalled by bipeds, had been unavailing in contest with that of the superior strength and fleetness of the raging animal. But, fortunately, it could not last; —it was expended in the distance, from loss of blood;—its exertions became more feeble;—the sacrifice of a deserted comrade had saved their lives;—they reached the camp in safety.

When sufficiently recovered, they reported the death of Glass, and their escape from the pursuit of the wounded grizzly bear. A large party was instantly in arms. It had gone but a short distance when the bear was discovered and despatched without difficulty. Glass, they found, was not yet dead; they bore him to the camp, still insensible from the shock of his dreadful wounds. They were considered mortal, but, of course, bound up and treated as well as their circumstances would admit.

A question then arose, how he should be disposed of; to carry him farther was useless, if not impossible; and it was finally settled that he should be left. Eighty dollars were subscribed for any two men who would volunteer to remain with him, await his death, and then overtake the party. A man named Fitzgerald, and a youth of seventeen, accepted the proposals; and the succeeding day the main party continued its route as usual.

For two days they faithfully administered to his wants; then their imaginations began to create difficulties in their situation; at least their inactive stay became very irksome; and as they considered his recovery as hopeless, they equally agreed to think their remaining longer useless. Thus wrought upon, and from innate depravity, they conceived the horrid idea of deserting him, overtaking the party, and reporting his death:—and they determined upon the prompt execution of their design:—nay more, these most heartless of wretches, taking advantage of his first sleep, not contented with the desertion of a sacred trust, robbed him of his rifle, knife, and, in short, everything but a small kettle containing water, and a wallet on which his head rested; and which fortunately contained a razor.

On awakening, how could he realize his situation! Helpless from painful wounds, he lay in the midst of a desert. His prospect was starvation and death. He was deserted by the human race.

But this act, which words cannot sufficiently blacken, perhaps gave a vital excitement. He muttered a mingled curse and prayer:—he had a motive for living! He swore, as if on his grave for an altar, his endless hatred, and if spared, his vengeance on the actors in so foul a deed.

Glass, when his water was exhausted, for fear he should become so weak as to perish for want of it, succeeded with great difficulty in crawling to the edge of the stream, where he lay incapable of further exertion for several days.

Few are aware, until tried, of their capacity for endurance: and the mind seldom shrinks from an exertion that will yield a single ray of hope to illume the darkness of its waste.

Glass did not despair; he had found he could crawl, and he determined to endeavor to reach a spot where he could better hope for succor. He crawled towards the Missouri, moving at the rate of about two miles a day! He lived upon roots and buffalo berries. On the third day he witnessed near him the destruction of a buffalo-calf by wolves;—and here he gave a proof of a cool judgment: he felt certain, that an attempt to drive the wolves from their prey before their hunger was at least somewhat appeased, would be attended with danger; and he concluded to wait till they had devoured about half of it, when he was successful in depriving them of the remainder: and here he remained until it was consumed, resting and perhaps gaining strength. His knees and elbows had, by now, become bare; he detached some of his other clothing, and tied them around these parts, which must necessarily be protected, as it was by their contact with the ground that motion was gained.

The wound on his thigh he could wash; but his shoulder, or back, was in a dreadful condition. For more than forty days he thus crawled on the earth, in accomplishing a five days' journey to the Arickara village. Here he found several Indian dogs still prowling among the ruins; he spent two days in taming one of them sufficiently to get it within his power: he killed it with the razor, and for several days subsisted upon the carcass.

Glass, by this time, though somewhat recovered of the effect of his wounds, was, as may be supposed, greatly reduced; but he continued his weary and distressing progress, upon arms and knees, down the Missouri River. In a few days he was discovered by a small party of

Sioux Indians: these acted toward him the part of a good Samaritan. The wound on his back was found in a horrid condition. It had become full of worms. The Indians carefully washed it, and applied an astringent vegetable liquid. He was soon after taken by them to a small trading-house about eighty miles below, at the mouth of the Little Missouri.

CHAPTER XX.

Glass slowly recovered from his wounds. He had been greatly reduced; he was, indeed, when found, a mere skeleton: but a vigorous frame and strong constitution, inured to constant exercise and rough labors, thus rendered iron-like, with little encouragement, quickly recovers from shocks that would be fatal to men of different pursuits. While in this situation, his curse, his oath of vengeance on the authors of half his misfortune, had not been forgotten. When in his feverish dreams he fought his battles o'er,—entrapped the wary beaver,—enticed to its death the *curious* antelope,—when the antlered buck was arrested in his pride by his skill, and weltered before him,—and when the shaggy strength of the untamable buffalo sank beneath his fatal rifle, the bear, the grizzly bear, would still disturb his slumbers; a thousand times would be imaged to his mind the horrid, the threatening grin of its features; now its resistless paw was suspended over his head, with nought to avert the death-inflicting blow—and now its bloody teeth mangled his vitals. And again it would change, and he was confronted by mortal foes;—and he felt a spellbound inactivity: goblin-like they danced before him; retreated, advanced, in mockery of the impotence of their intended victim;—and then he would see them afar off, with demon countenances of grim satisfaction, in leaving him to a fate they could easily avert, of studied cruelty, worse than death. Awaking with convulsive start, the "Great Nemesis" ever invoked by the unfortunate, would seem to whisper him, "Hast thou forgot thy oath?"

His oath of revenge was far from forgotten. He nourished it as an only consolation; an excitement to hasten recovery. Near two months had elapsed, when Glass was again on his feet. Nor had his ill fate in the least dampened the hunter's ardor: he the rather felt uneasy quickly to resume his adopted habits, which he had so long, so unwillingly foregone.

The pleasures of this roving, independent, this careless life of the hunter, when once tasted with relish, the subject is irreclaimable, and pines in disgust amid the tameness of more quiet occupations.

Glass had found sympathy among his new friends at the trading-house. Who could withhold deep interest from the story of such wrongs? He was destitute of clothing, the rifle, butcher-knife, &c., the means of the support, and even existence of the hunter. These they generously supplied him. A party of six of the *engagées*, headed by one Longevan, had occasion about this time to ascend the Missouri, in a Mackinaw-boat, with the purpose of trading with the Mandans, about 300 miles above; these Glass resolved to accompany; he was anxious to rejoin the trapping expedition from which he had been cut off; a great object, it may be readily conjectured, was to meet the two wretches he was so much indebted to.

The party set out in their Mackinaw in October; and near a month did they tug against the stubborn current of the Missouri: so slow is the progress of all boats but those impelled by resistless steam, that hunters have the greatest leisure to subsist a party thus employed. At the Big Bend, a half hour's walk across reaches the point gained in three days by the boatman's labor. Among the hunters, Glass was, as usual, conspicuous for patience and success. Many fat elk fell by his hand.

The Arickara Indians, driven by armed forces from their extensive village, had retreated up the river to the Mandans for relief. They had been overpowered but not vanquished; and their immemorial hostility to whites was but aggravated to fresh deeds of outrage.

Late in October, the Mackinaw had reached within twenty miles of the Mandan village. Nor had its party been more cautious than is usual on the river. Late in an afternoon, at this time, they unsuspectingly landed to put ashore a hunter; and, as it happened, at a point nearly opposite the spot chosen by the Arickaras for their temporary abode. Ever on the alert, the boatfull of white men had in the morning been descried by one of their out-parties; and a runner had informed the tribe of the glad tidings. So all was in readiness for the destruction of the unconscious objects of savage revenge. Scarce had the boat left the beach, and Glass, as the hunter (his lucky star still prevailing), gained the concealment of willows, when a hundred guns or bows sent forth their fatal missiles, and on the instant rose the shrill cry of war from a hundred mouths. Had a thunderbolt burst from the cloudless heaven upon the heads of the boat's crew, greater could not have been their astonishment, or its destruction. The appalling din was echoed from hill to hill, and rolled far and wide through the dark bottoms; and it was such as to arrest in fear the fierce panther in the act of leaping upon the now trembling deer.

But few guns from the boat sent back defiance to the murderous discharge; the shouts were but answered by the death-cry and expiring groans. The Indians rushed upon their victims, and the war-club and tomahawk finished a work that had been so fearfully begun. They rioted in blood; with horrid grimaces and convulsive action they hewed into fragments the dumb, lifeless bodies; they returned to their camp a moving group of dusky demons, exulting in revenge, besmeared with blood, bearing aloft each a mangled portion of the dead—trophies of brutal success.

Glass had thus far again escaped a cruel fate. He had gained the almost impervious concealment of drifted and matted willows, and undergrowth, when the dread ebullition of triumph and death announced to him the evil he had escaped, and his still imminent peril. Like the hunted fox, he doubled, he turned, ran or crawled, successively gaining the various concealments of the dense bottom to increase his distance from the bloody scene. And such was his success, that he had thought himself nearly safe, when, at a slight opening, he was suddenly faced by a foe. It was an Arickara scout. The discovery was simultaneous, and so close were these wily woodsmen, that but the one had scarce time to use a weapon intended for a much greater distance. The deadly tomahawk of the other was most readily substituted for the steeled arrow. At the instant, it flew through the air, and the rifle was discharged; neither could see the effect produced, but they rushed into each other's grasp, either endeavoring to crush his adversary by the shock of the onset. But not so the result; the grappling fold of their arms was so close, that they seemed as one animal; for a while, doubtful was the struggle for the mastery; but Glass, not wholly recovered from his wounds, was doomed to sink beneath the superior strength of his adversary, by an irresistible effort of which, he was rolled upon the earth, the Indian above. At this instant, the effect of his unerring shot was developed. The Indian's last convulsive exertion, so successful, was accompanied by a shout of victory; but dying on his lips, it had marked his spirit's departure. It was as if his fierce soul, sensible of approaching feebleness, had willingly expired in the last desperate effort and the shout of triumph, with which he would have ushered both their souls into the presence of the "Great Spirit."

Redeemed unhoped from death, Glass beheld at his feet his late enemy, not only dead, but already stiffening, with hand instinctively touching the hilt of his knife.

Brief was his breathing-time; he was soon rendered aware that the report of his rifle had been heard by the Arickaras; that his escape was discovered; he had instinctively reloaded his gun, and he renewed a flight of which his life was the stake. Concealment from his pursuers having become impossible, he used his utmost speed in the hope of soon gaining a shelter of such a nature, that he could end a race which could no longer be doubtful. Horses had been called into requisition.

We may suppose his hurried thoughts now turned upon his late narrow escapes, which he feared were of little avail; that the crowning scene was now at hand; or that he prayed that That hand, so often interposed between him and death, would again extend its protection.

Horses were of little aid in the thick bottom; but

shouts, uttered at occasional glimpses of his form, announced to Glass that his pursuers were thus excited to efforts that could not much longer fail of success; and his thoughts were intensely turned upon some desperate stratagem as his only hope, when a horseman suddenly crossed his path. In his present state of mind, any Indian appeared to his eyes, a blood-seeking enemy. He felt his death now certain, and was determined not to fall single and unavenged; he was prepared for his last mortal strife. But fortune, which apparently delighted to reduce him to the narrowest straits, but to show her freaks in almost miraculous reverses, had thrown in his way a friend. The horseman was a Mandan Indian on a visit to the Arickaras. Attracted by the noise of the pursuit, he had urged his horse's speed to witness the result; and, coming suddenly upon the object of it, he, at a glance, became aware of the state of the case; a hundred in his place, or he a hundred times to this once, though of a friendly tribe, would have sacrificed the white; but taking one of the sudden and unaccountable resolutions of an Indian, or, perhaps, thinking his interposition of almost impossible avail, at once entered into the excitement of the trial. Be this as it may, he motioned to Glass to mount behind him; it was instantly complied with,—when turning his horse's head, he urged it to its greatest speed. Better ground was sooned gained; and avoiding the Arickara camp, they that night entered the Mandan village in triumph.

Here Glass was well received; for the announcement of his presence was naturally accompanied by the recital of his escapes, which nought but the greatest prowess could have accomplished; and nothing is better calculated effectually to engage the interest and admiration of Indians.

And often are acts and events, which are set down to the score of fortune or good luck, the result of superiority in qualities immediately conducing to the result. Fortune is not so far removed from the agency of man, that a genius may not, by a happy effort, insure its favor and apparently dictate to fate. A true knowledge of all of Glass's career leaves a first impression on the mind, that it is a rare combination of *fortunate* escapes, of *lucky* accidents; but much of it may be explained as the more natural result of physical strength, cool intrepidity, and untiring patience.

After remaining a few days with the Mandans, Glass, nothing daunted by his past dangers, and equally regardless of new ones, resumed alone and on foot, his journey up the Missouri. The Mandan village is on the left or the northeast bank of the river; it was on the same side he commenced his journey, intending to leave the Missouri at the mouth of the Yellow Stone, about three hundred miles higher up; his object in following water-courses, being to meet with white men, and to run no risk of missing the trapping party under Major Henry, he was so anxious to regain.

His arms were now a rifle, small axe, and the ever necessary knife; his dress, a blanket capote, perhaps a flannel shirt, leather leggins and moccasins and a fur cap: he was, in addition, equipped with a blanket, spare moccasins, and a small kettle, composing a bundle suspended on his back. His route lay through a country infested with the Blackfeet Indians. The Blackfeet muster eight or ten thousand warriors; they live north of this part of the Missouri, and extend west to the mountains; and they are frequently upon the Yellow Stone. To their east live the Assinaboines, Mandans, and Minatarees; to the south the Crows and Sioux; and north and west the Mountain or British Indians. With these tribes they wage perpetual war; and to the whites, incited by British traders, they have been more dangerous than any other Indians. It was through the grounds of this people that Glass had to make his solitary way.

The country on the Missouri, from the L'eau qui-court up, is nearly bare of timber; the river bottoms are narrow, and on but one side at a time, changing at intervals of twenty or thirty miles, and sometimes there are none at all, the ground being generally high bluff prairies. This open, bare country is at times, as far as vision extends, in every direction blackened with buffalo; it is within bounds to say, that a hundred thousand may be seen at a glance. One of these vast herds, all taking the same course to cross the Missouri, detained Glass for two days, declining the perilous attempt to penetrate a mass, which, when in quick motion, is as irresistible as the waves of the ocean.

In two weeks he reached the mouth of the Yellow Stone, having met neither white man or Indian; here he crossed the Missouri on a raft made of two logs tied together with bark, and continued his journey up the Yellow Stone. This is a wide and shallow stream, emptying into the Missouri from the south; it is even more muddy and rapid than the latter river, to which it is believed to have considerable agency in imparting these qualities.

It was more than three hundred miles to the forks of the river, nearer than which he could scarcely hope to meet with any of the party, since it had set in very cold, which would cause the small detachment of trappers to be drawn into that point, where he knew they were to winter. Right weary did he become of his journey, inured as he was to the toils and dangers which surrounded him. Almost in despair, and having at times nearly resolved to retrace his steps and winter with some of the most friendly Indians, one morning in December he was overjoyed to discover a hunting party of white men. On reaching them, long was it before they could make up their minds to believe their eyes; to believe that it was the same Glass before them, whom they left, as they thought, dying of wounds, and whose expected death was related to them by two witnesses. It was to them a mystery; and belief of the act of black treachery, which could only explain a part of it, was slow in being enforced upon their minds. Overwhelmed with questions or demands of explanation, it was long before he could ascertain from them in return, that the party had rendezvoused for winter at the Forks, which was but a few miles distant; that Fitzgerald was not there, having deserted; and that the youth was still one of the expedition.

Fiercely excited with conflicting feelings,—the escape of the main object of his just revenge,—chiefly for which he had made so long a pilgrimage,—and the certainty of soon facing the accomplice of his crime, Glass hastened to enter the encampment.

Nearly the first person he met, was the unfortunate and guilty young man; and it so happened they came upon each other suddenly. All attempt must fail to describe the effect of his appearance upon the youth. Had he awoke from a deep sleep in the embrace of a grizzly bear, or been confronted at noonday by the threatening ghost (and such he believed of him) of a deeply injured enemy, greater could not have been his fear. He stood without power of any motion; his eyes rolled wildly in their sockets; his teeth chattered, and a clammy sweat rose upon his ashy features. Glass was unprepared for such a spectacle; and well was it calculated to create pity; for some moments he could not find words, much less the act of his purpose. He leaned upon his rifle; his thoughts took a sudden turn; the more guilty object of his revenge had escaped; the pitiful being before him was perhaps but the unwilling and over-persuaded accomplice of his much elder companion;—these, and other thoughts crowded upon his mind, and he determined upon the revenge which sinks deepest upon minds not wholly depraved, and of which the magnanimous are alone capable; he determined to spare his life.

With dignity and severity, but great feeling, he thus addressed the petrified youth, who but expected immediate death: "Young man, it is Glass that is before you; the same that, not content with leaving, you thought, to a cruel death upon the prairie, you robbed, helpless as he was, of his rifle, his knife, of all with which he could hope to defend, or save himself from famishing in the desert. In case I had died, you left me to a despair worse than death, with no being to close my eyes. I swore an oath that I would be revenged on you, and the wretch who was with you; and I ever thought to have kept it. For this meeting I have made a long journey. But I cannot take your life; I see you repent; you have nothing to fear from me; go—you are free—for your youth I forgive you." But he remained mute and motionless; his reprieve, or rather pardon, for such it must be considered in a country where the law has never reached, could scarcely allay the awe and fear of an upbraiding conscience. He was taken off by some of the witnesses of the scene, in whose breasts pity had begun to take the place of wonder and resentment.

Glass was welcomed as one recovered from the dead; one whose memory—such is our lot—had already been swept far upon the gulf of oblivion. His services, ever highly appreciated, were again engaged in the company, where we leave him, employed as the rest, in the sole labors of supplying provisions, and of self-defence from the extreme coldness of the winter. Only adding, that his determination of revenge upon the more worthy object of punishment from his hands, far from being abated, was rather confirmed; and that, what he considered a sacred duty to himself, though postponed to a more convenient season, was still nourished as a ruling passion.

CHAPTER XXI.

The varieties of human character, though infinite, yield to a grand division of the race into two classes,—those with much and those with little sensibility. It is impossible to tell which is the more fortunate organization: the one class chafes and frets at all it sees wrong, and experiences positive pain at every exhibition of selfishness, cruelty, or turpitude; but, with a lively perception of every natural or moral beauty, it has various capacities for pleasure and enjoyment. The other class is seldom troubled with emotions of any kind, and passes through life in a routine of sensual pleasures and animal pains. This mental and moral torpor I eschew, and prefer to hold intercourse with nature; to walk forth alone—nay, friend reader, if you are in the mood, bear me company. Let us take a stroll together this sunny afternoon; 'tis glorious October, that, with its gorgeous mantle of purple and of gold, sheds a "dying glory" on the parting year. Here is a deer-path through the hazel thicket: see how generously unfolded are the ripe nuts! Stop—listen a moment how the monotone of that gurgling waterfall harmonizes with the repose of nature! Here it is. Let us cross by that moss-grown log. We have no longer a path, but we will go up this noble hill; it is a natural park, and often graced by antlered buck, but in the majesty of freedom. Here we are out of sight of the "improvements" of man; so let us sit on this velvet moss; mind not the rustling lizard, it is harmless. What a glorious solitude is here! Before us is "a prairie-sea, all isled with rock and wood;" and beyond, like an ocean shore, a vast bluff, rocky and forest-crowned. And yonder is a glimpse of the river, mighty in repose; a zephyr hovering on its bosom sports with its tiny waves, which, dancing, reflect the dazzling light through those red and golden leaves. But the charm over all is a perfect REPOSE. Even the winds, whispering anon, seem to have folded their wings: and see yon leaf, in its "dying fall" —if there be a poetry of motion, behold its gently circling descent! That gray squirrel detached it. And look, *he* seems to slumber. Nature is taking a sunny sleep.

Oh, there is an invisible, unknown, mental link, connecting all sweet, and calm, and beautiful things. Who can view such a scene without hearing a natural music, or an echo of some long-forgotten tone, which thrilled the heart, without recalling the few blissful moments which shed a secret, selfish joy o'er the dreary void of life—the first conception of love—its tone from beauty and young innocence—the awakening from some sweet sleep to the sound of soft music, which was deemed to be not of earth.

Behold the thin blue smoke floating above those distant tree tops! It is the type of the little present, hovering between the great past and the mighty future. What! you too are asleep? Unkind! But 'tis well. Alone let me knock at the doors of old Time, and challenge the shades beyond. The spell is potent. I see dim figures, as in a dream; but they assume the forms of palpable and warm existence. They are paler than the Indian, but are not white. They seem to worship at a mighty altar, and it bears the emblems of war. How strange is all! Unknown animals are there, crouching among the multitude; beneath the white drapery of a vast pavilion, with flowing red streamers, the grave elders are seated in council. See, a noble youth arises; he seems to speak: he addresses the fathers. How graceful! how animated! His robe falls back, and he shakes aloft his arm. His is a voice for war: for behold that eager and trembling maiden! She drinks those flowing tones, inspired perhaps by thoughts of her. Love and ambition have carried him away. His spirit seems caught by the multitude. 'Tis ever so. Genius and enthusiasm possess a master-key to all hearts. The elders wave their arms, and seem to deprecate the rashness of impulse; but in vain; there are times when it is prudent to be rash, and they must lead or follow; for all seem resolved, and the assembly breaks up.

But lo, a change! They go forth to war. Song and shout uncouth, and strange forgotten instruments fill the air. Huge animals shake their heads, and bellow to the din of rattling arms. There is a band of horsemen, with shield and spear, and waving streamers: they seem clothed in white cotton mail. The orator is there, in highest command. His countenance now is filled with thought, and proud and stern resolve. See the mighty host slowly disappear, winding among the far hills.

Another change! Behold a vast multitude, "vast beyond compare," with signs of mingled mourning and lofty triumph. All bear loads of earth, and deposit them on that beautiful spot. How fast it grows. It has become a mighty mound. And now they disappear. But one, of all, is left. The same maiden; her face is spread with pallid woe; she weeps, and will never be consoled, till her ashes mingle with that monument of victory and of death —the tomb of her lost idol.

> "As swim
> O'er autumn skies the fleets of shattered cloud,
> So swam these scenes and passed."

What a moral was there! Not the air-built castles of the hopeful and ambitious of the extinct race have fallen into more immemorial oblivion than have their proudest and soberest realities. Their mountain tombs are their only monuments.

But the charm of this quiet existence, which had extended through several summers, was rudely broken. Even then the holy calm of nature was disturbed by the noisy bellowings of steam, which I had strangely imagined those of living monsters; and its echoes among the hills around me had a power to banish the sylvan ministers to my solitude. I felt my Arcadian dreams dispelled forever. I beheld the conquering struggle of man with the mighty Missouri, and felt that the type of a more active, troublous existence, in which the world demanded the performance of my part, was before me.

Soon all was activity and stirring preparation. Half of us were to go to another frontier, where alarms and bloodshed had aroused every element of commotion. But I was not included in the call. Nevertheless, I had felt that I was to go.

CHAPTER XXII.

A YEAR before—in 1831—there had been a military expedition to the Upper Mississippi, to remove forcibly the Sacs and Foxes from their old country in Illinois (their birthright, which they had sold for a mess of pottage): and now again, as if irresistibly and fatally attracted to the homes of their youth and the graves of their fathers, they had revisited, but peaceably, the forbidden land east of the Mississippi. The militia (that prosopopœia of weakness, waste, and confusion) had been called out; about three hundred, well mounted, had left an encampment on Rock River—it is said in a kind of frolic—under a Colonel S.; they came upon a few quiet and inoffensive Indians, and murdered several of them in cold blood; they afterward came in contact with a large body which they attacked; they were repulsed, and retreated at speed in utter confusion; *sixteen* Indians pursued them many miles, and speared eleven of their number; the rest, throwing away their saddlebags and flying before this force, did not draw rein for about forty miles: they reported that they had had a bloody battle with 1500 warriors! After bringing on the war in this style, the militia under Brigadier Whiteside retired to their homes.

To Brigadier-General Atkinson of the army, had then been assigned the conduct of the war, and the organization of an army of volunteers to co-operate with his regulars; he had established his head-quarters and rendezvous near the head of navigation of the Illinois River; and had sent an order for two of the four companies at Fort Leavenworth to join him there, with a view to their junction with six other companies of the same regiment then in camp on Rock River.

The two named companies of our battalion were ordered to embark as soon as possible. Believing that the time had come when gunpowder would be burned, I offered my services as a volunteer; and they were accepted.

We departed within twenty-four hours after the arrival of the steamboat, and in forty-nine more, were in St. Louis, taking on board arms and provisions: the next day we departed for the Illinois, and, in two more, disembarked at Gen. A.'s encampment at the rapids.

It is these rapid and exciting changes, with their uncertainties and hopeful anticipations, and these sudden and unexpected meetings with old friends and companions, under novel and enlivening circumstances, that lend a seductive attraction to the service, even in a time of peace: and, to that happy law of our natures which causes us to forget pain, and to remember and dwell on the bright points of the past, we doubtless owe those regrets and repinings which are said generally to haunt the minds of officers who resign their commissions for other pursuits.

However eligible and pleasant had been my situation at Fort Leavenworth, a seclusion of two and a half years had produced a longing for the *unseen*,—a desire for change; and what had not five days brought forth? A visit to a city,—the rapid motion of nine hundred miles, —and, contrasted with our former quiet, the bustle of a camp of several thousands of men on the eve of a campaign;—and above all, the unexpected meeting under these exciting circumstances, with many very dear and long absent friends! Those five days,—and above all, that last evening of my arrival, were worth years of humdrum existence:—over the long interval of years,—over the chaos of events, it comes back warm and bright with a pleasure which causes me to linger as I write!

Next morning I was in the midst of the multitude of citizen volunteers, who were as active as a swarming hive; catching horses, electioneering, drawing rations, asking questions, shooting at marks, electing officers, mustering in, issuing orders, disobeying orders, galloping about, "cussing and discussing" the war, and the rumors thereof. Here was a fine harvest for the humorous;—and one might have passed the day in giving quizzical answers to absurd questions;—there was no immunity; the General in his tent could not escape the intrusion of these raw fellows, who had no more idea of the first principles of military respect and subordination, than they had of Frederick's campaigns. "Are you Colonel of the artillery?" asked one of them of Lieutenant A., who was acting ordnance-officer. "No! I'm commander of it." "Beg your pardon, *General.*"

There was an unfortunate circumstance attending the organization and services of the Illinois militia;—important elections were pending; all candidates of course took the field, and unfortunately were candidates *there;* and in the execution of their duties, the enforcing of disagreeable regulations and constraints, were the subjects of this mistaken extrinsic influence. The strict and impartial performance of *duty*, is the basis of all military popularity.

A remarkable exception to the general censure, was the brave and indefatigable Colonel E., who, stern, exacting, and even harsh when it was necessary to be so, was a model of energy and endurance:—happily I can add, that he soon after received the highest of those civic honors, which so many aspired to: he was elected a senator in Congress.

My services as a volunteer were in the market; and I was offered the appointment of aid-de-camp to one of the three militia brigadiers, with the somewhat tempting rank of major; I did not fancy the connection: but I lent my unavailing assistance to one of his staff, who spent several days in abortive attempts to produce a morning report: he was then furloughed for the duration of the campaign (and doubtless has been well paid for his *ardent* services).

The organization of the volunteers was painfully slow, notwithstanding daily information of Indian ravages. But at last, on the 19th of June, one brigade was reported ready for service: it was very complete—on paper—for they even had paymasters and their mates;—it being well understood that they would never handle any but their own pay. The same day, this brigade and our two companies of infantry, marched with a provision train for Dixon's Ferry on Rock River: we were commanded by the gallant old General Brady; who had come as a volunteer, and was soon after assigned to the command of a division. We passed over a fine country of woods and prairie interspersed; but the soil was rich and soft; and our progress with heavy laden wagons was tedious.

The volunteers on this short march, gave us a fine specimen of what was to be expected of their services. They had been ordered to take on their horses some twelve or fifteen days' rations; on the second morning's march they raised the cry of "Indians! Indians!" when several hundreds without orders, or the least order, galloped out of the column, and scattered at full speed over the prairies;—on joining again several miles beyond, it appeared that they had all thrown away the incumbrance of provisions: it was said to have been a manœuvre for that object. We arrived at Dixon's June 23d. Here we found entrenched on the north side of the river, six companies of the 6th, four of the 1st, and two of the 5th infantry: the volunteers encamped on the south side, and we joined our regiment: I then received a staff appointment.

Here was another delightful meeting with my own regiment, and old 1st infantry companions at Jefferson Barracks; though delay was irksome, it was to me a delightful camp.

Rock River, here about one hundred yards wide and not fordable, is a beautiful stream; its glassy waters glide over white sand and pebbles; its rich and verdant banks present every variety of natural beauty; savannas, slopes, gentle hill and rocky bluff, prairie and grove, presented a varied picture, beyond all imitation or improvement of art.

It was not strange that such a country, bound to the very heartstrings of the Indian by all native associations, and all the pleasures of his free, sporting, and untrammelled life, should possess for him fatal attractions; fatal, when the dollar and cent interests of the unsympathizing whites demand the letter of the hard-driven, if not fraudulent bargain.

This was the point of final arrangements for the campaign; five days after us, arrived Alexander's 2d brigade, which encamped with the 1st on the opposite side of the river; the next day Gen. A., with his staff, and Henry's 3d brigade also, arrived.

The night after this junction, about nine o'clock, a heavy and continuous discharge of firearms took place in the militia camp; and soon after its commencement the horses broke loose, and more than a thousand of them ran scampering over the prairie hills. The roar of the firearms, and the flashes of flame which they gave out in the darkness, and which lighted up the river between us —the noisy rush of the horses over the hills—and the other adjuncts to the scene, which any one may well imagine, made us believe, as we hurried together, that the devil was certainly let loose amongst our militia friends. The firing was redoubled and became the regular discharges of battalions; the General, astonished and uneasy, despatched a company of regulars in a Mackinaw boat to ascertain the cause; the officers on reaching the camp witnessed a singular scene; a whole brigade was regularly paraded and firing in the air as regularly as they knew how, while their General, mounted on a tall stump, was endeavoring to argue them out of it; but their perseverance was not more extraordinary than their commencement; and neither was ever explained: their General finally damned them to all posterity, and resigned his commission in violent disgust. The firing came to an end, as all things must.

The next day was spent in hunting horses: many of which were injured by rushing in the darkness against

Dixon's fence. The Brigadier was induced to resume the exercise of his commission.

About this time, Galena was the scene of some extravagant proceedings; it was much exposed, and might with little difficulty have been captured and destroyed by the Indians, had they possessed a little more enterprise and daring; the inhabitants present were in a state of complete panic, and the most unbridled disorder; martial law was declared by the notorious Col. S., or one of the companions of his Hegira: but it may be presumed that the martial law entered as little as the civil, into their crude conceptions of order. They owed their safety to the timid inaction of their enemy.

Brigadier-General Henry having marched north to form a junction with Col. Dodge, who had raised a mounted battalion of the miners, the 1st and part of the 2d division of the army were put in march before the end of June, and ascended the left bank of Rock River. A day or two after, we passed the ground of Stillman's defeat and race; we saw parts of the scattered garments of the slain; in front of the creek on which the Indians had been posted, the ground was boggy; a circumstance peculiarly unfavorable to the action of horsemen; but militia, or Western and Southern militia, though they never become cavalry, will never turn out, it would seem, otherwise than mounted. The horse is an incumbrance in warfare, unless his rider is ready and skilful in the use of the sabre.

The army marched northward about a week over a fine prairie country, intersected by many bold streams, skirted with woods; crossing many well-worn old Indian trails, and passing the ruins of several ancient villages; seeking, I suppose, the fastnesses of the enemy, without any very definite information of his actual situation; although the mounted men were scattered far and wide by the General, in efforts to make discoveries.

At one time, indeed, some of the staff seemed to believe that they knew the exact position of the enemy; and on the information of certain guides, actually sketched a map of his stronghold, intrenched among swamps and morasses, the approach through which marvellously resembled the schoolboy puzzle of the walls of Troy.

About the 9th of July, at the noonday halt, the General called an informal council of war; having received information that Black Hawk and his warriors were strongly posted some eight or nine miles in our front; he proposed, we understood, this question: whether the army should then advance in the expectation of arriving much fatigued before the enemy, and near nightfall; or encamp, and advance to the attack very early next morning?

The army advanced; and performed a march of near ten miles, without passing water on the prairies; the sun was fast sinking, when we approached an extensive wood: and so soon as the advance had struck it, we heard and saw an irregular discharge of fire-arms; our pack-horses were immediately picketed in a body, and left under a guard; and the infantry hastened to advance in column, while we all were in the very pleasant belief that we were marching into a decisive combat: never were troops in better spirits, when it is considered that a minute before many seemed exhausted by fatigue and thirst;—on entering the woods under these circumstances, it became known that the fire had proceeded from a body of irregulars—chiefly Indians, in front of whom a deer had run a kind of gauntlet. Every circumstance had conspired to assure us of an approaching action; and slowly and unwillingly were all convinced of the truth; so that in the dispositions for the night-camp—which was established very soon after near a pond—some, in the blind obedience which discipline exacts of the most eager, only recognized the preparations for battle; and when I assigned to a company commander of the 6th his camp-ground, he inquired of me the position of the enemy!

We were afterwards strongly confirmed in a belief then held, that the Sacs and Foxes were that night encamped within two or three miles of us: in fact, two of us on this occasion offered our services to the General, to proceed on foot and endeavor to discover his position; but it was not approved of.

In this camp one of the militia sentinels was so nervously vigilant as to shoot a friend. This is not a very uncommon occurrence among them; and they are supposed by some ill-natured persons to be generally more dangerous to their friends than to their enemies.

Being near the enemy, and in the vicinity of his favorite retreats, the infantry next day moved to better position, which was near at hand, and the volunteers were detached in force in different directions to seek him: but they met with no success.

The day after, the army marched by Lake Koshkonong, and took up a strong position beyond on the bank of Clearwater Creek, not far from its junction with Rock River. Opposite was a very extensive and almost impenetrable tamarisk swamp: nevertheless a substantial bridge was commenced next morning; and evidently under the observation of the Indians, for two of our men were wounded.

Riding that day alone in a wood, a little distance in

advance of a column, my discipline was sorely tried; a noble buck approached me and stood several moments within pistol-shot; my hand, almost before I knew it, had grasped a holster pistol; but I resisted the temptation, only to hear, immediately after, some of the irregulars popping away at him as he ran past.

One day was spent in camp on Clear Creek; but the bridge was not quite finished, when the next morning the march was resumed; our course was up the Clearwater, as near as swamps, bogs, and some very difficult miry branches would permit. When these occur in a low prairie they require much labor to render them passable: if not bridged, the banks are dug, and much brush and long grass deposited; over these trembling causeways, each horse seems to consider his passage an adventure; and many a rider, too; their awkward mishaps repay in amusement the pioneers for their extra work; the streams are very deep, with abrupt quicksand banks, covered to the verge with sod. One of them I attempted to leap; but mistook for my point of departure, a tuft of grass for a substantial sod, and of course tumbled headlong in. I then, wet as I was, committed a double imprudence; first, in riding at a very slow pace—which was no exercise at all; and then, on getting into my tent, changing all my clothes; the consequence was a very violent cold;—almost the only one I ever took in camp.

I observed to-day a fair specimen of the great advantages which the front holds over the rear of a column of march; we passed some remarkable springs;—little grassy mounds in a savanna; the first comers drank of crystal and very cold water bubbling over the rim of something very like an immense emerald bowl; but before the last arrived, they had become mere mud-holes.

The whole march of some twelve miles was in view ot the tamarisk swamp. Our camp was pitched on a slight elevation near the Clearwater. A council of general officers was called, and it was decided not to cross and penetrate the swamp at this point; nor to move further in this direction.

Accordingly, on the following day, a countermarch was made; and the army retracing its steps, passed beyond the mouth of Clearwater, and encamped on the shore of Lake Koshkonong, which is an enlargement of Rock River.

The provisions of the army were very nearly exhausted, and the consequence was a temporary suspension of operations, until a further supply could be drawn from the nearest depot; this was Fort Winnebago, distant about sixty miles. The division of mounted volunteers was ordered to march thither and draw fifteen days' rations, which they were to transport on their horses: whilst a convoy was to be despatched to our camp.

A slight breastwork was thrown up round this camp; and the troops were also employed in building two block-houses, and a connecting picket-work to serve for a depot.

I do not attempt to give more than a mere sketch of the actual operations of this campaign: for, not having been on the General's staff, I was not "in the secrets of the cabinet:" I did not harass myself in seeking by cross-questions, scraps of intelligence; or, in eternally discussing and criticising operations founded on intelligence and exigencies of which the critics were generally in profound ignorance; or, in volunteering advice to any of supposed influence who would listen, as some one or a few officers did, and seemed to suffer as much uneasiness as if they had borne a load of responsibility equal to that with which many adverse circumstances seemed to overload our commanding General.

It was, however, impossible to mistake the causes of this delay, when a prudent General and an able staff were evidently blameless. It was generally reported, and not contradicted, that the volunteers had been improvident and wasteful to the degree of leaving in certain camps rations that had been issued, by the barrel in unbroken bulk! And again, the militia convoys were incredibly timid and unmanageable; provision trains could not be got on; one was abandoned by guard and drivers, within two or three miles of our position here, in consequence of their having imagined that they had seen an Indian or two: thus were good plans thwarted in despite of the great exertions of the quarter-master department; which was indebted to the militia for an active and energetic *head*.

Whilst the infantry lay here under these circumstances, I well remember reading in a National Intelligencer—which some express-man had brought to camp—a speech made by a Western senator, who branded the regular army as the "sweepings of cities," &c. &c., and extolled the frontier men—militia—rangers—(our friends, the volunteers), as infinitely superior; men who would be "here to-night, and to-morrow fifty miles off;" who would "*subsist* themselves," &c. Verily, your politician excels in humbug!

CHAPTER XXIII.

After a delay of four or five days in camp on Lake Koshkonong,—waiting as before stated for a supply of provisions,—and for the mounted volunteers to supply themselves at Fort Winnebago,—a provision train arrived under the conduct of the indefatigable Quarter-master-general March, and we were joined by one brigade of the militia. Next morning the army marched once more—in a heavy rain—over the same ground of its former march and countermarch. At night we had not advanced so far as on the first occasion, and we were forced to encamp on a piece of ground of slight elevation—a sort of island—amid the creeks and their swampy and overflowed bottoms. We were soaked to the skin; the rain still fell,—and fuel was scarce: I was in a small tent with the commanding officer, in rear of one of the regiments composing one front of the encampment; it was late and very dark; I had fallen asleep on my blanket. Perhaps soon after, I was aroused by a rushing, rumbling sound, as of an earthquake,—and quite as quickly as the consciousness of the dangerous cause, found myself standing astride our little fire, with sword and cocked pistol in hand; and saw,—hemming us in on all sides—the glaring eyeballs and arched necks of hundreds of horses, wild and trembling with excitement, and crouched almost in act of dashing over us; I stood at desperate bay, with finger on trigger: it was indeed a moment of great peril,—but it was passed in safety; and the horses became instantly calmer as they heard the voices of their masters; many of whom came boldly among them. They had been picketed in the other end of an inclosed parallelogram;—Indian yells had been heard, when they took fright, and rushed in the direction of our regiment, which, at the first alarm, had formed their line,—and as they came thundering on, had faced inward among their fires, which, glittering on their arms, had served to arrest their course, which had not acquired its full momentum; they were thus thrown round our tent, which, mistaken for a more solid barrier, they had managed to avoid in their first career, and we were saved. It was the custom in like cases to spring to a wagon or tree; neither was near us on this night: but an officer told me that he had sprung up one of the latter just in time to save himself, as the horses rushed under him and against his legs as they hung down.

Next morning many horses were missing, and others injured. In the course of the night, an express, which had pushed through under its cover from the depot at Koshkonong, brought to the General important information; and a second countermarch was ordered at daydawn. The General had been informed that in returning from Fort Winnebago, Brigadier Henry, in command of his brigade, and Dodge's mounted battalion, had discovered the fresh trail of the whole body of the Sacs and Foxes moving northward, and had marched in pursuit.

This day we passed Fort Koshkonong, in a cold and beating rain, and forded Rock River below the lake,—it was nearly swimming,—and half dead with cold and fatigue, encamped on the right bank.

This encamping after a weary march,—particularly in a rain, or when it is late,—is the most trying part of a soldier's life; the day's labors would seem but then commenced; every earthly comfort has to be worked for, as much as if they had never been obtained before; and one's labors are retarded, and depend upon the will and motions of others;—details are to be furnished; guards mounted; camps laid out; baggage unloaded,—and how often is it to be waited for!—delaying everything; tents are to be pitched; wood to be cut; water to be brought, frequently from a great distance; rations to be distributed, then cooked; arms to be cleaned; inspections made; but, above all,—with cavalry,—forage to be procured, issued, and fed; and horses to be groomed, and watered often in almost inaccessible places.

After urging my poor horse over all kinds of obstacles —assigning their ground to the companies—communicating orders to their commanders, and *hearing* the snarls of an occasional grumbler—I had still before me the duties of the regimental and grand guard parades. What wealth is there in a cheerful spirit! A good soldier never grumbles (if he can help it);—when his rights are invaded, he pursues the most quiet, firm, and effectual mode of redress.

Next forenoon we met expresses, who bore the news of an action on the banks of the Wisconsin, where the enemy was overtaken, and said to have been roughly handled; a gallant fight it was represented to have been. That evening we formed a junction with the brigade and battalion of spies, at the Blue Mounds; whither they had *retired*, after their glorious victory, to meet us. It would be difficult to give a full idea of the proud, but modest complacency with which they all agreed—for they *must* tell the truth—in extolling the intrepidity and coolness exhibited in the battle; how they had, for example, cried out in the midst of it, "Come forward, boys, and draw your ponies!" by which they had playfully expressed their intention of appropriating to themselves those little animals; (which the Indians found so useful that we could not learn they had been persuaded actually to part with any of them.) "Wisconsin Heights" fairly promised to prove a watchword, before which "Tippecanoe," &c., might hang its head;—"Pity it was, we had not been there;—but they could not help it,—how could they, if the Sacs *would* allow themselves to be used up?"

After all their boasting, the simple fact was, that Black Hawk, although encumbered with the women, children, and baggage of his whole band, covering himself by a small party, had accomplished that most difficult of military operations,—to wit, the passage of a river,—in the presence of three regiments of American volunteers! And they were now gone—the *victors* could not tell us whither.

The next day the whole army marched to resume the pursuit and cross the Wisconsin; it encamped at night at Helena, on the left bank of the river. Here a delay of a day or two occurred; arising from the extreme difficulties encountered by the commissariat of so large a force in an uncultivated country; and one very deficient in the means of transportation; and the only calculations that could be made as to the next operations were, that they would be in an almost impassable wilderness!

Between Rock and Wisconsin Rivers we marched amid the most beautiful scenery I had ever beheld; a varying succession of prairie and forest; of hill, vale, and mound, so various in form, abrupt yet smooth and green, that it might be imagined the sudden petrifaction of an ocean storm. Again, the soft face of gentle slopes, with groves and trees in the semblance of parks and orchards, and little prairie fields, presented the picturesque and peaceful appearance of a highly cultivated district, whence the dwellings of man alone had unaccountably disappeared.

On a nearer approach to the Wisconsin River there was more wildness and sublimity; we marched along lofty and narrow ridges and beheld everywhere broken and jagged peaks—dark and profound abysses (bearing evident traces of volcanic action)—vast rocks disjointed and scattered;—all seemingly in the confusion of some great catastrophe. But amid this sterile grandeur, we caught glimpses of green and sunny landscape, which seemed warmed and brightened by the effects of contrast. Descending as we approach the river, we followed a remarkable prairie valley, straight, level, with steep green sides or banks, presenting an extraordinary uniformity for five or six miles. Again, very near the river, we saw many isolated sugar-loaf hills, towering several hundred feet in the air; covered with grass; dotted with pines, and showing in places their rocky structure. Their summits commanded noble views; the bright and swift river winding among rugged mountains; and beyond, far away, its wide savannas and noble forests; all, in this wild and scarce explored region, filled our minds with the exciting ideas of the discovery of a new country, which, in its summer dress, seemed to greet our approach with smiles.

Such is the scenery of the valley of the Wisconsin, from which it was our ungracious errand to drive the original possessors, who, like spectres haunting the scenes of their nativity and warm attachment, were destined to atone in blood for their only fault or misfortune, that they loved not wisely but too well.

A post was established at Helena; and the army crossed July 28th, and marched in a northern direction, in the expectation, doubtless, of soon falling upon traces of the retreating enemy. If so, they were soon realized; for we were still in the low grounds of the river, when, being with the van, I witnessed the discovery of the trail, which led to a singular and amusing little scene;—suddenly I saw Colonel D.,—who was riding in advance with the General,—draw his sword and spur forward with great animation, riding hither thither—gazing on the ground, and uttering unintelligible exclamations;—the General, though evidently quite ignorant of the inspiring cause of this eccentric proceeding, in a kind of blind sympathy, galloped after the Colonel, following him quite closely in his course, which became a series of circles, narrowing down to a point, where, sure enough, was the plain fresh trail of the whole tribe. Imagine a pointer circling in search of the hole of a ground-squirrel with a young one following, nose to tail, in an attempt at imitation, and then imagine them metamorphosed into horses, and on their backs,—of one, a portly and grave Colonel sword in hand—and of the other, a dignified and still more portly General!

The column here turned to the left, following the new course, which led down the prairie bottom of the river.

We had now a good laugh on one of the General's staff (a fine fellow and a great favorite he was!) who, absorbed in geological researches, or in search of the picturesque, had ridden far in advance, and continuing the course which we had first taken, passed without knowing it, so large a trail (which we were seeking); and was then to be seen a mile or two off, on the summit of one of the singular conical hills of this country.

CHAPTER XXIV.

Now followed a march over a country which we found to present almost insuperable difficulties to the passage of an army; a march which was perhaps as trying to the perseverance and endurance of the troops, as some we read of as remarkable before and during the Revolutionary War, though, doubtless, surpassed in these respects by some performed by that "Hannibal of the West," General George Rogers Clarke. It was through a district said to have been unexplored by whites; and certainly remarkable for a combination or juxtaposition of the primitive, alluvious, and other formations, almost unheard of in geology. It lies between the Wisconsin, Pine, and Kickapoo Rivers; and was said to have been entered by Black Hawk in the belief that the army could not follow him; if so, he paid dearly for his mistake.

All but provisions and baggage of the first necessity, being left with every wheeled carriage, and taking, as it were, a temporary farewell of the sun and his cheerful light, we forced our way into the bramble and thicket of this gloomy forest. We followed the narrow trails made by the Indians through undergrowth which could only be passed by patient and painful effort. The first day we forded Pine River, all but swimming for horses, and in the face of such other obstacles that an ambush must have led to great disaster. Afterwards for several days we toiled over a seemingly endless succession of lofty hills, so precipitous, that it was frequently necessary to use the hands to assist the feet. After ascending such a hill, perhaps three hundred feet in height, we would find ourselves on the verge of an equally abrupt descent; then a valley from a quarter to a half mile wide, to the foot of the next hill; but in the valley we invariably found a bog, and a miry creek; half the army as pioneers would then, with axe, hatchet, and spade, labor at causeway and bridge; over which horses and mules struggled, making desperate but not always effectual efforts to extricate themselves.

At night our encampments, or places of rest, were on all manner of ground, and in every shape; fortunate the individual who found—if any did—a spot not too steep or rugged to lie on with comfort;—and the nights were very cold, though midsummer; once there was a frost.

I have not mentioned the flankers;—so necessary when the column was lengthened out, as if in a forty-mile defile;—their obstacles, which the instinct of the Indian avoided in making the trail, I will not enlarge upon.

What a situation—to which there seemed no end—for an army! How differently considered by the General and the subordinates who could laugh at personal difficulties and dangers; and who, if life even were endangered, were involved in no harassing responsibility, threatening reputation and honor!

How unenviable is rank and power thus (in our Indian wars) continually struggling against obstacles and the oppressive sense of responsibility! The exalted consciousness of well-used power, warming and ennobling the mind, is denied him; or is overpowered and depressed by a struggle against disheartening difficulties, which he *knows* his government and his fellow-citizens will not, and cannot appreciate. Even the pomp and circumstance of arms,—flattering to the minor feelings,—are denied him. To this picture there is no brighter side. Fame, glory, are not accorded to the conqueror of Indians! How *substantial* then, should be the government rewards of so much labor and suffering, in the cause solely and exclusively of the country! A leader of an army in a *fair field* of battle with a civilized foe, exalted by the hope of glory—which, like a bright spirit of the air, seems to beckon on!—by a happy effect, or a happier accident, occurring amid the confusion of battle, and beneath the smoke (which, oh! how often, obscures and veils forever the deciding stroke of some inferior), achieves a victory, and becomes famous.

But Black Hawk and his band! Unhappy tribe! Flying from their foes, did the warriors witness with stoic apathy their wives and little ones famished, exhausted, diseased, and left to die on the roadside! Every earthly tie severed—all humanizing feelings, attachments, and sympathies, outraged, embittered, destroyed;—every hope and passion merged in revenge;—why did not a desire to end a wretched existence in a glorious death, halt the red warrior on the hill-top? Appealing to the avenging spirit of his tribe, why did he not on his NATIVE hill-tops, make the acceptable offerings to liberty, of blood and of life?

Is this wretched love of the most wretched existence implanted in the human heart, an evidence of Unchangeable Omnipotent Will? Not so:—for the more elevated by faith, patriotism, love of glory, and the many ennobling sentiments of our most tutored and exalted state, then the less does this selfish influence control us.

But my subject;—do these fancies and fine words belong to that? Alas, I know not:—when the memory of that unhappy flight was recalled;—when I saw again all the evidences of suffering and starvation;—the corpses, not of warrior only, but of poor women,—lying as they fell by the trodden path,—how could I confine my thoughts, or their expression, to unmoved description?

Why did not the Indian chief leave a chosen body in these fastnesses, where natural obstacles could well-nigh defeat the progress of an army? That he had scouts that marked our progress, can scarcely be doubted; but why he did not avail himself of their information that we had, or act upon the strong probability that we would, venture among these morasses, dense thickets, and precipitous defiles, and oppose to us some small force, seems inexplicable:—at the Wisconsin he had covered well his passage; and when we overtook him on the Mississippi, we were met by a small body of keen warriors, who accomplished much with a similar object. Here a small force could have retarded pursuit at every step; could have compelled us to condense our march, and continually make deployments on ground almost impracticable for any manner of military manœuvre, and where the horses of the volunteers would have proved a great embarrassment; endless coverts must have kept us in constant ignorance or uneasiness, as to the amount of his force; an ambuscade might have been formed every mile. It may have been that he had calculated, with supposed certainty, our inability to overtake him east of the Mississippi; a want of provisions may have been an obstacle; may have rendered it impracticable to leave a large force;—though he certainly had many horses (some of which were eaten); and a dozen good men could have effected the purpose.

An ill-judged confidence of security is the stumbling-block of warfare. But there was certainly a great deficiency of natural abilities for war continually manifested by the Sacs. There has been many an Indian warrior—

unless they have been greatly overrated in our histories —who could with their means and opportunities in this campaign, have made us pay dearly for every success. (Though doubtless had regulars been opposed to them at the passage of the Wisconsin, a fatal blow would, have been struck.) A Philip, a Guristersigo, a Tecumseh, a Keokuck or an Ietan, would have destroyed Galena;—would have taken Fort Winnebago;—would, on many occasions, have run off and captured the horses of the volunteers;—would have taken or destroyed provision trains guarded by these gallant knights of the *whip*,—and finally, would have brought to this pass, a force sufficient to have fully covered a retreat of their families and all their baggage, far beyond the Mississippi River; if not to have inflicted a severe check to our arms. Very incapable would I have pronounced that captain of our army, who with a hundred men, could not have repeatedly thrown our army into great confusion, and have disputed for weeks the passage of these fifty miles.

It was stated that the General, for the four days during which we contended against these dangerous obstacles, with the whole Sac force but a few miles in our front, was in a state of great anxiety and apprehension for the result; and was anything but desirous of an opportunity of striking them on this ground.

We emerged on the 31st from these gloomy forests into the gladsome light of the sun, in an open pine grove, on the bank of a fine little river, which we scarcely knew then to be the Kickapoo. No great change of circumstances ever had a pleasanter effect upon the spirits of an army; vast high prairies were before us; the sun shone brightly, and gleamed from the crystal waves of the pretty river; the refreshing prairie breeze whistled merrily through the leaves of the pines; there were indications in the enemy's deserted camps, that we were close upon him; and probabilities favored the belief that we would engage him on the prairies; and in a fair field and open daylight, settle with him the long account.

And here it must be confessed, that all were in profound ignorance of our whereabout; as individuals, we were certainly all "lost;" and perhaps none knew the distance or direction of the nearest point of the Mississippi; but as an army, we were in high spirits, and only wished to *find* the Indians whose trail we were on.

Next morning we early commenced what promised to be a forced march; our course lay over high prairies, with but little timber in view; but they were broken by deep and abrupt, though grassy valleys; and in these ran streams and springs, bold, transparent, and of almost icy coldness; beautiful brooks abounding with trout, which we could see everywhere darting about in frolicsome security.

This march did indeed turn out to be a long and weary one of full twenty-five miles. We saw several corpses—in every-day dress—lying by the trail in the open prairie; and where pack-horses had fallen exhausted, they had been slaughtered; and nothing but the hoofs and the paunch were left. It was clear that the Indians had suffered from hunger; but could not have famished, while they retained horses—as they did—to take off much baggage. At sunset we arrived on the ground which they had that morning abandoned: the fires still smoked. Here I saw a dead warrior, who had been placed in a sitting posture, with his back to a tree; he had been painted red as if going to war; and—his arms folded—he seemed to bid us grim defiance even in death. Few might look on unmoved,—none could ever forget that dead warrior in his paint!

We learned that the magnanimous volunteers, being in advance and having discovered an old Indian in this camp, had extracted some information from him, and then coolly put him to death.

An army which in summer encamps at the going down of the sun, eats dinner and supper together about 10 o'clock at night; at 11, on this occasion, we received orders to march at 2 o'clock in the morning.

CHAPTER XXV.

After three or four hours of rest, we were roused on the 2d of August, and marched at dawn of day. The order for the early march had been received by the volunteers after they had turned out their horses: this explanation was made of the circumstance that they did not march this morning for an hour or more after the mounted spies and infantry.

The sun found us marching over very high prairie hills in view of a vast extent of country; there was a mighty valley, and the forests of its lower level indicated the great river. Soon we saw a long and devious bank of fog rising white as snow in the sunshine, and evidently marking its course. A bright rosy summer morn shone over this scene of beauty and repose—as quiet and as peaceful as if man had never been there: at the creation, there could not have been less indication of his presence, save the measured tread of an armed band, speeding on to awaken the echoes which had slumbered from eternity, to the sounds of confusion, strife, and bloodshed.

Soon we saw a staff-officer gallop past towards the rear, and heard him report that the enemy was drawn up in the open woods in front to receive us; immediately the men were ordered to leave their knapsacks, with the baggage, under a small guard; and the infantry were formed in one line in extended order, and again advanced.

Perhaps to the uninitiated no battle was ever intelligibly described; and perhaps none such ever gathered from a description, aided by drawings, a clear and full idea of the manœuvres and main incidents of a battle;—the greatest difficulty is to preserve the unities of time; but in fact, it is beyond the power of genius—whose main attribute is expression—to express that which was never fully formed in idea. Let us consider the obstacles in the way of the commanding general, who must generally have much the best opportunity of seeing or conceiving all the acts and scenes of those great tragedies. First, the extent of the lines—of the field of battle; second, intervening woods and hills, which must almost always conceal much that occurs; third, the smoke, the dust, and the distance; fourth, the simultaneous occurrence of distant and unconnected events, confused and complicated in their action; fifth, the impossibility of conveying an idea of the shape of the ground: and then there are many difficulties in making his description (report) of what he *has* seen or conceived;—a disinclination to tell the whole truth, which, in matters unimportant in the result, might be disagreeable to himself or others; details might render his narrative inelegant, or might establish a connection between unpleasant causes and agreeable effects. How many actions are decided by the original acts of subordinates! It is a merit in all commanders of corps to improve sudden opportunities or openings, which, it may be, there is not a possibility of the chief commander's seeing.

As to those officers who are more engaged in the fighting, it is next to impossible that they can have even a general idea of proceedings beyond their immediate sphere.

The General arranges and directs the first blows: but then amid the noise, the smoke, the dust—the thunder of cannon—the deafening rattle of small arms—the rushing of squadrons—the thousand commands, all uttered as loudly as possible;—in a word, the darkness and confusion of the combat, generals, colonels, captains, and sometimes lieutenants, sergeants, and even privates themselves,—all more or less act a part of their own;—the soldier in battle, is something more than a mere machine.

Gen. Henry Lee was a man of genius; a good scholar, a fine perspicuous writer; he had studied his profession, and was one of the best soldiers bred in the revolutionary war; he commanded an independent legionary corps; and yet he fails to give a definite idea of Greene's battles, in which he acted a conspicuous part—and where only two or three thousand fought on a side. Gen. Greene gives his account of them in his reports:—his enemy a materially different one; Lee differs from both; whilst the editor of his work—his son—undertakes to correct *him*, and differs from all.

The following is substantially an extract from the report of the skirmish which now occurred (2d August, 1832), on the bank of the Mississippi, just below the mouth of the Bad-axe; and which closed the "Black-Hawk war:"

"And at dawn I marched with the regular troops under

Col. Taylor and Dodge's battalion, leaving Posey's, Alexander's, and Henry's brigades to follow, as they were not yet ready to mount—their horses being turned out in the evening before the order to march at 2 o'clock was received by them. After marching about three miles, the advance of Dodge's battalion under Capt. Dixon, came up with a small party of the enemy, attacked and killed eight of them, and dispersed the residue; in the meantime, the troops then with me were formed in order of battle, the regulars in extended order, with three companies, held in reserve; Dodge's battalion was formed on their left. The whole advanced to the front, expecting to meet the enemy in a wood before us—Posey's command soon came up, and was formed on the right of the regulars; shortly after, Alexander's arrived, and was formed on the right of Posey—a position, at the time, considered of great importance, as it would intercept the enemy in an attempt to pass up the river. Not finding the enemy posted as anticipated, I detached Capt. Dixon, with a few of Dodge's spies to the left, to gain information, and at the same time sent one of my staff to hasten the march of Henry; soon after, another was despatched with orders to him to march upon the enemy's trail, with one of the regiments of his brigade, and to hold the remainder in reserve; finding the enemy to be in force in that direction, his whole brigade was ordered upon that point. The order was promptly executed by the brigade, having in its advance the small body of spies under Dixon, who commenced the action, seconded simultaneously by Henry.

"The enemy was driven across several sluices down the river bottom, which was covered with fallen timber, underwood, and high grass: the regular troops, with Dodge at the head of his battalion, soon came up and joined in the action, followed by part of Posey's troops; when the enemy was driven still further through the bottom to several small willow islands successively, when much execution was done. The main body of the enemy being in the bottom, and adjoining small islands, Alexander was ordered to move with his brigade to the point of action; but from the distance of his position, he came up too late to participate in the combat, except two companies of his brigade, that had previously joined the brigade under Brigadier-General Henry.

"The small body of spies of Dodge's battalion and Henry's brigade, from their earlier position, shared more largely in the combat than those who, from the distance they had to march, consequently, came late into the engagement. As soon as the enemy were slain and dislodged from the Willow Bars, the regular troops under Col. Taylor, and a company or two of volunteers were thrown on board of the steamboat Warrior that had just arrived, and were landed on two adjacent islands to scour them of the enemy, assisted by a detachment from Henry and Dodge's commands on the river bank. Some three or four Indians were found and killed."

This report shows, that sometimes in military affairs, "the last shall be first;" as witness Henry's brigade: while "Capt. Dixon, with a few of Dodge's spies," were looking for the Indians, the line of regulars—who were in the utmost impatience—were halted in the open woods near the edge of the bluff, for more than half an hour (it seemed an age): this was the ground where the Indian scouts, or rear guard, had been defeated and slain, as we saw. When we were at last ordered to advance, we threw ourselves down the high bluff, which was not quite perpendicular; and in the act of descending I saw the Indians below, scampering through the woods, and occasionally firing. After crossing on logs, and wading several sloughs, with a general discharge of firearms in our front, a halt was ordered, and a very difficult change in the order of the column commenced; for what purpose heaven does *not* know. During this strange delay, a staff-officer of this column—finding his words or advice had no good effect—went on, accompanied only by a bugler; following a path which soon led him to the river bank, he there found two mounted officers of high rank, of whom he inquired where the enemy was? He was told in an island opposite, and was further informed, that the water was fordable; this officer immediately ordered the bugler to sound "Relieve skirmishers;" hoping thereby to attract the brigade of regulars: and soon after he saw it marching past 200 paces from the river; he moved toward it, and with much difficulty made himself heard by its commander, to whom he gave his information; after a slight pause, he was told "it was too late now" (he was afraid of another countermarch), but was advised to take in the reserve which followed. And on he went due south. The staff-officer succeeded in securing the reserve—three companies led by a major—whom he conducted to the bank, and jumped in; and, though a tall man, found himself breast deep: the battalion threw themselves in after him, and waded to the island, where we lost five killed, and several wounded;—the best set-off possible to the claim which the militia were inclined to make, that (in consequence of our long halt) they had done all the fighting. The army just then was not popular.

In this island I rescued a little red Leila, whom I found in very uncomfortable circumstances. I felt some rising symptoms of romance; but the fire, mud, and water, or rather I believe her complexion, soon cooled them, and I sent her by a safe hand to the rear.

I was as much interested in a keen lad of a soldier (of the 6th), whom I had known of old, and had seen jump in upon a wolf at bay, when its eyes shone like balls of fire; he had now picked up a glaring Indian sash, and put it on; and behaving very gallantly, was probably mistaken for a captain, and was shot through. Six or eight weeks after receiving this dangerous wound, he left a comfortable hospital without leave, and joined his regiment six hundred miles off!

And now, above the incessant roar of small arms, we heard booming over the waters, the discharge of artillery; and lo! the steamer Warrior came dashing on! It was a complete surprise, and had a very fine effect; we had not dreamed of a steamboat, wandering so long through unexplored swamps and forests, where nothing so bright as the idea of steam had ever entered; nor had the party on the boat the slightest expectation of finding the army here. A captain went to the shore some distance below and waved a flag, when he was saluted with a discharge of grape, which covered him with a shower of limbs and leaves.

The fog had stopped the boat, or the whole tribe would have been in our hands; and wo had been unto them! I saw a wounded infant wailing over the dry dugs of a slaughtered mother.

At 3 o'clock, after breaking our fast with some crackers and butter, which we found aboard, the steamer was crowded with troops, and we steamed among the many islands, which result here from the mouths of two rivers —the Ioway being opposite;—and how well had Black

Hawk chosen his point of crossing, being destitute of transports. After dispensing grape and cannister right and left very impartially into the islands, we landed on the largest, and scoured it completely in extended order. Large numbers had evidently just left it; but we found only two men, whom the cannonade had driven into the branches of large trees. Instantly without orders, the volunteers commenced firing, and a hundred guns were discharged at them; I saw them drop from limb to limb, clinging—poor fellows—like squirrels; or like the Indian in the "Last of the Mohicans." A fine young Menominee, who was by my side, ran forward, tomahawk upraised, to obtain the Indian honor of first striking the dead—I lost sight of him;—a few minutes after I saw him stretched upon the earth;—he had been shot in the back by a militia friend! It was hard to realize; a moment before he was all life and animation, burning with hope and ambition; now, there he lay with face to heaven, with no wound visible,—a noble form, and smiling countenance—and but a clod of the earth!

He was buried with honors in the same grave with our soldiers. Our total loss was five killed, and eighteen wounded, including two officers; that of the Indians was reported "about one hundred and fifty men killed"—forty women and children, seventy horses, &c. &c., captured.

CHAPTER XXVI.

THE poor Sacs and Foxes were now the martyrs of a peculiarity of nature, generally attributed to dogs, but common to men. They were going down hill, and might have looked out for bites or kicks. The Sioux followed them after this defeat, and slaughtered one hundred and forty! The General very humanely issued orders to stop the further effusion of blood.

It was singular, but 'tis true, that the regular brigade had been unaccompanied by an army surgeon, since the opening of the campaign; a citizen physician alone attended us; fortunately, in the Warrior, came up Surgeon B., who immediately had his hands full; and an Indian child with a broken arm or finger was turned over to our doctor, whose treatment of it was laughed at.

It is to be hoped, that the women and children fell by random shots; but it is certain that a frontiersman is not particular, when his blood is up, and a redskin in his power.

The Sac band was broken up, root and branch; with their horses, very much of their baggage was lost; their valuable copper kettles; their knapsacks or "kits" of private effects; even their sacred war-gourds, containing the teeth of the drum-head fish, were left on the ground; a volunteer found $500 in specie in a bundle; taken probably from Stillman's men, in the saddle-bag retreat.

The steamer Warrior returned to Prairie du Chien, and again came up, before we left the ground of the action: it brought up, among other rarities, a stray dentist from the East; who gathered a rich harvest of teeth taken from the Indian dead;—doubtless some very fine Eastern personages now rejoice in savage ivories.

Never was a fine-dressed man so out of place—not to say out of countenance, as another passenger, whom we saw tripping about over our dirty and rugged encampment. It reminded one of the lordly messengers to Harry Percy: for, though few of us smarted with "wounds grown cold," the "outer man" among us had suffered terribly from brier, brake, and bog. "I say, Fitz, what 'critter' is that?" "It's Major ——'s nephew." "D—n Major ——'s nephew; what business has such a thing here?" How very ridiculous is a dandy in the woods!

Would that a Carle Vernet could have sketched our Indian pony auction;—the background of this picture, a Mississippi bottom, for such a pencil, would prove a rare and worthy subject: but the student of the human countenance — of passion, of suffering, despair, could possibly never have such an opportunity as in some women prisoners which I saw. I shall never forget the unmitigated expression of despair in a face at the same time in some sense utterly impassible. I verily believe she heard or saw nothing around her; her mind seemed to wander over a past and future, where all was blank or fearful.

On the third or fourth day we embarked, nothing loth, on the Warrior, for Fort Crawford, about sixty miles below. We had several Winnebago Indians on board; one I remember was a bit of a dandy, and had a taste for *personal* ornaments; he wore, for instance, crooked over his forehead, the finger of a fellow savage, secured round his head by two strips of skin which had once connected it with a hand and arm. As we rounded to, at Prairie du Chien, we saw some dead bodies, which had floated sixty miles, when one of these fellows was so eager as to discharge a rifle-ball close by the faces of a row of us standing on the guard; and among others, the General's, who exhibited a strong disposition to have him pitched overboard; the patch struck and blistered an officer's face. And then followed the exhibition of an awful specimen of human nature (if the nature of an old bloodthirsty squaw can justly be placed in that category): we saw several canoe-loads of these red fiends contend in a race to reach these dead bodies, for the satisfaction of taking the sodden scalps of corpses four days in water.

All knowledge being founded on experience and comparison, I believe the Infinite beyond human conception; but its nearest approach might be found in the contrast of a fair and refined woman to one of these hags;—one of these beastly excrescences of Nature, which for our sins, to teach the lesson of humility, or for some inscrutable purpose of the Almighty, are suffered in some slight semblance of humanity, to exhibit on earth the deformity of sin and hell.

We pitched our tents on the inhospitable sands which here abound, and awaited as patiently as we might the progress of events.

General Scott arrived with an aid. He had been sent from the East with a small division of regulars to reinforce and take command of the army in the field; he had met with terrible disaster and loss from cholera, on the lakes; and though not very distant at Chicago from our position at Koshkonong—when he announced to us his approach —he had magnanimously refrained from assuming a nominal command, which would have deprived General Atkinson of the credit of closing the war; of which the impracticableness of the militia, and the intrinsic difficulties of the campaign—for which no allowance was made by an impatient chieftain, wrought upon by the ignorance and criminal folly of demagogues—had thus well-nigh robbed him.

Hundreds of brave soldiers fell before that terrible scourge, the cholera; at that time many northern physicians confessed a total inability to afford relief. Gen. S. was on the lakes in a steamer crowded with troops, when the pestilence raged among them; and this confinement to a comfortless boat must have rendered it tenfold more trying; surgeons and officers alike—all that were well—devoted themselves to the care of the sick. Thus to face deliberately inglorious death, to avert which no exertion of courage or abilities can avail, tests more severely heroism of character, than the fiery trials of war.

The unavailing loss of so many good soldiers reminds me of the speech of an Indian. About ten years ago, the Pawnees of the Platte lost nearly half their population by the small-pox: they were visited by their agent, Major D., who witnessed the most horrible scenes. The poor wretches were utterly ignorant of any remedy or alleviation; some sank themselves to the mouth in the river, and thus awaited the death which was hastened: the living could not always protect the dying and dead from the wolves! Their chief, Capote Bleu, exclaimed to Major D., "Oh, my father how many glorious battles we might have fought, and not lost so many men!"

My old Colonel and myself were destined to another luckless adventure in our little tent on these treacherous sands. A violent storm of wind and rain rose one night, and aroused me by a severe blow on the head from a green ridge pole—and him, by blowing a wet tent in his face by way of counterpane. We thought it after midnight, and the prospect was blue enough. The Colonel fumbled for his cigars, and swore he would smoke off the rest of the night (the Colonel was a smoker). "It will never do," said I. "But it must do; we could never raise a light. Confound that tent pin! William!" (William, lucky dog, was at the fort, of course, gambling.)

"But we could find our way to the barge."

"D—n the barge—not military—we should break our

necks or be drowned. I tell you, sir, I shall sit here and smoke till morning." (The Colonel was a little Turkish in his philosophy.) I left him, not to his fate, but to seek the steamboat barge. After running over a sentinel (I forgot my own countersign), and falling down a sand-bank, I gained at length the barge cabin, when I found it was only ten o'clock. I ordered a berth prepared, and returned with a decanter of brandy; meeting with no difficulty in finding the Colonel, who was puffing away at a segar, which blazed like a beacon; my report, and the first fruits of my success, so mollified the old gentleman, that he suffered himself to be conducted to a comfortable bed.

Soon after, the regulars moved by steamboat to Fort Armstrong on Rock Island, where they encamped.

CHAPTER XXVII.

Here, after a short interval of rest and comfort, we were destined to face suffering and death in new forms, and infinitely more trying than any other to which we had been exposed. By the approach of the remnants of the eastern division, we were well convinced that we were to be exposed, and unnecessarily, to the fatal ravages of the cholera. In vain were arguments multiplied, as to non-contagion—conviction did not follow; and all we could do was to resign ourselves with what grace we might, into the hands of fate. After the pestilence had exhausted itself among these troops, they had been put in motion across the prairies for this post; when, the campaign being over, they could serve to swell the command of the new general commanding, and add to the pageant of the treaty, or settlement of the affairs of the now subdued and humbled Sac band.

They came; and soon after their arrival, the terrible disease broke out with new virulence; it was uncontrolled; there was no shield from the danger; science confessed itself at naught; temperance shrank appalled at its impotence, while drunkenness and exposure met swift destruction; all felt its effects; but to be seriously attacked was certain death: the first forty died to a man. Fort Armstrong was converted into an hospital, whence all that entered were soon borne in carts, and thrown confusedly—just as they died, with or without the usual dress—into trenches, where a working party was in constant attendance; and it is a fact that an officer in charge of it, making inquiry as to some delay on one occasion, was answered that there was a man who was moving, and they were waiting for him to die. Your messmate at breakfast—you heard with little concern for *him*—was buried at the going down of the sun.

A calm, unappalled heart,—a moderate use of brandy, with an unchanged diet, were proved to be the best reliance of safety. The first sensible check to the ravages of the disease, was occasioned by a man's escape alive from the hospital, to which he returned, and died, a day or two after; his appearance in camp—terribly shaken, and half flayed as he was with rubbing—by restoring confidence, had undoubtedly a most salutary effect.

'Tis strange how soon in such scenes the heart of man becomes callous. Self-love dries up the sources of sympathy, which under *ordinary* circumstances of bereavement, are ever ready to overflow.

As I wandered one evening among the half deserted tents, I saw two friends, who, about to retire, were bathing their limbs with spirits, and bid a jesting defiance to the king of terrors. Over one the angel of death then hovered, and had marked him for his shaft! Brave heart! that night were you stricken in the pride of youth and promise!

I remarked that certain men who had spent much of their lives amid the trials and dangerous adventures of the farthest West,—men who, led into such scenes by their enterprise, and there hardened in their bravery, and schooled to meet the worst emergencies with calculating firmness, now, when exposed to the cholera, were among the most timid; they found terrors in this new foe, which no bravery could defeat, nor skill could elude; to which the accustomed discipline of their lives could offer no barrier. One of these, who bore a character for insensibility to danger, was offered a high-flown compliment which he did not appropriate: "Mr. G. you are the bravest of the brave; you are under no obligation or restraint, and can fly if you choose; but you do not." "General,"—was the candid reply—"you are very much mistaken; I am devilish afraid to stay here; but more afraid to run for it, for if I should be taken on the way, I should stand no chance."

A certain Doctor from the mining districts, who happened to arrive here, fancied that he had cured many cases of the cholera, and could do so again. Well, he had certainly brought his talent to a good market; and General A. sent him with me to the hospital; he went boldly in, and, doubtless, was very ingenious and confident in his belief; but never was a poor fellow so suddenly undeceived, or quickly induced to confess an error. He was aghast; his nose seemed to grow blue, and his jaws to collapse; the use of his feet and hands was alone preserved to him; with one of the latter he seized his hat, with the other the door, and the benefits of his science were lost to us.

He is not deep in human lore, who will be shocked and surprised to be told that ere these scenes had ceased, their impression could not prevent nights being passed by parties over cards and brandy, amid all the exposure of irregularity and dissipation in a cold tent. Care for self, or for others, could not prevent the recklessness which grows out of such circumstances. And what is there so terrible or so painful, to which we do not soon become reconciled by force of custom?

General A. had offered a reward of twenty horses for Black Hawk; and accordingly he was soon captured by some Winnebagoes; and the old gentleman, with some other chief men, about this time came down in irons aboard a steamer. Great preparations were made to receive such distinguished personages; but the managers of the steamer had no taste for the Rock Island latitude; its atmosphere was not agreeable; and after much puffing and backing in mid-river, they gave us the go-by, and were off for St. Louis.

The Indian war and the cholera over, I felt a longing for other scenes. Fort Leavenworth again had attractions; and leaving the grand army to play its part at Indian councils, and to witness the usual one-sided treaty (in which the Sacs and Foxes ceded the best slice of Iowa territory as an indemnity for the expense and trouble of exterminating their friends, Black Hawk's band), in company of some others, I took boat and departed.

And now the accursed disease seemed to have spared me, when there was a chance of medical aid, only to seize me when there was none; its symptoms fast grew upon me; and there was not even a medicine-chest aboard. I hunted up some chance doses of medicine, and scraped out all that had the appearance of calomel, and swallowed it; but to little purpose. I landed in St. Louis in rather a precarious condition; one of the first persons I met in the streets was a physician, who was struck and seemed alarmed at my appearance; he immediately prescribed an immoderate dose and sent me to bed. Next morning he repeated it; he seemed bent upon trying his hand; and probably thought, that, kill or cure, it would be well to put a period to symptoms of cholera in a city with a clean bill of health.

However, I escaped from him and the disease, and quickly departed, having strictly charged a negro servant to burn all the woollen clothes which I had brought with me. This good intention his cupidity probably defeated, as I afterward accidentally learned he was one of the first victims to the visitation of the pestilence which soon followed us.

Returning from my visit to Fort Leavenworth before the end of autumn, I once more found myself with new duties and old friends, at Jefferson Barracks; a post, which the ever-varying policy of the government had shorn of its original glory, when it was a "school of instruction" (rather a *reserve* station) for several regiments, and had now cut down its garrison to a battalion of one.

The society this winter was small; and unfortunately some of it had found such attractions or connections at

St. Louis, as to destroy the unities of sentiment, motives, and pursuits, which constitute the happiness of a small community.

The winter quietly passed, and with the spring of 1833 new views, and the opening of a new career for some of us were the occasion of a severance of the old and happy ties of association and attachment to a regiment, whose fortunes for five years I had shared; among whose members I had formed and enjoyed the warmest friendships. It seemed the signal for a general breaking up in that honored regiment. Not long after, many, weary of the inactivity of peace, or disgusted with mismanagement, favoritism, and the discredit thrown upon them from sources whence they should naturally look for support and encouragement—mortifications and evils which they shared with the army—resigned their commissions, and entered the lists with the active world around them; and they failed not to meet with prizes; among which may be mentioned the station of General-in-chief in a sister republic. Wherever our fortunes carry us, few will cease to cherish recollections of our ancient association as members of the 6th regiment of infantry! And many have since shed their blood like water, and died upon the battle-fields of Florida;—their memories are embalmed in the hearts of their old comrades!

CHAPTER XXVIII.

Early in the summer of 1833, I was among the hardy sons of West Tennessee, seeking to infuse an ardor for service in a new regiment of Cavalry, one destined, we believed, to explore far and wide the Western Territory, and bear the arms of the Union into the country of many Indian tribes. It was a prospect that did not fail to excite the enterprising and roving disposition of many fine young men, in that military State.

Having previously met with indifferent success at Columbia, Dover, and Clarksville, I purchased a horse at the last place, in order to ride into the western district; having been advised to move in the "direction" of Reynoldsburgh, visit Perryville, &c. There was no road to Reynoldsburgh; but a candidate for Congress was kind enough to furnish me with a pencilled map for my guidance, in which he embodied a knowledge of by-paths gained in his electioneering explorations: he gave me also a letter of introduction to the hospitable Judge H.; whose house, distant about forty miles, I expected to reach the first day.

I found the country rugged and barren; abounding in iron ore, with perhaps wood enough to smelt it; in spite of the map, I repeatedly lost my way among paths scarcely discernible, on the hard and stony hills. Just as the sun, which had been all day obscured by sullen clouds, managed to give me a smile, as if to bid me good night, I had the good fortune I thought, to find a wagon road; and which without consulting the cardinal points very closely, I struck into right merrily; it soon led me to a rude dwelling, where I was informed that I was going exactly wrong; with reluctant conviction I turned about and was soon lost again. It was fast growing dark, when I descended a hollow way which the woods rendered exceedingly obscure and dreary; my hat was struck off by limbs, and I could but trust to my horse to keep the track; it soon led to a large creek, which I forded; but in going out naturally missed the road; and in attempting to ascend the bank, myself and horse tumbled back in reversed order. I succeeded in leading him out, and encountered a high fence, which forced me to turn to the right or left. I took the right, which I found to be wrong: we scrambled on through the brush between the fence and creek, until I heard the bark of a dog, and looking carefully, I espied a light very high and far to the left; this light I resolved to make my polar star, and to go to it, despite of all obstacles; the first was the fence, with lofty stakes and riders, which I patiently pulled to the ground and passed through; then another—and another, I know not how many; but each I laboriously overcame, ascending the while over ground, which I could but wish had been more smoothly cultivated. At last I reached a snug-looking house and sought admittance; but, directed by the sweet sounds of a piano, I unceremoniously pushed on into a parlor, and recognized the daughters of Judge H. I had lost my letter; of which I informed the Judge, when he soon after came in, with a manner which indicated that I attached but little importance to it, under the circumstances; and related to him my own misfortunes and those of his fences; with which I suppose—as an hospitable man and careful farmer—he equally sympathized.

I certainly passed an agreeable evening: and listened to the sweet music of an accompaniment of the flute by the father to the piano of his daughter.

My kind host, after a good breakfast next morning, gave me particular directions for my further journey, which, however, was not performed without being repeatedly at a loss for my course. As the sun set, I found myself on the bank of the Tennessee River at Reynoldsburgh, whose "direction" I had carefully sought for two days; this I considered quite sufficient; for a more miserable hamlet I never saw; a half dozen houses composed it, and their occupants seemed victims to fevers; the river, which gushes from the Virginia mountains in swift and beautiful streams, here, like a sickly sluggard, had lost its youthful promise; but even the springs, I was told, are here poisonous; I took boat, crossed the river, and slept in a tavern on the southern bank.

The following day, by selecting such bridle paths as promised the best direction, I reached the neighborhood of Perryville, and slept in the log-house of a small farmer; who, like all his class in this country, entertained travellers without the expensive formality of a license and sign-board.

Next morning early, I arrived in Perryville, the county seat of Perry County, and situated a few hundred paces from Tennessee River. Soon after, guided by a horrid cacophony to a brick court-house in the centre of this wretched village, I there witnessed an astonishing scene. The room was filled—a stand of some elevation in the midst was occupied by a Baptist preacher, who addressed the audience in the most impassioned manner—ever turning and inclining lowly his person to the dying cadence of his song: for in a kind of monotonous tune he delivered himself of a wild rhapsody, of which the constantly repeated words, "morning star," were almost alone intelligible to me: but the painful part of the exhibition was, that he totally exhausted his voice or breath at every sentence which he sang out; and caught it—as he raised his body—in a prolonged, shrill wheeze, like that of persons with the hooping-cough; or like an exaggerated paroxysm in a broken-winded horse. I got no further than the door; and asking some one why they did not take the poor wretch away, I escaped, full of wonder that so many reasonable beings could complacently witness so painful an exhibition of disease and unintelligible fanaticism.

At my tavern I was duly installed, as a mark of distinction, in a separate chamber; this was a space about twelve feet square divided from a large loft, by a partition of thin boards which reached a little higher than my head: above, was the roof, which proved a sorry protection from the heat of a scorching sun.

Terrible was a week's sojourn in Perryville. The only inhabitant who—by virtue of a title of lawyer—laid claim to intellectuality, was in reality a loafer; he had by one act, established here a lasting reputation; this solitary and distinguished achievement should be commemorated; he had in some quarrel, thrown at his adversary's head a pitcher!

I once sought relief in a walk to the bank of the river; but the sight and stench of its green slime caused a precipitate retreat. I next tried gunning; and returned covered with thousands of the almost invisible seed-tick. They could only be removed by undergoing the martyrdom of a thorough fumigation by burning tobacco.

But I succeeded in engaging some hardy recruits, whose imagination inflamed them with the thoughts of scouring the far prairies on fine horses, amid buffalo and strange Indians; so much so, that they scarce listened to any discouraging particulars, which they would persuade themselves were only given for discouragement sake. A man's wishes can always blind and deceive him: these fellows, in some after moment of disappointment and discontent, would be ready to accuse another of what their own folly had caused.

I next visited the pretty village of Lexington, where I remained three days. The evening before my departure, in paying my bill, I perceived an extravagantly dishonest charge, made in consideration of my having endeavored to insist on a separate room. I gave mine host a piece of my mind, which led to some altercation. Immediately after, an elderly personage whom I had never seen before, called me to a private place, and saying nothing, very mysteriously commenced baring his breast, and directed my attention to certain scars, which there and elsewhere, told of many a wound; upon my showing signs that his pantomime was a riddle, he found his tongue, and thus addressed me—"I came to this country, like you, young, fiery, and impatient; and these are the consequences—take a friendly warning." Verb. sat. I had *heard* of "eloquent wounds," but perhaps never before had realized the full force of the expression. The morning after, I was to set out very early for Jackson: I was so much disturbed, long before daylight, by noise, that I arose and dressed myself. I discovered that it was made by a gentleman, who, it appeared, was on a circuit electioneering for the office of brigadier-general; he had taken the rather extraordinary method to recommend himself, of getting drunk before daylight: but as I afterwards found him a very intelligent person, I have no reason to doubt that he understood his own interest.

It proved we were to travel the same road; and probably owing in a measure to some sympathy between our profession and pursuit, a kind of intimacy grew rapidly between us. As we rode off together before sunrise, we saw a splendid horse ridden at a little distance, which I had before attempted to bargain for: the temptation was now strong, and my companion aggravated it. "Look *at* him, Lieut.," said he: "take him Lieut.—what's a few dollars? I'll lend you the money, if you hav'n't it to spare," &c. &c. It was irresistible; and at sunrise of a Sunday morning—I grieve to say—I changed saddles and bridles—and exchanged horses and purses, mine being much the heavier—and rode on my way rejoicing.

At breakfast my new friend, from force of electioneering habit, over-persuaded me to join him in a glass of whiskey, which our host recommended as particular; saying, "Good G—, stranger, don't drink *that, this* is three weeks old;"—of a truth it was detestable; and proved I believe *de trop* for my companion; for after riding a very little way, in a terribly hot morning, I observed him attentively examining the landmarks for a certain fine spring; and his discourse turned upon the virtues and delights of cold water.

In a sequestered spot, beneath the cool, dark shade of a noble forest, we found it; and his praises were all faint in describing that glorious fountain. There it was before us, with its crystal and icy waters welling over the brim of a moss-grown gum; delicious was the draught we took! and renovating the bath to our fiery temples! Had the romantic old De Leon found such a one in Florida, he had cried *Eureka!* and asked no proof that the fountain of eternal youth was before him!

Much refreshed, we pursued our ride; and after the privations of some weeks, my companion, without great difficulty, persuaded me to make a divergence of a few miles to the house of his father-in-law, who, I found, was the father of an old army friend.

I spent there several very pleasant days; it was a noble plantation, and had a most hospitable owner. At parting, my friend, the brigadier, and myself, exchanged tokens of our singularly commenced friendship, and have never since met.

I found Jackson a lively, thriving little town: I observed it under the exciting circumstances of a Congressional election; and the successful candidate was no other than the celebrated Davy Crockett.

Having accomplished my mission, I set out on my horse for Nashville, and made the journey in three days. I spent about a week enjoying the hospitalities of this pleasant and flourishing western city; after which, with another officer, I departed in a keel-boat with our company of recruits: this tedious mode of navigation was occasioned by the lowness of the water in the Cumberland. At Paducah we took a steamboat for Jefferson Barracks, where we arrived without other incident than a detention and change of boat; the consequence of a boiler being worn out: so much so, fortunately, that it would not bear a pressure sufficient to lead to a dangerous explosion.

CHAPTER XXIX.

Those persons who may at times have felt symptoms of envy at the fortunes of officers preferred to new regiments, might console themselves if they could but realize the amount of labor, care, and vexation, attendant upon the task of enlisting, organizing, disciplining, and instructing a new corps,—of producing order from chaos: and much the more with cavalry, where the amount of duty, instruction, and responsibility, may safely be considered as doubled in the comparison with infantry. And this, without consideration of the extraordinary fact, that cavalry tactics were unknown in the army; and, with the whole theory and practical detail, were to be studiously acquired—in a manner invented—by officers, before they could teach others.

It is not a little astonishing, that our government should have so long deprived the country and the army of the services of so very important an arm as the cavalry; that it should have suffered all knowledge and experience of its organization, equipment, and manœuvres to have become extinct.

Circumstances have ever been unfavorable to a general and just appreciation of the power and importance of this arm of military organization.

The insulation of Great Britain has been there an obstacle to a fair test of its uses and capacities; which, otherwise, their fine breeds of horses would seem to have much favored. An inferiority in this respect, and other reasons which might be easily shown, caused it to be neglected in France and other nations of the continent; while in Egypt, in Asia, and in the Ukraine, the nature of the institutions have, for want of instruction and discipline, rendered in some degree abortive the individual pre-eminence of their armed horsemen. (Not forgetting, however, that the Moslem cavalry conquered half the world, and were only checked at the gates of Vienna by the Polish cavalry of Sobieski.)

In the decadency of chivalry, the first introduction and improvement of that essential arm of infantry (which in reality is the *body*, of which cavalry and horse artillery are the *arms*), led to such extraordinary, though natural success, that in the progress of reaction—with the common use of gunpowder—men naturally fell into an opposite extreme.

The great warrior of this age perhaps over-estimated, in the comparison, the importance and effects of artillery, which he brought to great perfection. But in Egypt, the undisciplined Mamelukes extracted from him an exclamation of admiration; and after a pause of far-reaching thought, he gave utterance to a deep regret that he could not render himself *irresistible*, by the command of such men, *disciplined!*

But the discouragements to the excellence and use of British cavalry (which must be transported by sea, to be used), have not prevented the truth from forcing itself upon the minds of some of their officers; and Col. Mitchell, who, with all his prejudices against Napoleon and his warriors, and the use of the bayonet, may come to be considered a military reformer, has *proved* the irresistible though unappreciated power of cavalry.

In support of these views, and of this assertion, I shall here give some extracts from Col. Mitchell's "Thoughts on Tactics," which may prove acceptable to the reader, who has not an opportunity to examine that interesting work.

"Though cavalry formed, in general, the strength of the armies of the middle ages, yet as the genius of chivalry tended more to acts of individual prowess and exertion, than to combined efforts, from which striking results could alone be expected, little or nothing is left to glean from that dark period.

"The introduction of firearms, which by degrees brought infantry back to the field, diminished even the efficiency which the cavalry derived from the energy of knightly spirit and enterprise; for they not only took to the use of the pistol and arquebuse, instead of the sword, their only arm of strength, but gradually covered themselves with such heavy armor, that a dray-horse alone could carry the weight of a man-at-arms completely accoutred. Thus mounted, the cuirassier was just able to sport his clumsy and unwieldy figure, as if for show, up and down the ranks of war, to exchange a few miserable pistol-shots, or, at most, to run a course, with lance in rest, over some hundred yards of perfectly level ground.

"At the battle of Hohenfriedberg, the dragoon regiment of Baireuth drove over twenty-one battalions of infantry, took 4000 prisoners, 66 stands of colors, and five pieces of artillery—an action, of which Frederick says, truly enough, that it deserves to be written in letters of gold. At Zerndorff, Seidlitz decided the fate of the day, by hewing down with the cavalry the masses of Russian infantry, before which the Prussian infantry had already lost ground; thus gaining one of the most sanguinary victories of the Seven Years' War. At Rosbach, twenty squadrons,* led by the same heroic commander, headed and crossed the French line of march under cover of the hill that separated the two armies, wheeled up in front of the hostile columns, and then,

'Like ocean's mighty swing,
When heaving to the tempest's wing,
They hurled them on the foe,'

driving the whole of Sonbise's army, 50,000 strong, in utter 'confusion from the ground.'

"'At the battle of Belgrade,' says this great soldier (Marshal Saxe), 'I saw two battalions cut to pieces in an

* Three thousand men at most.

instant. The affair happened in the following manner: A battalion of Lorraine, and one of Neuperg, were posted on a height that we called the battery; and just where a breeze of wind dispersed a fog which had impeded our view, I observed these troops on the brow of the hill, separated from the rest of the army. Prince Eugene asked me if my sight was good, and who were the cavaliers coming round the hill? I replied, that they were a body of thirty or forty Turks. These men are lost, said the Prince, measuring the two battalions, though I could not perceive that they were attacked, or likely to be so, as I could not see what was beyond the hill. But I galloped towards it at full speed, and at the moment I arrived behind the colors of Neuperg's regiment, I saw both battalions make ready, come to the present, and, at thirty yards, fired a volley at a body of Turks who were rushing in upon them. The volley and the closing, were one and the same thing; the two battalions had no time to fly, and were all sabred."

"Combat of Avesne le Sec, Sept. 11th, 1793.

"A corps of 8000 French, mostly infantry, having marched out of Cambray, in order to make a demonstration in favor of Quesnoy, then hard pressed by the allies, were overtaken near the village of Avesne le Sec, by Prince Lichtenstein and Count Belgrade, at the head of four Austrian regiments of cavalry. The French, seeing that an action was inevitable, formed two large squares, between which they placed the whole of their artillery, consisting of twenty-guns, and thus posted, they firmly awaited the charge. The Austrians realized everything that could be expected from brave horsemen, for without awaiting the infantry and artillery, that were still far behind, they instantly charged, and though saluted with grape by the French artillery, and received with a volley of musketry, fired at less than fifty yards, they overthrew both the squares at the first onset. Two thousand men were taken, and most of the others cut down, for only a few hundred stragglers reached Bouchain and Cambray; the twenty guns, together with five stand of colors, also fell into the hands of the victors." Austrian loss, "only two officers and seventy-nine men."

"Action of Villers-en-Couche, 24th April, 1793.

"On the 23d of April, 1793, the French, to the number of 15,000 men, advanced in three columns from Bouchain towards the Salle. They were met on the following day by General Otto, at the head of ten British and four Austrian squadrons. While part of this force dispersed the French cavalry, four of the allied squadrons, two British and two Austrian, attacked the infantry, consisting of six battalions, who had formed themselves into an oblong square, broke them, killed and wounded nine hundred men, captured four hundred more, together with five pieces of cannon; the allies themselves losing only ninety men in killed and wounded."

"The following is the account he himself (Blucher, then colonel,) gives, in his journal of the campaigns of 1794, of the affair near Kaiserslautern: 'As soon as I had assembled about eighty hussars and dragoons, I commanded, march! at the very time when the enemy's infantry, at least six hundred strong, were crossing the plain. The officer who commanded the enemy's battalion, showed much countenance; he was on horseback, and kept his men well together. But nothing could intimidate our brave horsemen; we stormed in upon the enemy, and though he opposed us with the bayonet, and made a most determined resistance, we nevertheless broke in, &c.' "The entire of the French party were either killed, wounded, or taken."

" Action of Garci-Hernandez, 23d July, 1812.

"Captain Riegenstein, who commanded the second squadron, finding the French cavalry had already been defeated, and hearing of the gallant and successful charge made on one square of their infantry, proceeded immediately to attack the other, which was as completely overthrown as the first, and with considerably less loss—a brave example once set, soon finds followers." "In following up this success, the third squadron, under Captain Marshall, together with half the squadron, came upon a third square of infantry. Victory ruled the hour, and these new foes were no sooner discovered than charged and broken." . . . . "Properly stated, the case stands thus: four squares of the best French infantry, for a rear-guard would, of course, be composed of the best troops, amounting at least to three thousand men, were attacked by three squadrons and a half of cavalry, that could not, at the most, count three hundred men, and three of the squares were defeated with a loss to the infantry of nearly two thousand men, while the victorious cavalry lost only one hundred men.

"If the cavalry, in charging infantry, do their duty, one of three things must follow as a matter of course; either they must fall by the fire of the musketry, be arrested by the bayonets, or they must overthrow the opposing ranks. Now, without again reverting to the few musket-shots that tell, as shown in the first part of this essay, we know very well, that, to the utter astonishment of many officers present, entire volleys were fired at Waterloo and at Fuente-de-Guinaldo, without apparently bringing down a man, however many might have been hit. We also know, that not a single one of the enemy's horsemen perished on the bayonets of the kneeling ranks in either of these actions; and it is, of course, perfectly evident, that a horse at full speed, if killed even by the projecting bayonets—which is possible, though not probable—must still, by his very influence, overthrow all the files opposed to him, and thus make an opening for those that follow.

"It is no doubt a splendid sight, when bugle-sound and trumpet-clang send onward to the charge a gallant line of horsemen: their plumes wave, their sabres gleam, the very earth is shaken by the thunder of their horses' hoofs, and, like the tornado in its progress, they seem destined to carry everything before them in their way. But the infantry to be attacked is prepared; the close and serried mass, bristling with arms, from which the fires of death are every moment expected to flash, is imposing; and the motionless stillness, with which tried soldiers wait the attack, has an air of stern and confident resolve that is chilling to ordinary assailants. The horsemen, not expecting to succeed, see only death before them; and busy fancy pictures at such times, even to the most wretched, stores of future happiness about to be sacrificed in a hopeless contest. The heart cools, and the speed is gradually slackened, instead of being augmented as the charge advances. If the dread of dishonor still keeps the men from turning back, the belief in certain destruction also prevents them from going on; but the middle way, so dear to mediocrity, whether of talent or of courage, is at hand, and no sooner does the firing begin than the whole of the plume-crested troop, vanquished before a shot has told, open to the right and left—fly, with brandished sabres, in wild confusion round the square, instead of rushing down upon it—receive the fire of four sides to avoid the fire of one, and, without striking a single blow for victory, resign with loss and disgrace a contest that, by courage and confidence, might have been successfully terminated at the expense of a few bayonet scratches.

"I appeal to the officers who were present in the squares at Waterloo, Quatre Bras, and Guinaldo—whether this is not an exact history of the best of the charges made by the French cavalry in those memorable actions. I say the best charges; for, on many occasions the horsemen actually halted, or turned, as soon as the fire began, leaving a few individuals to dash forward and shake their sabres at the adversaries with whom they dared not close. And yet this is called charging, and by such foolery is the power of the cavalry to be estimated, and the infantry of England, the gallant and the brave, must still trust for victory only to the chance of similar conduct on the part of future foes, instead of trusting to those high qualities, that, backed by an efficient system of tactics, would insure them success in every species of contest."—(From pages 76 to 107.)

In no country of Europe, nor in Asia, can horses be so numerously and so cheaply supported as in the United States; and our plains and prairies plainly indicate that cavalry is the most suitable military force. In the Revolutionary War we had a small force of admirable cavalry on the plains of the Carolinas, to oppose that of Tarleton, which was the terror of the whole country; and it was of paramount importance. General Greene's celebrated retreat before Earl Cornwallis, but for Lee's legionary corps, could scarcely have been attempted; they were at once the shield and the right arm of his army.

Whoever has studied the American military history, knows that cavalry have been the scourge and peculiar dread of Indians. Not to mention the conquest of Mexico—how wonderful were the achievements of De Soto, with his little band of Cavaliers! They outdo romance. He encountered numberless brave Indians, but his horses gave the victory. The Indians triumphed greatly more in the death of a horse, than of his armed rider. Infantry never could have accomplished his march.

Near the close of the war of the Revolution, the powerful nation of Cherokees made an irruption into South Carolina. In "Lee's Memoirs of the War" we find the following account of its results: "Pickens followed the incursors into their own country, and having seen much and various service, judiciously determined to mount his detachment, adding the sword to the rifle and tomahawk. He well knew the force of cavalry, having felt it at the Cowpens, though it was then feebly exemplified by the enemy. Forming his mind upon experience, the straight road to truth, he wisely resolved to add to the arms, usual in Indian wars, the unusual one above mentioned.

"In a few days he reached the country of the Indians, who, as is the practice among the uncivilized in all ages, ran to arms to oppose the invader, anxious to join issue in battle without delay. Pickens, with his accustomed diligence, took care to inform himself accurately of the designs and strength of the enemy; and as soon as he had ascertained these important facts, advanced upon him. The rifle was only used while reconnoitering the hostile position. As soon as this was finished, he remounted his soldiers, and ordered a charge: with fury his brave warriors rushed forward, and the astonished Indians fled in dismay. Not only the novelty of the mode, which always has its influence, but the sense of his incapacity to resist horse, operated upon the flying forester.

"Pickens followed up his success, and killed forty Cherokees, took a great number of prisoners of both sexes, and burned thirteen towns. He lost not a soldier, and had only two wounded. The sachems of the nation assembled in council; and, thoroughly satisfied of their inability to contend against an enemy who added the speed of the horse to the skill and strength of man, they determined to implore forgiveness for the past, and never again to provoke the wrath of their triumphant foe." Page 383, to which there are the following notes: "John Rogers Clarke, colonel in the service of Virginia against our neighbors, the Indians in the Revolutionary War, was among our best soldiers, and better acquainted with the Indian warfare than any officer of the army. This gentleman, after one of his campaigns, met in Richmond several of our cavalry officers, and devoted all his leisure in ascertaining from them the various uses to which horse were applied, as well as the manner of such application. The information he acquired determined him to introduce this species of force against the Indians, as that of all others the most effectual.

"By himself, by Pickens, and lately by Wayne, was the accuracy of Clarke's opinion justified."

"The Indians, when fighting with infantry, are very daring. This temper of mind results from his consciousness of his superior fleetness; which, together with his better knowledge of woods, assures to him extrication out of difficulties, though desperate. This temper of mind is extinguished, when he finds he is to save himself from the pursuit of horse, and with its extinction fails that habitual boldness."

I will only add, that, after all the terrible inflictions of the whites, the Indians have almost invariably expressed, in two words, their sense of the most dreadful peculiarity of the superior race, in naming them—from the sabres—the "Long Knives."

CHAPTER XXX.

We found excellent stables at Jefferson Barracks, and everything convenient for the prosecution of our laborious undertaking; and we looked forward with pleasant ardor to the formation of a uniform system of tactics, and of the various duties connected with this new arm of the service. No one dreamed that the government could waver in this obvious policy of concentration and quiet preparation, so essential to these important objects; (the more so, that many of the new appointments were not military men.)

The result was, that, before all the companies were mounted, an order was received to march some five hundred miles, to Fort Gibson.

* * * * * * *

If the reader will imagine six dreary months to have passed—*so* painful and cheerless that I shrink from reviewing them progressively even in thought,—and will wing his mental flight over the rugged Ozark Range, he will find me beyond, under a canvas shade, on the verge of boundless prairies; their cool green adorned with rich unknown flowers, and waving to the breeze, which had wandered, unobstructed by hill or forest, from the snowy summits of the Rocky Mountains. Thus, in the sweet month of May, 1834, I sat in my tent, giving the fresh impressions of the bleak interval, amid the pleasant scene to which I have introduced you.

I wrote as follows:

"The distractions of a camp are so manifold, that it is an effort of no small fortitude to undertake a subject, which a feeling of slight, but just excitement, so fatal to comfort in this burning climate, clearly indicates will swell under my hands.

"One of our first military writers has made the reflection, in substance, that it costs more blood and treasure to defend a country by militia, than to maintain a standing army, sufficient at all times for its defence. This position I believe to be incontrovertible, and indeed unanswerable. Now, far be it from me to wish to make deductions unfavorable to the contrary policy, originating with the sages of our Revolution, adopted by the wisdom of their successors, and sanctioned by a nation's voice. But it stands an abstract truth, modified in practice by considerations which it is not my intention to discuss.

"In 1829, owing to the absence of the garrison of Fort Leavenworth,—who were protecting the Mexican trade,—a necessity arose, owing to the conduct of the Iowa Indians, of calling out the Missouri militia. In 1831, owing to the smallness of the regular force on the Upper Mississippi, a large draft of Illinois militia were called into service. In 1832, under the same circumstances, about 3000 mounted Illinois militia were for months in the field.

"What amount of treasure has been thus expended, the guardians of the treasury can best answer: those conversant with militia claims, can perhaps estimate:—to what purpose, with what gain to the nation, military men might answer if they pleased; but all conversant with figures can demonstrate that the militia operations of 1832 cost a sum that would support the regiment of dragoons for ten years; to say nothing of an immense loss arising from a general neglect of business, more particularly farming. Now, none can doubt that the regiment of dragoons, had it been then in existence, would have prevented, or would have been fully competent to carry on this Sac war, without the aid of a single volunteer, or even, perhaps, the regular infantry.

"Guided by the sober light of experience, Congress, acquainted with the most prominent results of this course of affairs, and with the necessities of the emigrating system further south, have taken a course founded upon a very few simple principles of political economy. The first symptoms of the adoption of a true policy, was the passage, I believe, unanimously by the Senate, at two different sessions, of a bill to mount a portion of the infantry. Experience, here still in advance, made new demands on the witnesses of the proceedings of the Black Hawk campaign of 1832. Congress answered by the creation of a corps of mounted rangers. Of this corps (in justice not so formidable to its *friends*, as a certain brigade of Illinois volunteers of notorious memory), after a few remarks on its *personnel*, none more readily than myself would pronounce its *requiescat in pace.*

"There was a time when our frontier's-men were the most formidable light-troops,—to speak technically,—that the sun ever shone upon. But what made them such? The constant exercise of arms; the stern necessity of untiring vigilance; a capacity for endurance, resulting from ceaseless exercise and warlike toil. These prime requisites of the soldier were created amid scenes of real danger, whose experience exceeded infinitely any result of the drill, or the mimic war of regular soldiers, by which they are prepared to become veterans. These were the scenes of the 'dark and bloody ground,' and these the actors, whose type was Daniel Boone (the sire of our worthy captain of dragoons). These were the unaided pioneers of an infant nation; these were the antagonists of the untamed Indians of the woods; who, singular enough, are as much more formidable than those of the prairies, as were the ancient Gauls and Britons than the slothful nations of the Asiatic plains.

"Where, now, are we to look for such a class of men? The government, gathering strength like a young giant, has taken these matters into its own hands. The strongest nations of Indians have been subdued to utter helplessness; others, awed and controlled. They have felt the strong hand of the government over and among them; they have been tamed. The infantry at outposts have long since succeeded to the heritage of border men. These last, from the slayers of Indians, have become the foes of timid deer; from the hunters of the bear and panther, have degenerated to those of the playful squirrel.

"But, it is the old-received,—once well-founded,—notions concerning this class, which naturally linger in the minds of a succeeding generation. To these we must look to account for the apparent preference of Congress for irregular troops, and their reluctance to substitute dragoons. It is on such foundations that, in moments of excitement, members have indulged the remark, that a company of men on the frontier are worth more than our whole army, 'composed of the sweepings of cities.' A twofold calumny! That member had every opportunity of knowing, when he uttered it, that a regiment of infantry had been, for near ten years, stationed three hundred miles beyond the most remote settlements, in constant contact with the Indians.

"Under these false impressions, did a certain honorable

and *intelligent* Senator from the West, state during the discussion of the Ranger bill, and the campaign of 1832, that the frontier men, then out in the field, soon destined some of them, to become rangers, were infinitely superior to the army, to the poor infantry (whom he would seem to reproach for not being mounted): that they could *subsist themselves*, 'be here to night, and fifty miles off by morning.' What must have been the feelings of officers on reading this, as they did, inactive in a wilderness—a swamp—delayed by these same boasted volunteers, who had marched to a fort for provisions,—it being notorious that they had thrown away their rations, to avoid the trouble of carrying them.

"Convinced by the experience of late years, of the necessity of a mounted force, to cope with mounted and other Indians, Congress passed the bill to raise a regiment of dragoons, on the 2d of March, 1833. The officers were forthwith appointed from the infantry and mounted rangers. They were immediately ordered to recruit for the regiment, and were restricted in their enlistments to persons between twenty and thirty-five years of age; native citizens who, from previous habits, were well qualified for mounted service. The officers were authorized to inform candidates for enlistment that they would be well clothed, and kept in comfortable quarters in winter. Five companies were soon completed and concentrated at Jefferson Barracks. The recruits had generally disposed of nearly all their clothing, in anticipation of their uniforms, on their arrival at that station. In this they were destined to be sadly disappointed. At the approach of winter,—in November,—before any clothing or their proper arms had been received; before two companies had received their horses; just at that season when all civilized, and, I believe, barbarous nations, even in a state of war, suspend hostilities and go into winter quarters, these five companies received an order to march out of theirs,—to take the field! By great exertions, and numerous expedients, a quantity of clothing nearly sufficient to cover them, but of all qualities, colors, and patterns, was obtained. The march to Fort Gibson was commenced on the 20th of November. On the third day, they encountered a severe snow-storm. On the 14th of December, they reached their destination, having marched five hundred miles. Here they found no comfortable quarters, but passed a severe winter for any climate in tents; the thermometer standing more than one day at 8° below zero. There were of course no stables, and but very little corn, and the horses were of necessity turned loose to sustain a miserable existence on cane in an Arkansas bottom.

"In what originated this march? Was any important public end to be attained? Was it to repel an invading foe? Was it to make a sudden and important attack upon a foreign enemy? Did the good of the service in any way call for it? To these questions there is but one answer—No! There has been assigned, as the only and great motive, *that the corps having been raised for the defence of the frontier, would be disbanded if it remained inactive so far in the interior as Jefferson Barracks.* What! has it come to this? Has Congress so firmly established a character for illiberality, inconstancy of purpose, want of intelligence, that the true public interest is to be sacrificed to appearances glossed for their eyes? Is their ignorance of military affairs so great as to become a matter of calculation? Is it attempted to flatter them with the possession of magical attributes?—

that, at their mighty fiat, the laborious and tedious process of enlisting, clothing, equipping—of discipline, of dismounted and the doubly difficult mounted drill, that has hitherto been considered the labor of a year, nay, of years, is all to be accomplished in a day? It is difficult to say; some mighty object has doubtless been in view; for men have been caused to suffer such hardships as the defence of country and liberty has not *always* been sufficient inducement to endure.

"The question may well be asked, has the Government of the United States constancy of purpose equal to the creation of a single regiment of dragoons? Our legislators must be aware that the officers appointed in the dragoons, were of necessity, infantry officers; that they knew nothing of the service of cavalry; that time is necessary to overcome these difficulties, and the opportunity of peace. The service of cavalry had become with us a forgotten and unknown branch of military knowledge; something to be read of, as we do of the Macedonian phalanx. There are but two copies of cavalry tactics, founded on the system followed, in the possession of the dragoons: the officers have been drilled in squads, in order to teach the men.

"Jefferson Barracks was doubtless originally selected as the station, where the regiment was to be set up after a uniform system, before it was to be thrown into actual service, operating in detached bodies among widely scattered tribes of Indians. This might have been done nearly as well at an outpost,—if the people are really so anxious that their lot should be cast beyond the pale of civilization—and they would have been spared the disasters of a *change* of policy.

"Rome was not more rigid in exactions from her armies

and their commanders, than are the United States—this most pacific of nations! Rome, whose very birth was amid the throes of a measure of military violence, whose population, wealth, and power were, step by step, the growth of military success, whose fame and history are but military annals. Marius was thought to have taken the first great step towards the ruin of the republic, when he permitted the richest and most powerful citizens to serve *by substitute* in his African wars—the first instance recorded. Such a nation might well exact of its armies *immediate* action and success, when every individual had been raised to arms.

"It is unnecessary further to waste words, on a subject that enforces conviction on every reflecting mind. The great change I have shown to have taken place in the character and habits of our frontiers-men, those pioneers of the civilized, was in part attributed to a corresponding change in the character of the Indians. But let it be here remarked, that all those who have had the opportunity have observed, as a trait of character common to *all* Indians, that none so instinctively appreciate the advantages of regularity, obedience, &c., in regular troops; it is apparently combined with a superstitious feeling, which inspires them with awe at the sight of a completeness and uniformity, so superior to themselves, as to appear mysterious. Owing to this, and the great changes in the circumstances of the Indians, and our relations with them, it were easy to clearly demonstrate that the regiment of dragoons is better calculated for service among them than any irregular troops, even of the old border caste, did they now exist. In the first place, it is well known that the Indians, having been driven back generally to the plains, the prairies, act now almost universally on horseback; of course; all operations of attack against them must correspond; now our border-men, rangers, &c., use their horses for the sole purpose of locomotion; they dismount to use their rifles: thus encumbered with the preservation of their horses, it of course is left optional with the Indians to attack him with advantage, or to avoid engagement by an indefinitely continued flight. But the main object of our troops, as I understand it, is in these times, to awe the Indians,—to *prevent* depredations and war; and to repress their morbid inclinations for internal aggressions; to *preserve peace*, and further the design of civilization. An irregular, ill-armed force, composed of individuals who have never acknowledged the common restraints of society; who confound insubordination with a boasted equality; who cannot endure the wholesome action of discipline, or even obedience, cannot be considered comparable for these objects, with a force whose perfect discipline insures an absence of all offensive irregularities, whose complete and perfect arms are the tokens of strength; whose accurate evolutions, responding to a guiding will, are emblematic of power; whose very uniforms have an imposing moral effect, investing them to Indian eyes, with the character of direct representatives of a great nation which they dread.

"It has been intimated in the national legislature, that the dragoons can and must build quarters and stables. There seems to exist a great want of information on every point of this subject. Now every officer of dragoons, every intelligent man acquainted with cavalry service, will unhesitatingly pronounce, from the force of an honest conviction, that this is impracticable, without great deterioration, beside a total loss of their services for the time being. Do gentlemen reflect that the dragoon is almost constantly occupied with the care of his horse? of the horses of the sick? of absentees from all causes? and until stables *are* built, his horse is tenfold an object of attention? To come to facts at once;—the dragoon horses at this post are *held out to graze* the half of each day. This, with watering, grooming, and feeding, the care of his various accoutrements and arms, and the drilling absolutely necessary to keep up but a moderate degree of perfection in his duties, occupies nearly every moment of the time of a dragoon soldier.

"The PERSONNEL of the army has heretofore been complained of; called 'the sweepings of cities,' &c. Young men, fit for the service required of dragoons, cannot be enlisted, with any such prospect of building, of hard labor, held out. If they are inclined to work, they can easily obtain at home double and treble the wages of dragoons. Some experience has been had on this point; and it was readily discovered, that the main, if not sole inducements of those enlisted, were a craving for excitement, and romantic notions of the far West, &c., operating upon enterprising, roving inclinations.

"The Regiment of Dragoons has had, so to speak, *bad luck;* which on some points is a charitable conclusion. The winter at Fort Gibson has been one of unexampled severity; the corn crop of last season had been swept away by an unparalleled rise of the Arkansas River. This was, however, or might have been, known before they were sent here.

"The river has been this spring, and is now, unusually low. Some of the clothing arrived in *February;* after having been, with the sabres and pistols, sunk in a steamboat. The guns made for the dragoons, and some of the clothing, have not yet arrived. Their sabres and pistols are not those intended for the regiment; but of a very rough, inferior quality."

CHAPTER XXXI.

THE other five companies of the regiment were enlisted in the course of the winter, and afterward organized at Jefferson Barracks. They were then marched to join us at Fort Gibson; they arrived in June; and were hurried off like the others, on the 18th of the month, quite unprepared for an expedition. Nevertheless the regiment marched full six weeks too late, when it is considered that we were to traverse the burning plains of the South: and the thermometer having previously risen to 105° in the shade, there was every prospect of a summer of unexampled heat.

It is painful to dwell on this subject. Nature would seem to have conspired with an imbecile military administration for the destruction of the regiment. On, on they marched, over the parched plains whence all moisture had shrunk, as from the touch of fire; their martial pomp and show dwindled to a dusty speck in the midst of a boundless plain; disease and death struck them as they moved; with the false mirage ever in view, with glassy eyes, and parched tongues, they seemed upon a sea of fire. They marched on, leaving three-fourths of their number stretched by disease in many sick camps; there, not only destitute of every comfort, but exposed with burning fevers to the horrors of the unnatural heat—it was the death of hope. The horses too were lost by scores. In one sick camp, they were in great danger of massacre by a horde of Camanche Indians, who had established themselves near by; and were in all probability only saved by the judgment and determination of the officer in command, the lamented Izard: and he was fortunately indebted to his experience on the Santa Fe expedition. In the face of overwhelming numbers, he kept every man who could possibly bear arms on constant guard: and opposed at the point of the bayonet the passage of a single Indian over their slight breastwork. He knew the influence of dauntless boldness over Indians, who dread every loss, and seek the attainment of their ends by cunning and management: thus on friendly pretences they sought admittance singly, with a view gradually to obtain the power to crush the small force at a blow.

General Leavenworth and his aid stopped. They both lost their lives. Colonel Dodge, with 150 of the hardiest constitutions, persevered and overcame every obstacle; they reached the Tow-e-ash village, in a picturesque valley, amid mountainous precipices and rocks; such he discovered to be the name of a numerous tribe, who altogether with Camanches, Kiawas, and Arrapahoes had hitherto been confounded under the name of Pawnees.

There, perhaps within the boundary of Mexico, was made this first though feeble demonstration of the power and ubiquity of the white man. Some breath was expended in an effort to mediate peace between these wandering savage robbers and their red neighbors of our border; as availing as it would be to attempt to establish a truce between the howling wolf of the prairie and his prey.

But in return for two female prisoners which the Osages

had captured, and by some accident had not killed, and which we carried with us, the expedition had the merit of rescuing from barbarism and restoring to his mother, a lad whom the Tow-e-ash had captured a year before. On that occasion the Indians had killed his father, a Judge Martin; who thus paid the forfeit of a very vagrant disposition, which must have led him to intrude upon these savage regions.

The shattered and half famished remnants of the regiment were gathered together at Fort Gibson, in August. The thermometer had risen in the shade to 114°. There, in tents and neglected, many more suffered and died. After a short breathing-time, the larger portion of the regiment marched for two other posts, distant many hundred miles, on the Missouri and Upper Mississippi; and this last, they had to establish and build. Thus, in three distant positions, the reader must imagine that the squadrons of this illtreated regiment, found some leisure to invent and practise as many different systems of tactics and duty.

PART II.

CHAPTER I.

Oh reader! "gentle" or not,—I care not a whit,—so you are honest—I will tell you a secret. I write not to be read, and I swear never even to transcribe for your benefit, — unless I change my mind. All I want is a good listener; I want to converse with you; and if you are absolutely dumb, why I will sometimes answer for you.

Hundreds go and come at my word; none are my "equals," so none are my *social* friends. I have much to do; very much;—if I nod at my post, some one, or some interest suffers;—nevertheless, the race of hermits is extinct, and man requires companionship; there are some moments unoccupied, sometimes even hours, and you shall be my Friend, and I will talk to you.

How dreary must be a great Commodore,
Alone in the cabin of a seventy-four!

Be not alarmed! I make a rhyme but once a year; the idea came in that shape, and you must take it as it comes.

Oh, wide and flat,—shall I say "stale and unprofitable"—prairies! I have traversed thy loveliest and thy most desolate wilds for three lustres; and I am not weary of *you*, but of the terribly monotonous jingle of the rusty accoutrements of Mars! Here Venus never smiles; nor Bacchus grins; nor beams the intelligence of Mercury. Oh, gentle Herald, that I could fly with thee! Well!—a pretty salmagundi I shall have of it! But amid my flights, I shall often be sober, serious, if not sublime. We will talk on all subjects, from the shape of a horseshoe to that of the slipper of the last favorite—say the "divine Fanny," from great battles, or Napier's splendid pictures of such, down to the obscurest point of the squad drill—from buffalo bulls to elfin sprites.

"So," said he, "so there is not a bandit on the road; we are going for nothing,—to wait on these ragged-rascal greasers. It will ruin the regiment! There has been expense enough for the trip already to break it down. I had rather be in the infantry." At that moment I was in a small prairie "island," "reposing from the noontide sultriness," reclining in that choice part of the shadow of a fine oak that the bole casts; had been reading about the hot red rays of the sun not being reflected by the moon;—gazing listlessly through the gently rustling leaves into the sparkling depths of ether, and wondering why the sun himself could not dispense with some of these same red rays in such very hot weather. "Suffering for country," thus, in the easiest possible attitude, I could not grow angry, and the very idea of talking, *then*, was heating; so I only thought. "Friend," thought I, "to obey orders is duty; and it is honorable to do duty. I would not undertake to think for my superiors, if it distressed me so much. Doubtless, there is expense, and if you, and some others, had your way, you would try the experiment of feeding the regiment on a straw a day;

and, gazing complacently on the skeleton, I doubt not you would expect praise or promotion for your services. I can even imagine you addressing twenty millions of people (who all eat meat three times a day) as follows: 'Behold, how faithful a servant am I; how much expense I have spared in this terrible regiment of dragoons!' And the 'sovereigns' would growl out, 'You had plenty of money; why did you spare anything to make them fat and efficient; we want to be well served; if we had noticed at all, we would have had several more regiments.'"

Oh! ye hypocrites,—demagogues,—who swallow a million squandered on a fraudulent contract, or an Eastern palace, and strain at a cent for the protection and peace of the simple border States!

I received a letter from the old General, who said, "If in the discharge of this duty you should find rough and perilous work, the meritorious services of your officers, and your men, and yourself, shall be affectionately remembered by every true-hearted soldier and statesman of our country; and more especially of those great and growing States of the Valley of the Mississippi, and more especially by your General and friend." I read this to another:—"Meritorious services," said he, "to stag after these negro Mexicans; what falsehood, what folly!" I was struck all aback. "Have you no merit in doing your duty?" "No, none!" Oh, Truth! thought I, how often wilt thou forsake the mighty, and choose companionship with folly! Surely, a man will seldom estimate his own value too low.

Where were we? Did I not tell you, my prairie friend, we should talk "*de omnibus rebus et quibusdam aliis.*" Do not be frightened at the latinity (I hope it is right). I seldom offend in that way,—I am like the "General" in this, and was never very deep beyond Cæsar. "General," said he, "you forgot the Latin;" the General took off his hat, made another bow to the multitude, "*E pluribus unum, sine qua non!*"—"That will do, General." So much for Major Downing.

"Beyond Cæsar!" What a singular schoolboy phrase for a soldier! I take Cæsar for my model in dealing with savages;—*seriously, he* was the greatest warrior that ever lived—up to the period when Alexander Hamilton is reported to have said, "The greatest man that ever lived was Julius Cæsar."

Where were we? Where *are* we? We are on a pretty hill near the spring and grove of a nameless tributary which meanders the beautiful valley of the Kansas River;—a hundred miles from any place; and it is in the dog days of 1843, and there have been three of the hottest I have felt; the unusually light breeze has been right behind, and only felt in bringing with us our dust. "Dog days?" Oh Sirius! thou brightest and nearest sun;—the centre,—it may be of many a more happy planet, "more social and bright" than this;—how, bright star, didst thou get thy name?

Talking of the dog star, on the Santa Fe Road, reminds me of a General, who, a longer time ago than I would care to tell a lady, sent an express to a command out here that I belonged to; and when an old woman at Leavenworth remonstrated at the danger (the man *was* killed), replied: "No! every Indian, from the Mississippi to the Rocky Mountains, shall tremble at my name." On hearing this, I made the following impromptu (the only one in my life):

"Immortal man, brave General ——!
The darkling dog star at thy birth
And fiery comet,—portents of fame,—
Gave warning that thy awful name,

Uttered in wrath in valley plain,
In echo should the mountains gain,
To teach each man of Indian race,
From river bank to mountain base,
To TREMBLE!

The idea of *publishing* a book is terrible; no military reputation could stand it; we, who of all things, seek distinction, should be most careful how we mingle with the vulgar herd of—book makers! But, if some "kind friend" should ever introduce thus my scribblings unamended to the world, I warn him to trust them only to an artist of the press; let one art help out another; not one in a thousand can *venture* in the guise of the "cheap literature" of the day, unless, indeed, it be a newspaper extra (subscribed for in advance). There is virtue in fair wide margins, and pictorial embellishment.

Truly, the Republic of Letters has become a rank democracy! In the olden time when literature was more exclusive, none wrote who felt not the call, and the inspiration strong upon them; and whatever is very difficult, and rouses the energies to accomplish it, is better done. Compare Eastern agriculture with that of the Great Valley! Compare the flower gardens of Nashville (city of elegance and hospitality), which is built on a rock, with those of any city on a rich soil!

Friend.—But you were talking of books.

"True, but I have none—Macaulay's Miscellanies, Stevens' new book, pshaw! even my manual, Napier, were forgotten and left; so it is necessary to *make* one; that is, fill up with our conversations this blank bound 'book.'"

"After all, it would be ridiculous to publish Irving in the cheap form, in the brown paper style; (won't the time come, when a salesman will wrap up a parcel—say a pound of tea—in a new novel, thrown into the bargain?) They have spared Irving: his liquid sentences flowing through glittering margins of fairest typography,—to what can we compare them, but to a crystal streamlet purling amid flowery savannas and sweet shady groves; and anon delving into cave-like clefts,—romantic recesses, where, of old, the fairies sought shelter from the glare of day. "And the smooth surface of the Bay presented a polished mirror in which Nature saw herself and smiled." Were I an Eastern monarch,—who had stuffed the mouths of poets with sugar and gold—how *could* I have rewarded such a writer?

"Could all the private wealth of England,—could all the hands of Birmingham and Manchester multiply the 'Last of the Barons,' for instance, as in the days of the polished and literary Greeks—in manuscript—to equal one week's supply! Published in London—and in two months a wanderer in the Rocky Mountains will pass the sultry noon, poring over its pages! Oh, Steam!"

Friend.—Let us take a walk.

"With all my heart.

"Behold! the prairie, which late I saw in its fresh and budding, yet immature beauties, has now put on a golden garniture; and its green velvet is decked as with precious stones; the fair rose—like virgin's blushes—has faded from its cheek; but here are its pink apples, that look like the cherry lips of beauty. Look at these magnetic weeds; from their young green leaves have sprung stout stalks as high as your head; and they have put forth other leaves which point, or *edge*, more truly to the poles, than the first; they have a yellow flower. See these beautiful red blossoms—but here is the queen of flowers! a sensitive plant; its leaves are as beautiful as diminutive; and its tall stem is full of sweet flowers of the most delicate yellow; it is the type of modest Beauty! even its slender, smooth, translucent stem is pretty."

Friend.—What is this, so like the locust, but which seems a bush or shrub?

"I am convinced that it is the Mezquit; which is not known to exist in our prairies; their frequenters have no name for it that I have heard, except perhaps, 'bastard locust.' Here is the milkweed, with its small white blossom;—and here the 'red-root;' it makes a good tea; soldiers all over the Far West know and use it. Yonder the prairie is golden with tall but miniature sunflowers—how rough the dark green leaves; turpentine is oozing from them, and from the stalk; the polar plant is full of it too—it may be a species. At the joint here, you see a collection of white foam; remove it, and there is an embryo fly;—yes; the true, troublesome horsefly; look, it is no longer an egg, but the little wretch has motion. Whence this moisture, and its mysterious continuance for days in the hot sun? Was the plant punctured that it might flow out for the protection of the egg? This turpentine seems necessary to produce horseflies; the triangular looking *earfly* is hatched on young pines.

"Botany—like all knowledge ennobling, what a treasure were it here! But how many are there who penetrate the pedantic surface? I care not for a little more or less. I know that 'male and female created He' also the flowers and plants; and I have seen some admirable hybrids. Ah! if I could go forth with Zanoni, and could penetrate the hidden virtues and the vital mysteries of a single square foot of the boundless waste around, then could I rejoice above all other men!"

Friend.—You are wandering again. What could have caused that strange circle in the grass there ?—it is forty feet across, and, sure enough, it is of the rank sun-flower.

" Why, my friend, if you were imaginative you could people it with the fairies which have been frightened from the old continent by the clink of gold, and have here found refuge—pretty far too from the sound of dollars."

Friend.—But seriously—it cannot be accident; in fact, there are many of them; could they have been caused by the circular dances of the Indian! The desert here is scarce a refuge for them.

" True !—you remind me though, how *one* might have been caused if that weed is fond of Indian-trod ground. When the cholera, girding the unhappy earth, reached Council Bluffs, a friend of mine was there and some Indians whom he knew ;—Big Elk, the distinguished chief of the Omahaws, and his party fled from the houses, where they saw it, to their native prairies, and fell upon this plan to puzzle the fiend—to throw him off their trail. They trotted around in a circle of about this size, uttering songs and incantations, until they wore a path; then, as agreed, one flew off with a wide leap in a tangent, and with steps as 'few and far between' as possible, disappeared; soon after another at a different point made his eccentric exit; and so another and another—all—the brave and sagacious chief the last, fled howling over the far hill-tops—the pestilence fiend was baffled and never found their trail."

Friend.—But was I right ? Are these supposed to be memorials of the poor Indians ?

"No ;—of their friends, the buffalo; when the wolves audacious from famine, threaten the calves, their mothers huddle them, and circle round on the defensive; and thus stirring up the ground with their hoofs, excite the growth of particular weeds; of this there is little doubt. So much for travelling for knowledge!

"But I am sure here is buffalo grass!—it is indeed;—quite a patch of it;—but close to the road where it may be *trodden:* which seems a condition, I mean a proviso, of *its* growth. I thought there was none so far to the east;—but look into my 'journal' for that subject. The dew is falling fast—let us get some of those fine plums, and so end our walk."

CHAPTER II.

SEPT. 1.—A fine rapid clear stream this! Six miles from Council Grove—famous as Council Bluffs. It is a tributary of Grand River, more prettily and distinctly called by its Indian name Neosho (water-white or clear; the Indians, like the French, give you the adjective last).

We will wait here in this shady grove, and let the horses eat the luxuriant wild pea-vine until the wagons come up. This baggage is to an army what a wife and children are to a man—a soldier at least—a necessity and a comfort, whilst a trouble and an embarrassment.

Oh, my books! my favorite authors, how I miss you! My call is to "spirits from the vasty deep." Not even Shakspeare; and Walter Scott,—what a camp library would his works be. Professedly an imitator of the great and philanthropic Edgeworth, he dated a new era, built up a new school, and then—ruined it: for he reduced authorship to a trade. Yet, who can but admire his enthusiasm of old age; his faith (and industry) which did remove a mountain—of debt!

And James, his follower,—his almost rival in the race of usefulness and fame; he never equalled Ivanhoe, but has written perhaps more books, and never descended to the level of Castle Dangerous and some others. The author of Attila and Philip Augustus must rank with the first.

Friend.—Do you not think his Black Prince and Last of the Barons may be classed together, whether as historical or romantic?

"Decidedly so, without pronouncing on their comparative merits; the last, though admirable, is too voluminous and heavy for a romance. Your remark might have been more just if the philosopher, his daughter, and her plebeian lover had been left out; and the work better for a more artistic unity."

"And D'Israeli, the younger, the sparkler! whose first book is his best and immortal. I read an odd volume of Vivian Grey every year.

"And Lever!—the bright coiner—so they say—of other men's ore!

"And Cooper! the American Scott, who still more than his model, wrote his brain as dry as a broken inkstand!

"And Willis! the Irving of 'periodical literature,' and the poet.

"And thou, immortal creator of Little Nell! whose genius could make classical the name of Twist!"

Friend.—He, too, founded a new school—of "serial" writers.

"And it bids fair to complete the work of literary deterioration. Oh, Dickens! the Atlantic was thy Rubicon; on its broad waste thou didst shipwreck much fame and honor. Wonderful indeed that thou shouldst, in a day, turn two millions of admirers, friends, into despisers! Whilst the arms of millions were outstretched to receive thee, and their eyes glistened with welcoming pleasure, in thy heart thou betrayedst them, and sold them to a publisher!"

Friend.—A dip into a good author, old or new, is often a mental shower-bath; it sets one's ideas in motion; is in some sort a substitute for the active emulation of the world!

"But that is essential to real progress. Something may be learned from every one we meet; an ox-driver may teach us some point of philosophy."

Friend.—Not mechanical philosophy; for all wagoners live and die in the belief that small fore-wheels make a wagon run lighter!

"By meeting and conversing with new people we gain new ideas, and are set a-thinking; that is the greatest benefit of travel. It is the throwing the ideas and experience of a multitude into a joint stock, that make such world wonders as London."

Friend.—Allow me to say that you are to-day quite as interesting—as original.

"Well, shall we '*talk prairie*' alone? Shall we discuss whether this beautiful purple flower, the bulbous root of which overflows with balsam, would bear transplanting into a flower-garden—a lady's bower! No? Well, give me another trial for something new on my subject. Man's improvement depends upon his being gregarious or not; which circumstances control; in Mexico, Peru, &c., where kinder climates multiplied the Indian, I attribute their great advance in civilization solely to their living in crowds, villages, cities. Our sparse hunter-tribes seem incapable of improvement; our own race, when they have fallen into the same circumstances, have grown barbarous."

Friend.—True enough, perhaps; but New Mexico, to which you are wending your weary way, owes its name to its superiority, when discovered, to savage tribes to its south, which long kept back its Spanish colonizers; they were then manufacturers of cotton cloth, and in fact improved very little on the slight Spanish infusion to the date of this trade.

"Which is of precious little advantage to any one else. I will give you a better than the usual answer to a stumper—'the exception proves the rule.' Their circumstances were very peculiar. Nearly isolated by wide deserts on every side, their arid and barren country only admitted the occupancy of valleys, where they must have congregated; and, in fact, were found in villages; excluded from these shelters, wild animals were repelled from their country, and they then became, perforce, herdsmen, instead of hunters. So much for these native Americans."

Friend.—"Americans." Can that name continue to distinguish the citizens of the United States? It has been suggested, that even now the name of the continent may be (and should justly be) changed to Columbia, and that we may thus secure our appropriate title.

"It is impossible to give so general and pervading a motion to the human mind as to change the name of a continent! Could vast bodies be easily set in motion, their momentum would soon overwhelm the world?"

Friend.—Are you reading there the Book of Regulations?

"Yes; they are changed and added to so often that it seems no one pretends to know what they are. Here is something on courts-martial; it is copied from the British."

Friend.—Do young officers become your judges as well as jurors, by instinct? I believe no examination into their qualifications is required before they are allowed to sit in judgment?

"No—it is a sore spot in our system. Something might be made of your idea."

Friend.—The Attorney-General (or a Judge Advocate General), an Inspector General, and a Professor of *Ethics*, might make a good Board?

"We have no Judge Advocate General; there is a Judge Advocate, I believe; but there being no law for his appointment, he keeps as close as a mouse. I rather incline to a radical change; the trial of all important cases by a kind of Circuit Court, of few members; officers of rank and experience, selected and appointed to perform this duty exclusively for a term of years."

To-day we arrived at Council Grove, and were received with "presented arms" by a company of dragoons—which makes a fourth. What a collection of wagons! there are hundreds, and nearly all have Mexican owners; look at their men! they show ivories as white as negroes; they are Indians, but New Mexicans as well, and speak Spanish. There are herds of mules in every valley, on every hill, and hundreds of oxen too. It is unhealthy here; many who have stayed a week are sick; the dragoon company has been waiting three days, and they are already suffering.

The sun set this evening with a phenomenon of marvellous beauty; from purple and blue clouds, gorgeously edged with gold, or rather celestial fire, shot up a "glory" —a fan of pencilled and colored light, expanded to the zenith; and joining there, another in reflected symmetry converged to the eastern horizon!

Council Grove is a luxuriant, heavily timbered bottom of the Neosho, of about one hundred and sixty acres; and there are several rather smaller in the vicinity. I can perceive no trace of fortifications, or other antiquities, which some fanciful writers have discovered here, though the ground is very uneven. It is a charming grove, though sombre; for we love the contrast to the vast plain, hot and shadeless.

Here we shall fairly launch into the green waste of the "Grand Prairie." Behind we have had a sparkling rivulet every few miles.

Friend.—Yes, far sweeter than this dark forest, fit haunt for Druids! There, were bowers, fragrant with rich wild blossoms, vocal with the songs of birds! Under their arching vines the eye enjoyed a picture where the light danced upon bright leaves, shaken by gentle airs, and which the smooth green hills and distant groves completed!

"No fancy picture either! But I am not in that vein. How long will the bowers, scanty though they be, escape the Vandal axe? How long will law, the parchment defence of the weak red man, resist the Saxon? I foresee that agriculture will soon make here its mark (and perhaps just here it may pause again). The migratory wave will extinguish the prairie fires, and corn-fields and young forests will make these beautiful prairies a memory!

September 3.—Diamond Spring. A true "Diamond

of the Desert," a Pearl of the Prairie—were pearls but as transparent as its cold and crystal waters!

Friend.—You were too busy yesterday at the Grove to ride with me and enjoy the beautiful scenery; there is an unusual variety; even rocky cliffs are not wanting. I saw, too, much wild flax, with its pretty blue blossoms, and sage, and sun-flowers twelve feet high, but with very small flowers.

"Busy! Sixteen hours of labor! I only chanced to notice the extraordinary repetition of the same strange and beautiful sunset, but not so brilliant as the night before: lightnings played among the darker clouds, and with rolling thunders gave portent of the stormy night we had, and the slippery roads to-day."

Friend.—Yes, truly, and when will all those five-ton wagons come up? I saw, that in the midst of your work of organization, examining papers, writing last letters, &c., a committee of Mexican owners waited on you.

"I told them that I must and would come to-day. Many of their men—half-starved wretches!—are ill. It was time for action, to escape the malaria of those bottoms which were lately overflowed. They said they had some expectation of meeting an escort, but that we would be well received, if we went to Santa Fe, which is more than doubtful."

Cotton-wood Fork, Sept. 6.

Marching this morning in a dense fog, about 7 o'clock, before the caravan,—as I thought—I soon discovered, like spectres, the dim outline of a seemingly endless column of wagons which had glided ahead of me; nine miles it took me to get in front, on the well-beaten road.

The breeze now rattles merrily overhead through the

tall cotton woods-which shade my tent; the light clouds of the broken storm fly like shattered fleets before a gale; now and then are heard distant cheers, or unearthly yells, and volleys of whip-cracks from the Mexicans, who are driving their overwoked mules up the steep bank at the ford.

I find Mr. Robidoux here, with a dozen light horse-carts; he has a trading house three hundred miles beyond Santa Fe. The snow-storm of the 8th of last November fell upon him in this vicinity; more than a hundred horses and mules perished, and indeed one man; he had lost his only axe, or he could have cut down cotton-woods for food to save his animals.

Robidoux undertakes to give me the boundaries of the buffalo grass, which extends to the Missouri River, and within eighty miles of the State boundary; he says, "that throughout New Mexico, where the buffalo do not keep it down, it grows a foot high; his cattle and sheep live on it exclusively, and keep fat in winter; and improve in size on the original breed; the mutton is superior in flavor to ours."

This man prays for the annexation of New Mexico, as necessary to develop its mineral riches: he asserts, "that he knows districts where, for twenty miles, it is impossible to find a handful of dirt without gold."

"Why in the world have you not made your fortune collecting it?"

"I sunk," he replied with a true Frenchman's shrug, "eight thousand dollar."

September 8th. *Friend.*—You appear to be uncomfortable?

"To ride in rain is common enough, and a man or woman either, can stand it without much inconvenience;

but this cold September rain is doubly unpleasant, when the reflection is made that it is twenty miles to the first tree or bush for fuel, and that heavily laden wagons must bear one company; but it is the villain musquitoes that fill the measure of 'discomfort;' you perceive they take refuge from the rain within my greatcoat collar, and beneath the pent-house of my regulation visor, although it is not large enough to cover the end of my nose."

Friend.—Perhaps they seek its atmosphere? it looks fiery.

"True: from yesterday's sun and high wind. This 'Turkey Creek,' which I left this morning, should have a truer name; it is a cold and rainy place, without fuel, and no turkey or other living thing did I ever see there, save a squad of horse-stealing Indians, which we once surprised at dark, after a forced march. Three months ago we had nearly frozen there in a rain; and I observed last night, 'we shall not find it as cold here in September as in June,' when suddenly a north wind belied me."

Friend.—But this grumbling! it is worse than your late discussions of mules, oxen, sheep—but above all buffalo grass!

"Bah! one cannot sink the shop; but you must know that this grass is my hobby. I have attempted to introduce it at the East. Yesterday's infamous roads and this rain are worst in the prospect of the great detention they will cause to the caravan; it will prove equal, I fear, to the Walnut Creek loss of twelve days in June; but now every hour counts, and is one nearer to frost and snow."

Friend.—You got some orders to go to Sante Fe and winter in the Rocky Mountains at your first camp; was additional clothing all you sent back for?

"Sir, I saw how matters would go, and the moment I

was put in charge, some twelve days beforehand, I took measures to double the outfit which had been ordered. I knew the Southern Department would not furnish an escort capable of relieving me. So, against advice and opinions of ——, and protesting quartermasters and other small fry, I kept my steady course."

Friend.—But what if you had complied with the letter of the order; which could only have been expected, considering you had just come back from a long and tedious march, and with "worn down horses," as even those acquainted with such matters thought?

"Nearly three-fourths of the horses are the same. But I will tell you what would have been the consequence—I should either have had to march back to Fort Leavenworth when I got the new order, and attempt to make a new outfit, or have come on and utterly failed of means to accomplish the objects of the expedition. I am now certain that the first alternative was impossible; for as it was, I was just in time at Council Grove."

Friend.—Well, failing to accomplish the object of the escort, you would have pointed to your orders?

"Yes, but *success* is the military test, touchstone, talisman! If disaster had occurred, a thousand judges with goosequill in hand and printing press at elbow,—if they had noticed,—would have condemned me unheard: the soldiers of a Republic have a narrow path to follow, and answer to two tribunals—the Government and the people."

Friend.—What are these beautiful animals.

"Antelopes—the first we have seen. There are four of them; two are this year's fawns. What fidelity in brutes! They are a family. It is here we first saw some in June,—I dare say they are the same."

Friend.—What singular tails! They look like bunches of cotton as big as my hat.

"It is two bunches or spots of white hair adjoining the tail which you see. They are a rare animal; I have never seen them in the States! they are the link between deer and goats."

Friend.—Have you ever eaten their flesh?

"Often: it is venison with the least taste of mutton; they are the fleetest of prairie animals; but are so curious, and so faithful to their young, that they are easily killed. An Indian brought one into our camp near here, in the summer, a singular-looking little pet, with a spoon-shaped nose and muzzle and a black tongue; its bleat was exactly the note of a penny trumpet; its legs of the size of your finger, ridiculously long; but the eyes were beautiful as those of the gazelle; it sucked sugar and water and flour; but we turned it loose."

Friend.—It is a wonder how these young animals, not to say the old ones, escape the wolves.

"It puzzles me; the wolves cannot be numerous here; even as much so as near the forts and settlements. Poor devils! like the Indians, they follow the buffalo."

Friend.—What! are they their victims? Will they attack a grown buffalo?

"Not in *prosperity*. I have observed numbers of the largest wolves familiarly mingled with buffalo, which were utterly careless of them; but besides accident and sickness, how many are killed and crippled by hunters! but when the wolves are famished, they do attack and kill stragglers; they eat also grasshoppers."

Friend.—What a beautiful plant with the striped white and green flowers!

"Those are the leaves; the flower—look closer—is

diminutive and of a delicate white; it is a species of milk-weed, and is called, I believe, the variegated euphorbia. But yonder is land to leeward,—as a sailor would say—(the flat, wet prairie is usually like the sea; a little further on, and it is salty). It seems a city! those white sand bluffs and forests mingled; a beautiful city with spire and dome, and cottage too! all *white*, and mingled with shade trees. How pleasant the first far-off view of the Arkansas! for there are its hills of shifting, impalpable sand. Those dark green spots far in front, are a few trees on the Little Arkansas: a big name, in fact, for a branch a few feet wide and inches deep; it *imitates the Great*, however, and is treacherous at bottom."

Friend.—Look at that gentleman! he has an ague; what a day, and what circumstances for a sick man!

"Bad enough; I must force him to get into a wagon; it is hard to make him give up: he has caught the accursed disease by his four nights at Council Grove. And that too puts a 2d Lieutenant in command of a squadron. I was years a Captain before I commanded one even on exercises."

Friend.—That was pleasanter than this: and what is the *honor* here?

"Pleasure and honor are somewhat matters of imagination or fashion; but there is *danger* here;—danger of dishonor,—that is, disaster, at least."

Friend.—'Fore Heaven! what from? Can't you see the 'ends of the earth,' and all a plain, naked as barren?

"You are a novice on the prairies, and I hope will remain one, as to its dangers, whilst in my company; but Cooper could tell you better than that. Why sir, an Indian will personate a wolf, and spy out your weak points over a distant swell of the seemingly level surface.

In '29 it was so; and we saw nothing—marching for months. Few would credit that there were human beings within a hundred miles. Well—one day four discharged men set out for home; they had gone about twelve miles when they were surrounded and one slain on the spot. About that time, a little off our guard, the cattle were suffered to graze a mile from camp, when lo! 500 Indians ready mounted sprang forth as from the earth and captured most of the cattle and horses, slew a man, and were only beaten off by grape shot and our determined face. The prairie is very deceiving. Kendall tells of a chasm, 800 feet deep, and not very narrow, which they did not perceive in open prairie, until within a few yards."

Friend.—I remember that; it was on the unfortunate Texan expedition against Santa Fe.

"Yes: they might easily have captured it, as there was great dissatisfaction against the government, if they had only had discipline. It shows the difference between the bravery of bowie-knife broils, and that high courage which supports one amid a long train of difficulties and disasters—which braves the wear and tear of adverse circumstances, famine, fatigue, and continual dangers: these only inspire the veteran with heroism! They had one such among them. Armijo has confessed that *he* could have succeeded well backed by a hundred men; or, as Robidoux said the other day, 'if they had fired three guns.'"

Friend.—Is there no end to this trudge through mud and rain? It seems to me we are always the same,—in the centre of a great circle of dank, flat, and changeless prairie.

"I have been thinking very seriously to what this infernal march may lead us. 'Circle,' indeed! and having escaped from that of incessant fierce winds, we have duly fallen upon the 'third circle.' "

——" della piova,
Eterna, maledetta, fredda a greve."

Friend.—Of rain eternal, accursed, cold, and heavy—it is a wonder Dante left out the musquitos!

"Yes; but our Cerebus has three *hundred* wolfish throats which bark and howl at us."

Friend.—Well, I think it won't do; you have fetched hell too far.

"Only come here in the dogdays, and if you can't imagine yourself around the edges of a more than poetical hell, it will be because the eternal winds are scorching, instead of cold."

September 9.—All day it has rained again. We have been lying still, trying to keep dry and warm, on the bank of the Little Arkansas. There are a few green trees and bushes, but little fuel. Worst of all is the case of the poor horses—they are starving and freezing before our eyes, for the grass is very coarse and poor; they have shrunk very sensibly in twenty-four hours.

Fiercer and colder rages the storm; faster pours the pitiless rain: it does us more injury than a forced march of sixty miles;—and the traders! where are they? What obstacles are in their way! What a great detention there must be!

Late at night.—The cold north wind, laden with ceaseless rain, moans dismally through the dank cotton-woods: dark, deep beneath, through its slimy banks creeps the sullen stream; the earth, our bed, is soaked; the tall, rank grass seems to wail to the watery blasts. 'Twas *here* that a cry to God, wrested by human fiends from a brother man, fell unanswered,—echoless on the desert air. It was here, in this solemn wilderness, where man, it would seem of necessity, must sympathize with his fellow,—that human beings, eight or ten, fell upon a friendless one, and for vile pelf slew him! Here, without a tear, a word, a look of human sympathy, was poor Charvis deliberately murdered. The famished howling wolves do not tear their kind! Ah! it was enough to freeze into palpable shape the ministering spirits of the air. Oh! methinks I hear *his* spirit moaning in the midnight storm. Yes, moaning for his kind. One tear of sympathy! there, you have it!—may your spirit rest.

Oh! how much better to die *thus*, than that there should enter into the soul, the hell which must accompany the conception of such a deed!

CHAPTER III.

SEPTEMBER 11.—If "time waits for no man," heaven knows what this chronic rain stays for. We wait on it; but if anathema or any kind of curses, sacred or profane, could avail, it had inevitably gone to—the driest place we read of.

A squadron of dragoons came last evening from the South; according to *their* order, to relieve us; but they are broken down and on the back track. Having pretty thoroughly exhausted the prairie plum crop, and the buffalo being washed away to far hilltops—they were now prone to the land of pork and beans.

What with inspections, reorganizations, writing reports, &c., I have worked sixteen hours to-day; and it is the least in the world singular, that I should be now writing for my own amusement; for any other's, quite absurd! There must be something *dry* about it for recommendation. Oh! expressive and honest Saxon monosyllable! —dry!—thy very sound is pleasing—the idea rapturous! Only think, though it *be* extravagant, at this hour of inevitable repose, of a dry blanket! think too of dry wine!

September 12.—Even until this morning did the cold rainy weather hold out. Now, it is gloriously clear, and the wind settled at the northwest. The Falstaff company have gone, except a platoon I have retained; and after a general forced contribution, one of them lacks a wool jacket.

This is the fifth day that the caravan has been coming forty-three miles, and I know not where they are, but have sent to see.

I set all hands to drilling this morning, and took an invigorating gallop along the bluff tops of the Little Arkansas; beautifully fresh and green looked the groves and trees on its banks. But ah, the killing frost must soon come; and then, where shall we be?

Strange, indeed, that of ten young officers, not one brought a Don Juan into the wilderness. Is it possible that already the torrent of *steam literature* has cast Byron into the drift? How many verses of the sublime, of the beautiful,—of love, of hate, of joy and grief, of pathos and most comic bathos, does that name bring crowding on my memory.

How wonderful is the contrast of true greatness and even sublime genius. Washington stood among mankind as the Apollo among statues. No other man has exhibited his perfect proportion, his sublime symmetry of character, of public and private virtues, of mind, manner, and person. (Too perfect, I imagine, for the sympathy of human love.)

September 14.—Owl Creek. A bright noonday, a fresh breeze rattling among the shining green leaves overhead, belie the ill-omened name.

Having built for them a causeway, the traders have managed to bring up to the Little Arkansas about one-fourth of their wagons: forty-three miles in six days! A wintry prospect.

Friend.—You have neglected me since your *new* friends have come.

"Excuse me; they have helped much; two came at Council Grove, and two more the other day; and men with heads. But, in truth, this inactivity stagnates my faculties; and you forget I have still newspapers to read. I am bringing up, as from daily mails, the daily news of some two weeks, which I had not time to read at the Fort. I have them snug in layers—strata—as to date and character too. What a study—if one stopped to study—a detailed history of the world for a fortnight! One hour I read the National Intelligencer, full of sanguine Whiggery—grave, dignified, with an occasional streak of cream in an ocean of milk and water. In the next, I am attentively perusing the abusive, yet vigorous, the self-important Globe, which has got a way of late of frequently stumbling upon truths. Again, I am absorbed in the able and interesting columns of the New York American; but there is a certain obliquity about the paper I do not like. Sometimes I am amused at the Herald; that strange compound of originality and enterprise, weakness and strength, and egotism so excessive as to reach within one step of the sublime! I read, too, occasionally, a St. Louis Republican, which ranks high from age and commercial support; it resembles the Intelligencer, substituting a little abuse for a little ability. You see, sir, I read both sides and neutrals, and promise to become a knowing politician—*for the Prairie!*"

Friend.—Admirable!—in one quality,—their fondness for the sound of their own voice.

"Frank as a bear hunter! Let us change then the subject."

Friend.—No! I tried to get in a word, some time ago. Do you call severe cavalry exercises twice a day, and an almost daily change of camp, inactivity? a reorganization of your command too! I fear it is slothful inactivity of *mind*, which has made you neglect me in the leisure I admit you have had.

"It may be so; but it is a tempting recreation to recline against the shady side of one's tent, to smoke, and watch the curling cloud ascend with fantastic grace, until lost in the blue ether—to dream dreams too transparent and airy, or too selfish for other's uses."

Friend.—Bah! Better continue your catalogue *raisonnée* of newspapers. What immense sheet is that?

"The Weekly Louisville Journal; an excellent farmer's paper. Prentice has a characteristic quality which now needs a name—better than *repartee writer.* But, heaven and earth! he is the best abuser too of his time—an exotic in a genial soil."

Friend.—I like a man hearty in everything; and he seems a favorite of yours—though hard to please.

"Bad luck to him! I don't know why he should be; he lost for me my last copy of a political pamphlet I wrote when I was a lad."

Friend.—When a lad! What was it?

"Oh, some Utopian scheme for curing the dishonesty

and rancor of national politics; but masses cannot reason, though they may grow corrupt. The idea, I remember, was for each party to elect three: no, it was to elect three persons to draw lots for the Presidency; but the most interesting particulars I now remember are, that it cost me half a month's pay."

Friend.—And not even thanks in return.

"I read the other day in the Journal, a very pretty account of a ramble or voyage to the Falls of St. Anthony. I even remember an idea, or sentence—'a new and virgin moon was just hung out like a coronet of pearl on the brow of evening.'"

Friend.—Beautiful!

"We frequently meet with a gem amid newspaper rubbish. It sends a modest ray to tremble a moment in a troubled atmosphere, and then vanish forever."

Friend.—May not the figure apply also to books? I read one a long time ago called the Vestal, which pleased me very much; but never have I seen it since, or heard it spoken of. An author of renown writes on the same subject—borrows largely, for what the world knows—and produces "The Last Days of Pompeii," which the world is fully prepared to laud in advance!

"Here is another newspaper gem: N. P. W.'s letter about Glenmary."

Friend.—Yes! by-the-by, he has imparted of late a spicy flavor to the National Intelligencer, which must have increased its readers, if not subscribers.

"Willis has an inexhaustible fund of novelty and originality in him; he is a sparkling and polished writer—but sometimes of nonsense."

Friend.—"The Adventures of a Younger Son," by Trelawny, is another instance; a book which I have read twice with delight; but it is out of print; I know no one who has read it.

"Excuse me, but *I* have,—and laughed till my sides ached. What a keen sense of the ridiculous. An original work altogether."

Friend.—And how superior to the sentimental tribe of heroines, is the Arab bride; and Van Scalpvelt is a jewel.

"Yes, the eccentric and inhuman martyr of science; he is food for much laughter."

Friend.—De Witt and the nameless hero, are every inch sailors and soldiers too.

"Do you remember the Malay chief and his red horse?"

Friend.—Remember them! It is a splendid picture of glorious bravery—of heroic action!

"And now, sir, your eloquence must not detain me from 'drill.' There are a half-dozen fine young fellows here who have not had even so good an opportunity as this to put in practice their theoretical knowledge."

September 17.—We have had some luck in incidents on this desert; or, the "trace" is growing a frequented highway. The day before yesterday eight horsemen approached the camp from the west. I thought they were Indians, or possibly, part of a Mexican escort. Before they were recognized, another column of horse, apparently, rapidly approached. I was much urged to prepare. "To horse!" was just breathing into the trumpets, when, catching sight of wagon tops, I prevented the "alarm." They were the spring caravan on their return; and a drove of mules were the column of horse. They bring the first certain news of their having reached Santa Fe in safety. They returned by Bent's Fort, and so can give us little information of the dangerous part of the direct route which the present caravan is to follow. They had unexpected success in disposing of their goods, the Governor of Chihuahua having brought to Santa Fe a thousand troops in consequence of the alarm of the Texans in June. No escort to relieve me had been heard of; and so my going on seems settled. They departed yesterday morning, as I marched hitherward; and one of them will offer five wagons for return freight, which would relieve some of the overladen wagons in the rear.

Soon after leaving Cow Creek we saw buffalo; and on our approach to Walnut Creek—where the camp now is—they were, as usual here, numerous. One was chased and killed by an officer. Very sweet, after a nine hours' ride, was the meat; it is certainly superior to beef.

Last night, for the first time, was warm; and I bathed in the stream, which is four or five feet deep. This morning the wind came rushing down from the north as the sun rose, and instantly it was quite cold.

A careless poor fellow of the guard, just before I marched from Cow Creek, shot himself; his carbine chamber was sprung and thus it was discharged as from a pocket pistol; the ball was deeply buried in the shoulder, and it is feared has injured the joint.

I have been reading an article from the London Literary Gazette, excusing Americans for using the expressions, "a tall time," "a loud smell," as stated by Dickens; it gives instances among the English and French of somewhat similar misuses of words, as a *long* man, for a *tall* man, &c. The English it would seem *cannot understand* us. (Dickens had no disposition to do so, or report us correctly.) It is very probable he heard many such expressions, but he criticises with ill-natured seriousness a mere fanciful exuberance of spirits, or slang affectations intended as small wit to amuse. An Englishman judges the well-fed, careless, jolly, *poor* American by the standard of his overworked "operative," for whom to be alive to small fun of this sort, in sober moments, would be almost a miracle indeed; there is very little joke, I imagine, in his composition.

September 18 (Arkansas River).—*Friend.*—Ah, why so dull? For a good half hour you have sat in your tent under the cotton-wood, with book at your knee and pen at hand, ready to take down in short hand a conversation, yet have not had life enough to bid me welcome.

"True, most welcome friend! true all—I am as dull as the leaden wheels of the motionless caravan. What on earth is there here to excite an emotion, or even a solitary idea? A vast expanse of prairie bottom with clouds of mosquitoes; there is a river close by, but it cannot be seen for tall grass; these half dozen trees would not, to a stranger, mark its vicinity. The day is warm, not a creature, not even a solitary buffalo dots the flat surface of the earth. I waited five days, and in five more, marched but forty-five miles, and still the traders will not come up; the clouds and northeast wind this morning threw me into despair. Another rain, and they peradventure would never cross this soft bottom."

Friend.—Pshaw! Cheer up! You will soon have new scenes; perhaps will be able to give a picture of the much talked of Santa Fe.

"That is the sore point; if I had got my present roving commission in my spring campaign, what a pleasant, easy matter to have gone there and returned; but *now* if I go I shall stay until it sickens us to the heart of its barbarous dearth of all mental and creature comforts;

for five or six months would some of us think of little but home! No! I shall accomplish all the public objects of my mission, and *return* by some hardworked expedient."

Friend.—But still you will see the Rocky Mountains.

"At a respectful distance Pike's Peak perhaps. I had a terrible disappointment yesterday! My daily allowance from the strata of newspapers, turned out I thought a prize, a number of Chuzzlewit; with the accustomed anticipations of pleasure or amusement from his writings, I lay down to read it. Martin had just arrived in New York; never were my feelings so revolutionized; on the dull prairie I could have relished novelty or wit at the expense of my very friends; even moral poison, if it were tart; but, lo! it was dull and disgusting; I could scarce wade through it; as the essay of a nameless author it could never have paid the printing; it has proved the very Muzzlewit to Dickens."

Friend.—Talk of dulness! and you are half asleep, and have just made a pun; which I consider deliberate and malicious dulness.

"You remind me of an excuse once made for shabbiness,—that a patch was premeditated poverty. But I plead guilty; to what can I attribute so *extraordinary* a circumstance? Perhaps, it is extreme fatigue, from an attempt to chew the coating of the hump rib of a late bull; or more likely it results from having read through a Philadelphia weekly.

"Farewell! We shall see the Pawnee Rock to-morrow, and perhaps have a cow chase!"

September 21.—Coon Creek. Phœbus! what a name. There is a tribe of them: long, crooked, shallow beds, with a string of pools in each, and if it be a dry time, they are rendered undrinkable by the buffalo; this is the "same coon" where there was no grass in the summer; but now it is better; it is buffalo grass, and has taken its second growth since the fall of the grain in July, and the late rains.

Friend.—Ah, please describe no more this barren region with a solitary animal and vegetable production —buffalo and buffalo grass.

"Prairie dogs and grasshoppers?"

Friend.—Pray, do not interrupt me. You described it more than sufficiently in your last journal. You dismissed me abruptly three days ago?

"In the accursed camp of swamps; it made us all sick; and next day, in a mile—of the best road we have had—three wagons broke down; singular that? One was repaired and sent home empty; so I had letters to write, yesterday, at the Pawnee Fork."

Friend.—You forget the Pawnee Rock!

"True—it is a natural monument inscribed with the names of all the fools that pass this way."

Friend.—But its name?—

—"Came from a siege there, once upon a time, of a small party of Pawnees by the Camanche hordes; the rocky mound was impregnable; but alas for valor! they were parched with thirst, and the shining river glided in their sight through green meadows! They drank their horses' blood, and vowed to the Wah-condah that their fates should be one. Death before slavery! Finally, in a desperate effort to cut their way to liberty, they all met heroic death; ushering their spirits with defiant shouts to the very threshold of the happy hunting grounds! The Camanches, after their melancholy success, were full of admiration, and erected on the summit a small pyramid which we see to this day."

Friend.—Pure fiction!

"Inspired by a supper of two pounds of the fattest cow that ever—"

Friend.—And worthy of its source.

Do you really think this meat better than fat beef?

"As superior as a young grouse to a long-legged chicken; and I might as well say infinitely at once."

Friend.—What is that! it seems an echo to your Elysian shouts.

"Ha! another; something is wrong out there! By heaven, those buffalo will be on us! and the squadrons are just unsaddled:—here they come! shout! fire your guns or our horses are gone! They stop on that swell—they turn to the right. Here they *come* right on! A general shout and discharge of some arms—again they pause. One shake now from that veteran's shaggy front and they will dash over us:—a new movement, see! to the right and left; that bull has lost the lead;—how they roll at us their fierce eyeballs as they pass—the very earth trembles. The horses are frantic—the men can scarcely hold them! But we have escaped!"

Friend.—That's right! pepper them well; a lucky shot! that fellow will pay us for our fright. I assure you I did not breathe!

"They caught us at the weakest moment; though the videttes should have been out. What a tremendous momentum! We are fortunate. I have repeatedly seen a single bull charge through men, horses, and wagons."

Friend.—Is not this near the scene of your wonderful bullfight in June?

"Yes; a few miles back; wonderful it was to think that a bull, after being wounded and stunned by a twelve-pound shell, should rush upon a great column of horse, and heedless of a hundred shots and twenty wounds, with a bull-dog to his lip, should toss a horse and rider like a feather! They all fell of a heap! Before the dust cleared up the man, who had hung a moment to a horn by his waistband, crawled out safe—the horse got a ball through his neck while in the air, and two great rents in his flank."

Friend.—And *then* ran off! It was time! But you have told me this before.

"Well, good night!"

CHAPTER IV.

SEPTEMBER 22.—Delightful, truly, to escort two hundred wagons with twelve owners, independently disposed, and sharply interested in carrying out different views of emergencies; the failure of water, grass, or fuel.

Want of water pushed us yesterday far ahead of them; want of grass set us in motion this morning. We had not made much headway,—against a beating wind,—when it was made known that Indian dogs had been in camp, and a rather doubtful horseman seen. Fifty sabres and a howitzer were immediately sent back with a roving commission, as whippers-in of these tardy merchant-*men*.

We were then on a very brown and very smooth desert; a table land with just enough of the hill about it—insensibly curving out of sight, with nothing below the sky to relieve or correct the eye by comparison—to create the sensation of immensity, and of vast height, as well; it is a very rare conformation, and the effect difficult to describe; the beholder suspects an illusion, but he is doubtful whether optical or imaginary. We were passing for ten miles, apparently over this hill-top, before a shallow pool, which we might dispute with the buffalo, enabled us to encamp.

Alas for hungry humanity! Alas! that the blood of six fat bulls cries in vain from the prairie against stomachs without consciences. So it is—the Saxon soldier goes that "entire animal," and still craves a piece of the *hog*.

Sept. 23.—Here we are opposite Jackson Grove; a point near unsurveyed and unmarked national boundaries:—it was named by an officer who was called upon very suddenly to decide to which of three nations it belonged; there depended much individual, if not national interest:—some half a million of property and the amount of blood that might be risked for the capture or retention of so much. The *decision* was right (by some four seconds of longitude, as it has proved in 1844): the *act* was to dash across the wide river, swimming in places, and with quicksands nearly everywhere, in the face of one or two hundred Anglo-Saxon prairie rovers (to soften two consonants into one) armed to the teeth.

Oh, Mark Tapley! thou strange brain-conception. To-day wouldst thou have been content, and have taken credit for cheerfulness. Caught twenty-five miles from fuel in a thirteen hours rain—"such rain as *is* rain,"—for fifteen miles we soaked, and mayhap sulked; in vain was excitement offered in the shape of the most convenient herds of buffalo; cows, calves, in fat family groups, kicking up the mud as they ran past almost into our faces:—a cape saturated to board-like stiffness, thrown back—a sodden holster-cover half raised—a horse urged to a deeper splash or two—and then, reaction brought us to the cold stage again!

Fifteen miles!—and flesh and blood—mule flesh—could stand no more; the column's head, followed by all its drill-cemented joints, was turned to a quarter where a "woodman's" faith in the "mariner's" compass was confirmed by the greater convexity of the treeless plain, that it would more suddenly dip to the hospitable meadows of the Arkansas; I knew, too, the hydraulic paradox, that in the low, flat bottom we should find dry ground; for it is composed of sand; but for fuel, the poor fellows, after their wet, cold ride, had to wade waist-deep, and over tedious quicksands, a quarter of a mile through the river to the grove, and return with the soaked sticks upon their shoulders; and the weather has turned cold. Pleasant passage, that, of military life!

Sept. 26.—*Friend.*—You neglect me! and for several days past you have had little to do.

"True; but how depressing the circumstances!—rain and frost, in a desert without fuel;—forage fast going the way of all *grass;* and no power to recede or advance, for the caravan is again stuck in the mud."

Friend.—I have heard of winter marches, but always, I believe, when the poor soldier with his single blanket, could have a good fire. Was there really a frost?

"Last night there was a severe frost, and the winds are very high, and low enough, as you see, to flare the candle under the tent, and cover me with dust; but let us change the disagreeable subject. You should have seen our buffalo-hunt yesterday as we marched up the river-bottom; or rather bull-baiting; an officer chased him toward the road, and gave him with his pistol a fatal wound; the column halted, and eleven officers approached and commenced firing, and two had carbines; the animal was at bay, and would dash at any one who came within fifteen or twenty paces; the fire was kept up for near a quarter of an hour; I was practising my new horse, but took deliberate aims; the furious beast must have weighed as he stood two thousand pounds. He had many wounds through the lights; one ball struck his spine or paralysed it, and he trotted dragging his hinder parts! but he recovered from that. Never did I see such a picture; his eyes glared terribly, his compressed breathings were snorts of excessive rage; every muscle of his body was rigid, or working with effort to vent his anger; his tufted tail stood like an iron rod; the blood from lung-wounds spirted from his sides at every breath—at least fifty balls had struck him,—he never flinched! deliberate shots were fired at his eyes, he seemed not to feel them; at last he sank upon his knees, and after many unavailing efforts to rise, as an experiment, I shook a great-coat over him; his rage then inspired him with strength, he rose and dashed after me! Several more wounds were inflicted before the poor brave beast fell and expired. How strange! I have not exaggerated. Usually on receiving a single wound, such as first given in this case, if undisturbed, they will lie down and soon die; whilst now and then such an animal as this is encountered, that seems deathless; of course the excitement must give strength and keep them alive."

Friend.—The excitement and motion prevent a fatal coagulation; are not the cows the best game now?

"Yes, but we seldom get them, they herd separately; the men are on half allowance of flour and bull meat; the bulls are now most dangerous; by-the-by, one of the young officers fell and dislocated his shoulder the other day; his horse, at speed, trod in a dog hole—that spoils his sport for the season."

Friend.—Are there no signs of your old friends, the Camanches?

"The animal itself; a vidette on the little hill behind the camp, saw this afternoon a horseman in the sand hills over the river—seeing is believing, but few will believe he saw him."

Friend.—Unwilling men—for it gives them trouble and labor—will only believe what they see, and while they see it; such have constantly to be taken care of.

"And grumble at the care."

Friend.—To be constantly on the defensive, and the strongest, is not the best school for strategy or military caution.

"True enough, though cavalry is always weak on the defensive, and peculiarly so without grain; on the offensive also, our town-bred soldiers can only be efficient on the prairie through speed, bottom, and superior strength or audacity. A surprise or concealed manœuvre, would scarcely be a practical method; a forced night-march would be their nearest approach to it."

Friend.—What then becomes of the common idea that a level plain is the ground for cavalry?

"It is mere ignorance; of practicable ground, a flat plain is perhaps the worst for an attack by cavalry; and it is an arm that always strikes—even when it shields a retreating army. I would choose hilly or rolling ground on which to attack infantry; but especially if I was unsupported by artillery:—and this ground serves for shelter from the enemy's artillery; and cavalry cannot *rest* under its fire."

Friend.—The Indians then have advantages in attacking?

"Decidedly, in their usual method by surprise; their

perfect knowledge of the ground enables them to use the concealment of long swells which we would scarcely perceive; they have no roads, and are never in danger of wandering from their object; their knowledge too, enables them to form ambushes, a favorite resort of partisan cavalry; they have no jingling arms, their horses are better trained, and will endure much more; and they lead them without tiring when concealment is necessary."

Friend.—And they can operate better in the night!

"They could—but the prairie Indians never do attack in the night; and foolishly enough, very rarely, if ever, attempt to drive off our horses, or even merchant teams."

Friend.—Nay! to the D—l his due; that is chivalry!

September 28.—"The 'Caches.'"

Yesterday we marched here for fresh grass. I expected a part at least of the caravan; but lo; this morning an express to Taos for mules! It reports the whole caravan still water-bound at Cow Creek.

Friend.—And I think *you* are getting into deep water, as Oily Gammon says.

"A sea of troubles at least. What is to be done with Uncle Sam's cavalry? the elite of six companies of her sole regiment of mounted dragoons. I was ordered since I marched, to go on to Santa Fe, then leave New Mexico and winter somewhere about the head of the Arkansas. I replied, you know, that I would either winter in New Mexico or return to Fort L."

Friend.—With an eye to the Senoritas!

"To save expense; I calculated on an average season!"

Friend.—And it is an extraordinary one. So much for penny-wise notions. Capitalists great enough to be self-insured, must be "pound foolish," *in appearance* to you small-fry operators.

"Who could possibly have foreseen when I last wrote, that in seventeen days we should progress but ninety miles! Now will the rations come?"

Friend.—You have made it a question, and you *must* answer! You may starve man as well as horse, or be crippled in your power to act, in circumstances as changeable as the weather in this desert, where the fickle winds have never a bush to stay their fury!

"When one, after close calculation, has announced an undertaking which wiseacres pronounce impossible; then to find the scroll of fate unrolling obstacles which experience could not anticipate, is a severe trial; and almost with anguish we anticipate the triumph of folly!"

Friend.—And the eternal, "I told you so, uttered by friends, those prophets of the past."*

"I have sent an express back to the officer in command of the company with the caravan, to learn if they will demand escort beyond the boundary; and how far?"

Friend.—Well, keep cool.

"A cool mind in a wet body! only a free translation."

October 1.—The night before last was, to the human body, almost freezing cold; there was a storm of raw, searching wind, from which blankets seemed no protection; the fires were all *blown out*—off—extinguished! Bent has come and has ten loads of rations behind, but anxiously awaits my decision, whether I shall give him the required notice to reduce his contract in a great portion of flour and beef, not yet purchased. Yesterday afternoon the express returned with a letter from the traders, answering me, that they require my escort to "Red River"—nearly to Santa Fe. Immediately after came their interpreter, with a confidential message that

* See quotation, Don Juan, canto xiv, stanza l.

they could dispense with it *much* nearer, *provided* Bent and his people could be kept in complete ignorance of any intention of returning; fearing it would be communicated to enemies; nests, they say, of semi-trappers and semi-brigands, who harbor not very far from B.'s establishment, and not far from a point of their route. Now, during this conversation, Mr. B. (and suite) walk up impatient for my final answer, for which he had very inconveniently waited a day, involving more or less this very point! A writer of scenic representation of the burlesque, could hardly contrive a prettier comic climax, than this pinnacle of the difficult!

My detachment has rejoined; Bent has gone. Some of the caravan are in advance of others,—none can say when they will come. And now shall I despatch an express to Fort L. for a light load of medicines and other necessaries for eight months in the wilderness,—time being precious,—or shall I wait for the small chance of the Mexicans dispensing with the escort at the Lower Semaron Spring, sixty miles in their country, in which event the command should certainly return?

Fair and bright dawned the first of October! The fierce chilling blast has sung a fit requiem to the infernal September; with its cloudy wings it has taken its eternal flight—may *such* another never revisit poor people so helplessly exposed to its dreary influences! Seven of the Mexicans have died under its inflictions, and twenty more of the comfortless wretches are prostrated with disease.

October 5th, 9 o'clock, P.M.—There has just gone forth from the hilltops, on the wailing north wind, the wildest chorus that I ever heard; a swelling unison of many tones and a dying cadence! It is music—natural concert music—performed by brutes under the influence of this dark hour, which heralds the dread footsteps of winter. And did you not know that wolves howl in concert? Did you never see them under the pale moon sit in circle watching their leader as bipeds do?

All nature is musical; the birds hail the dawn, and when the god of day touches with his pencil of light the lovely landscape picture, their glad voices swell to harmonious glees of praise. In evening twilight, or when the silvery moon (like Memory) casts the homely in shadow and brightens every point of beauty, that Beauty finds a voice! Like a sigh of happiness, Zephyr swells, and falls, and rises again, till the answering foliage rustles with music; the myriad insects—whose life is a song—led by sweet katydid, hum a mellow and soothing concord. Now and then this monotone is relieved by the dream-notes of some happy bird, or solo of whip-poor-will, whose song expresses the very Poetry of Night. Ah! *then*, how happy those who hear that music of all,—the *voice* of love!

Nature is full of music, and for every ear that harmonizes with all smiles and tears:—the sounds attuned by man can only accord with the transient mood; he can thrill the victor with the brazen-mouthed voice of triumph, or echo with plaintive flute the lover's sigh.

The wolves then harmoniously howl their plaints to Nature, and soothe their pains with music; it is the natural expression of the hour and its influences, and it strikes in the human breast the chord which they have strung.

It may be singular—I can scarce account to myself—but I *never* heard without pleasure this voice of the Night—the more if it be stormy and threatening—whether in the "witching" midnight hour, or in the lonely morning watch by the feeble guard-fire,—their wild and mournful howling has been *ever* welcome. This instant! listen! It comes to my soul far more intelligible music than those extravaganzas of sound triumphantly "executed" by men and maidens.

* * Blessed IDEAL! rosy realm! Welcome resort of sad and weary souls! *welcome*, as to the fainting, lost wayfarer, struggling in darkness, the rising sun.

Dear friend!—spirit oft invoked!—Sweet Inspiration! that leadest me ever with winged joy from the dreary present to the fountains and groves of Memory—Beautiful Presence!

A voice.—Dreamer, awake!

"Scoffer! Who art thou, so near?"

Friend (*entering the tent*).—Thy monologue I endured, whilst it touched of earth; but when self-forgetting, thou transformedst thy true friend to a spirit minister of hardly dubious sex,—who methinks, would wander *here*, from no comfortable abode of earth or sky—

"Enough! And may not the actor be dreamer too? Ah! dreams, dreams! And why not thus live o'er the few rosy hours?—taste again, if may be, the one sparkling drop of 'misery's cup?' "

Friend.—Pshaw! *That* cup, if you please, at your elbow, and let's have a drop of *creature* comfort. Things are changed?

"Yes; destiny has now shuffled the cards of our small fates; they had been stocked by some attendant imp, who was leading us (and tickling us the while, with exciting chimeras), to the d—l."

Friend.—Nay, stick to the *surface* now; only "to the d—l" with your double-refined poetry and romance.

"Well, I must submit, to please you, and attempt a lower level."

Friend.—Where I fear you will scarce be at home to-night. But do give me the news?

"Two nights ago, I at last got together the caravan merchants; they insisted upon my going *on*—so I marched fifteen miles next day; and as I approached a camp ground on the river bank, a man ran out and told me that there was a Mexican escort, waiting a few miles above, at the crossing! This sudden and—of late—wholly unthought of news nearly took my breath. Joy, and disappointment—of wild and dreamy adventures—had an agitating struggle in my breast; but home-feelings soon reconciled me to Destiny; the brain—"

Friend.—Can master every passion?

"Cool and philosophical as a woman (of *whom* it may be true); but the passions not only increase in force with the power of the brain, but in a higher ratio."

Friend.—No mathematics either, if you please, they are *infernal.*

"I assure you (it is a secret of mine) that nothing else known among *men* can cope with feminine logic; but *that* is magical; the d—l can as well resist holy water. Well, at this news, it was remarkable and quite a study—speaking of ratios—that the faces of the married men were lengthened in proportion to the length of their married life."

Friend.—Scoffer!

"Fairly hit! Return we then to our sheep,—I should say our Mexican escort. They were 50 lancers—an advance party, a 'forlorn hope' of 150 more, who would not trust their carcasses on this disputed ground further than the Cimerone. They all left Santa Fe a few hours after the arrival of a courier from the City of Mexico.

Next morning, leaving the baggage, I marched to the

crossing in my best style; on our approach we saw the Mexicans beyond the river saddle and mount; but on our dismounting they were dismissed. The adjutant rode over to make inquiries and invite them to cross and spend the day with us. Their commander declined, with the pointed excuse that he was ordered on no account to cross 'the boundary.' There can be no doubt that the Mexican minister, seeing General G.'s published letter, announcing our return and intention, for 'free trade' sake, to visit Santa Fe, hastened to inform his government; and that President Santa Anna sent the express with orders to despatch an escort 'within an hour' after its arrival in Santa Fe. They were just in time!

"Receiving their hint with a good grace, as soon as the caravan was over, we mounted in order of battle, and as a significant salute, fired a round from the howitzer battery; the shells were directed in ricochet down a fine reach of the river between us, and after a dozen of beautiful rebounds, exploded under water—to the manifest astonishment of some of the aborigines amongst our suspicious allies. Then, turning our faces homeward, we filed off,—returned and slept in the camp where we had left our baggage."

Friend.—Which to-night is twenty-five miles behind you; it is a subject for gratulation, *for you will accomplish your undertaking!* I leave you to your slumbers, and—your wolves.

CHAPTER V.

October 7.—If I can write with gloves, here goes! for the sun has risen only high enough to illume the crystals of frost with which the grass is studded—and here and there a glassy pool.

Yesterday I left the road—which we will not strike for several days—to follow more closely the bend of the river: I had to leave the "bottom" but once; when, with a direct course of several miles over the hills, I struck it again at the extremity of a beautiful, level, and smooth savanna three miles by two in extent; the hills forming the chord of a graceful sweep of the river,—its whole course marked by its sky-reflecting waters, or an irregular fringe of cotton-woods; what a glorious spot, we exclaimed, for a chase! And we had one, worthy of the scene.

Far in the bend of the river, we soon saw a large herd of elks. Several officers made a wide detour to get between them and the water: I had just run my horse over broken ground in the hills after four does, which seemed to glide away from me like spectres, encumbered as I was with great-coat and sabre; but the previous night—singularly enough—I had read in the Spirit of the Times an account of the habits and peculiarities, and best manner of chasing the immense herds of these animals, found far to the north;—so, I saved my horse, edging down quietly, expecting a part of them at least, in their confusion, to run toward me.

The noble creatures, with a whole forest of antlers, taking the alarm, first began to trot round loftily, with heads tossed high in air—the men swore they were wild horses; now we see the officers, putting spurs, suddenly dash among them; we see two, three, four little blue puffs of smoke, and hear the explosions; but no elk falls! Now there is a rush for the river,—they have turned again!—some are in the water;—see! a hunter is following there that immense buck, the patriarch of the herd!

Bravo! I was not deceived; the herd has dispersed in confusion;—one gang has taken the wind, and quarters on our coast;—one hunter follows at a goodly distance! —he is firing into their rear, but does not appear to gain on them; these elks, without much show of motion, scud along at a telling rate, and keep a long while at it. Now, I tighten my belt, and lightly costumed, brace myself in high excitement; yet cool enough still to manœuvre on their flank at a sweeping trot:—Now, to work!—And somewhat late, for I soon find myself in their rear. Exquisite the excitement of race-horse speed, and the near approach to these grand animals, straining every muscle, in *powerful* motion, their cloven hoofs sharply rattling! —and for the first time! What novelty of sensation!—what astonished curiosity!—my horse snorts, and shares my joy! Thunder we on! Now, my noble Brown, take the spur. Wildly excited he dashes into the herd, and I am rushing in ecstasy in their very midst, their large eyes flashing fire, their antlers sweeping the air above my head. But Brown reminds me he brought me not there for fun alone; and so I fire my pistol into the nearest buck, and take a pull on the willing horse. My elk—poor fellow—seconds my intent, and soon we are motionless on a profoundly silent plain.

Now, my fierce excitement subsides. I observe curiously—almost timidly—a magnificent animal, large as my horse, but of a loftier crest. Ah! what beauty and what suffering! With majesty in all his bearing, he violently grits his teeth in pain or defiance; but in his beautiful eyes I imagine that rage is yielding to a mournful reproach.

And now I suffer a reaction. We are alone with Death, which my hand has summoned to this peaceful solitude.

The still erect but dying animal faces me at six feet, and painfully heaves. I stare dreamily into those fascinating eyes: his dignity of suffering seems to demand of me an explanation, or, a conclusion to the fatal scene.

At length, with a sigh, I finish my work; and with another ball end his pains forever!

After supper.—The hunter in the mouth of his tent reclines, with a pipe, upon a glossy bearskin;—before him, a desert expanse of grass and river;—his attention is apparently divided between the moon, suspended over the western hills;—the flickering blaze of a small fire, and the curling smoke which he deliberately exhales. His friend stirs a toddy, reading with difficulty a crabbed manuscript. *Loquitur.* "When I saw you yesterday, beside your usual duties, acting as guide, surgeon—(for you have effectually cured the snake-bitten horse)—as hunter, or butcher"—

"Say commissary!"—

"I conceived hopes of you,—that the poetic spirit was *laid;* and when at supper to-night you ate so heartily of the elk-steak, I little thought you had been indulging again in such pathetic"—

"Pshaw! it serves for a gilding to life's bitter pill! The delicious supper should have mended your humor: for I stake my reputation on it—as 'guide, surgeon, and hunter' "—

Friend.—And butcher—

—"That the flesh, cooked as it was with a little pork, cannot be distinguished from that of the fattest buffalo cow that ever surrendered tongue and marrow-bones to hungry hunter."

Friend.—Bravo! I *have* hopes of you! Kill your meat with a good conscience, and, daily labor and excitement over, solid indeed is the hunter's comfort! With grass and bearskin bed, his toddy, and his soothing pipe —the musical ripple of the river sparkling in the moonbeams—I mean—

"Fairly caught! I little thought when I heard you abuse my pathos over the noble beast that had yielded his life to my sport, that mere creature comforts would thus inspire you! Dear critic, and lover of *bathos!* hast thou found poetry in a full stomach?"

Friend.—The devil's in the moon. And there goes another wolf "concert"—

"With the thorough bass of a thousand bulls."

Friend.—All as thoroughly musical as the donkey braying in the caravan camps. I wish you a very good evening, 'and a little better taste.'

The hunter, gazing apparently upon his ascending smoke—as if of incense—indulges in soliloquy.

"My Friend leaves me to the silent Night—and solitude as profound as when 'the Spirit of God moved upon the face of the waters.'

"Incomprehensible scheme! Oh! thou beautiful and wonderful Nature!—mother and moulder of the forms, and minds as well, of our wayward race. Now, she smiles in brilliant moonbeams on the grassy meadows, which wave with answering gladness to the whispering air. And the strong river flows as gently as an infant playing on the young mother's breast;—its murmurs as softly musical as that infant's voice! The air, methinks, is fanned by seraphic spirits on their winged errands of Peace! My heart swells in adoration and beats in harmony with the holy eloquence of the hour.

"But strike another chord.

"Lo! floods burst their bounds with cruel wreck.

Darkness appals, and Storm howls o'er its victims! Passion, Vengeance, and black Crime rear their crests—Dismay and Chaos rule the hour."

Oct. 7.—Mark this day with a white stone! After travelling sixty or seventy miles off the road—encamping each night on the river in comparatively good grass, and with driftwood fuel too, I this morning, as guide, took a course for the crossing of the Pawnee Fork, and struck it to a degree! Then, in the beaten dry road, the mules were much relieved. As we passed over the hills we saw to our left countless buffalo:—last night we heard them crossing the river incessantly, in single file—which indicates their migration; with a constant utterance of their very peculiar sounds, which may not be better described, than as something between the grunt of a great hog and the low bellowing of a bull. This afternoon, as we approached a beautiful camp-ground, on Ash Creek, a large herd came rushing by our front. Five of us dashed after, and each killed a cow, or young bull; and all within a mile, and as near to our camp ground! Mine I shot with a pistol at six paces, at full speed:—it fell as if struck by lightning, and never moved. Very rarely does that happen! Glorious sport it is! To rush along in the very midst of herds that blacken the earth with numbers, and shake it with momentum; and richly, too, it rewards the skilful hunter's hungry toil!

This has been a true October day—delightful and magnificent October!—and with but little of the high wind, which here so generally prevails. But this was all too sweet, and must have its bitter. A luckless wretch of the guard allowed his horse to escape—"all accoutred as *he* was," and he has not been recovered, or traced.

Diamond Spring, Oct. 17th, '43.

Ours is a true retreat!—a retreat from frost and starvation,—the starvation of horses and mules. Water has frozen a half-inch thick almost every night; and sometimes there was no fuel:—horses have begun to drop by the roadside.

At Cow Creek I made my last buffalo chase, which had a singular incident. Just as I was *closing* on eight large bulls, on the level bottom, they utterly disappeared, without my seeing or conceiving whither! Nothing could equal my astonishment whilst I ran twenty yards;—then my horse, by a powerful effort, which very nearly precipitated me over his head, stopped on the square brink of a deep slough, where my phantoms reappeared,—and in great bodily power, were making desperate struggles to clear the mire, and the opposite bank, equally vertical, and set to the edge with tall grass. This narrow chasm could not be seen till right over it; and the bulls had pitched in, whilst—I suppose, without knowing it—my eyes were for an instant averted.

We encamped on the Little Arkansas, in a high wind: the grass was tall; and I gave a very special warning to all to beware of fire. Nevertheless, about the time we were fairly settled, I heard a sharp alarm! All rushed to the spot with blankets and whatever they could lay hands upon; a hundred men fought it desperately—exposing themselves without stint—for provisions, baggage, everything, depended on success; but it was a doubtful struggle, until happily, a barrel was found, to roll over it. And this fire had not spread thirty yards! Such is our sole forage.

Friend.—Very interesting, this dry grass and frost! Has the idea of home banished me from your thoughts?

"Ah, no! I am a bit of a philosopher; and take this October marching very kindly—particularly, after thawing of a morning; and riding ahead, I kill a grouse occasionally with my pistol."

Friend.—What would you give to see a late paper?

"You have me there! I have a weakness for a damp newspaper;—let me see—it is now eight weeks since we have had news. But I discovered a copy of James's False Heir with my baggage; that, in my mental famine, has been quite a feast."

Friend.—Do you like it?

"I think he has exhausted his best powers: the plot turns solely on a worn-out incident; the real or pretended substitution of infants. James has at last committed the folly, which, first or last, all the British authors seem to fall into—I mean a sneer, or slander, on us Americans. Strange, indeed, that a writer who has made friends of the readers of a great nation, should without any good object turn their finer feelings into contempt or anger, by a few motions of his pen. Ah! deliver us from the temptation of a sneer! But *this* is coolly and deliberately done."

Friend.—And what is it?

"I say Americanism advisedly; for republicanism is a very different thing, and does not imply a rejection of refinement in the higher classes of society."

Friend.—He pins his faith then upon the mercenary class of tourists; for he has never visited us. Did you ever remark that his valets are often the most intelligent and quickwitted of his characters?

"It is the case in this very work. The hero is a lad

of seventeen; old enough to fall in love, and but little else. St. Medard is a mere abstraction, De Langy a cipher, Artonne a riddle, Monsieur L. a man in a mask who puts himself in the way sufficiently to give some interesting trouble and help out the plot. In the most commonplace manner, he has thrown the hero and favorite characters into difficulties for the transparent object of a final triumph; he disinherits the hero, shipwrecks his best friend, St. Medard; confines Artonne in prison for murder, and last, not least, sends his best-drawn character, Marois, to the galleys!"

Friend.—James has an extraordinary habit of making his spokesmen repeat the first sentence of their speeches, thus—"I don't know, sir; I don't know, sir,"—"That's a pity—that's a pity!" Since I have noticed it, it always makes me nervous!

"One of the last announcements I read before I left home, was, that he had engaged to write a 'serial' for the Dublin University Magazine; sorry I am, but such is the accustomed drivel of exhausted minds."

Friend.—After all, James has been a most effective moralist; and we owe him much.

"It is excessively cold! And if I sleep to-night, I shall say, blessed be the man that invented—wool!"

"110 Mile Creek."—Welcome as palm groves to the desert traveller,—as the bearer of glad tidings to the anxious soul,—welcome as home to the troubled and weary spirit,—so welcome thy forests, thy waters and grassy glades, oh, "Hundred-and-ten!"

Thus far safely, over the desolate and bleak prairies; but with what pains! How pleasant to regain, one by one, the summer camps, homeward bound! But how mournful the blackened plains, and the freezing winds to which the solitary trees bend with shrill complaint.

I have risen after midnight where there were none—and with a few fragments of barrel staves, kindled a little fire in a hole, where some one had managed to heat a coffee-pot; and with a blanket over *all*, sought a renewal of vital heat!

With what extreme care have we nursed our horses and mules! sharing our blankets with them, and giving them flour mixed with the dead grass chopped with our knives. At the hospitable shelter of Council Grove, a few of the most broken down horses and teams were left to rest, and await the succor I had long written for; the first of which—a wagon-load of corn—we have met here—forty-five miles on.

Leaving the Grove, as we passed over the lofty prairie hills, all the world seemed afire! The unresisted winds seemed to riot with fire, which they drove to madness! Black clouds and columns of smoke were wildly tossed in the tempestuous air; whilst the flames now darted with lightning speed and glare,—now flickered with baleful illumination and stifling effect over our hurried path. Thus desperately I pushed on for two days—regarding nothing—with a will fixed upon this haven of shelter and relief.

And now, our horses browse at will throughout the forest; our log-fires crackle under the noble arches of boughs and foliage; we read our letters and news; our repose is home-like; and as we gaze at our forest-roofs so cheerfully illumined, we indulge in extravagant anticipations of winter enjoyment at Fort L.

Fort L.—Two nights and a day were thus spent; and when, almost unwillingly, we ventured forth again from the pleasant forest, the scene and the actors were changed!

Autumn—so long our tyrant—pursuing us with frosty breath on wings of flame,—in the last act had met a master; and shrieking over the desert had fled—like a blusterer—to the south. Stern Winter had come with his pure winding-sheet of snow, to cover the blackened scars of the conquered and dead year.

In three days we reached our homes, and our air-castles have sobered down to highly-appreciated comforts.

But dear "Hundred-and-ten!" we shall never forget thy hospitable oasis;—there was little more poetry in it, than in thy singular name (and thus both were highly satisfactory to my matter-of-fact Friend, with whom I there parted, with hopes of a future meeting). But, with charred deserts behind—and forgotten; and snow-storms before, but unforeseen,—we embalm in memory thy friendly shelter, and the calm repose of thy homely forest!

CHAPTER VI.

1845. A RIGHT pleasant company we are! Duty has borrowed the attractions of novelty and adventure. All are bent joyously upon scaling the crest of the broad continent; leading and protecting those pioneers and missionaries of civilization, the Oregon emigrants; the rude founders of a State. Self-exiled and led by a human instinct—inspired, and superior to reason; neither pilgrims nor of broken fortunes, but unconscious workers of National *Human* Destiny, they *seek* the perfect independence of savage life, aided by some invented powers of civilized art.

They scorn all royal paper claims to this virgin world

of ours! The best diplomatists of us all, they would conquer the land as easily as,—Adam lost Paradise.

Such military expeditions as ours will sufficiently protect this migration of families; intermediate posts could be maintained only at an immensely disproportioned expenditure: for nature has furnished no facilities for transportation through this wilderness.

On a bright May morning, turning our backs upon lovely Fort Leavenworth, we set forth to march twenty-four hundred miles before we shall return. We followed for two days the trails of previous marches, guiding us through the intricate and broken, but picturesque grounds which border the Missouri. Right beautiful scenery it is; with its winding green vales, its irregular but grassy hills, all dotted and relieved by dark oaks and cedars; in the distance, some bold blue highland of the great river, —or, itself revealed in far off silvery sheen. The third day we struck out boldly into the almost untrodden prairies, bearing quite to the west. The sixth day—having marched about ninety miles—we turned toward the south, crossing a vast elevated and nearly level plain, extending between two branches of the Blue River: thus, without an obstacle for fifteen miles, we reached and encamped upon its bank. We had the company of an afternoon rain, which lasted the night. Thus to sleep *wet* is "perchance to dream," for young campaigners. In the morning something was heard of the joke of "seeing the elephant;" but an amateur, whose horse had disappeared in the night, was understood to have expressed the opinion that it was a poor one.

We had fortunately struck the Blue where it was fordable; and the pioneers soon prepared a way for the wagons. This is a serious undertaking, to lead three hundred heavily armed men beyond communications, for three or four months. It is not thus the European marches, or goes to war. Foresight and experience is necessary; and we are encumbered with seventeen wagons, although the rations are shortened, cattle driven, and some dependence put upon buffalo.

The seventh day, leaving the Blue, and turning to the northwest, between two tributaries from that direction, we soon espied on a distant ridge, the wagon-tops of the emigrants—dim, white spots, like sails at sea. Gradually converging, in a few hours we met.

Here was a great thoroughfare—broad and well-worn—the longest and best natural road perhaps in the world. Endless seemed the procession of wagons; mostly very light, and laden only with children and provisions, and the most necessary articles for families; and drawn generally by two yokes of oxen; some three hundred wagons or families, they said, were in advance. Here was some cause to tremble for our sole resource for forage: for the grass is backward and scanty, and these foster children of the Missouri *bear*, as we know, like all partially civilized nomades, are accompanied by herds of cattle; and we cannot, like Abraham and Lot, take different courses.

Having marched about twenty miles, we turned off for water and a camp, to a small branch of the Blue, where we found our friends ahead had made their mark. There we had a frost.

That little stream had made a section of about twenty feet through a bed of yellow adhesive clay; at the base was found a mammoth tooth: there can be little doubt of the skeleton being near; of the grinder being—to borrow a mineralogical expression—nearly *in situ*.

On the 26th we were off betimes, highly desirous to

"head" the very leading "captain" of this vast migration, for we found that, worse than the myriads of locusts we saw east of the Blue, they would make a clean sweep of the grass near all the spots where it is necessary to encamp for water. After a very long march a camp-ground was sought at a small branch—fringed as usual by a few trees, which seldom indeed deceive the water-seeker upon prairies. But the grass was consumed, and we were forced to retrace our steps for a half mile. Then had the soldiers, weary with the long, slow march, in addition to the usual toils of tending horses, unloading wagons, pitching tents, cooking, &c., &c. (making their extemporaneous settlement in the wilderness), to go afoot this long half mile and return burdened with wood and water. Such is a peace campaign; but cheerfulness makes all light. We had halted at noon at one of those crystal streamlets, which in meandering, protect and foster little green islands in prairie seas; sweet groves, where every shrub, and vine, and flower seem to seek refuge, and joyously to flourish, in defiance of the flame-storms which subdue all around:—like fairy bowers they are in summer season; their cool recesses are vocal with happy birds; they refresh and charm every sense, which fatigue and privation make keenly alive to enjoyment. An hour—almost of happiness—passes, and we take up our burdens and part forever! Our camp mayhap will be an inhospitable waste,—and such is the type of a soldier's life. Indeed, it gives it all its zest: the excitements of change and uncertainties; the unlooked-for pleasure, and the difficulty overcome.

Friend.—Never was there such an escape! In fact, you did not quite escape, and nearly spoiled your honest but faint description of natural beauties by a lamer flight.

Your "almost happiness!"—and "burden," of *life* did you mean? for I never saw one lighter mounted on a finer horse! But I really congratulate you on arriving so safely in a sober "camp" in the midst of this very flat earth.

"Amigo mio! Didn't you desert me on the eve of a snow-storm, like many another friend of so honest mouthing! And is a touch of poetry a bad companion in difficulty and trial? Never a bit; it was the boon of a God —*Wisdom* was ever feminine."

Friend.—Phew! The fit is on! Sorry I said a word! I supposed frost and starved horses,—the sight of poor women to-day trudging the weary road,—the driving poor beef instead of the spirit-striving chase, would have tempered you to the philosophy of a very materialist (male or female).

"Poor women, indeed! Three weeks ago they parted from every comfort—severed ties of kindred, even of country, and their journey is scarce begun—a short 150 miles with 1800 more before them! What privations are here; what exposure to bad weather, cooking unsheltered; they must unsex themselves and struggle with all the sterner toils which civilization happily casts upon the harder and rougher male."

Friend.—Is it possible that many of them *willingly* follow thus their life's partners for *all* the "worse?"

"Heaven knows! we passed an old lady of sixty whom I have often seen kindly dispensing a comfortable hospitality, and I *cannot* believe that she is content to give up the repose which her years, her virtues, and her sex entitle her to; but strange! she wore a cheerful smile, and said her health improved."

Friend.—And that child—that poor little boy, who

barefooted limped along, holding to the wagon, how pitiable he seemed.

"Ah! but he may be one day the 'gentleman from Oregon,' who arrived in last night's cars, and to-day takes his seat in his arm chair in the Capitol."

Friend.—Did you hear of the wedding last night?

"Between three days' acquaintances! a fine girl she for a new country! Such are our best diplomatists for Great Britain."

Friend.—But how cool you are; I thought it would kindle your romance. I'll wager my meerschaum to those Sioux moccasins, that you make a goose-quill flight of it yet. We shall read of a wild and wilful—a bright-eyed nut-brown maid of the prairies, and her loves with a bold horseman of the mountains,—of the eagle feather nobility, whose love-tokens are scalplocks—perhaps a dusky rival.

"Hold! I accept the wager; hand me the ink-horn; here goes for the *poetry of matrimony* (*writes*): 'Marriage on the Prairies—A driver of oxen—a homespun matter-of-fact lad, not a "leather-stocking," but clad in dirty woollens,—having for sometime observed with longing eyes a fair friend of the company—that is, for three nights they had made their solitary beds on the banks of the same streams,—and that she was the possessor of a red blanket, an extra blanket; and he, the wretch, all cheerless, and cold o'nights (and that accursed frost!) with nothing between them and the damp earth but a worn and well-singed rug;—forlorn and tempted by such splendid attractions, and struck too with the obvious truth that two can sleep warmer than one, bluntly proposed; the kind she consented, and their fates (and blankets) were united!' As usual, a *marriage de con-*

venance, and I defy you, friend critic, to make more or less of it."

Friend.—Well done! But I can make *more* of it; did you not hear the sequel?

"Upon my word I have not; what can you mean?"

Friend.—Pshaw! This actually occurred. It seems that they had no taste for "stars for nuptial torches," and had no "cave for bed," and so, unluckily converted a wagon into a marriage chamber. Well, they had hardly gone to rest, when they found the wagon in motion!—faster!—faster!—which, all in the dark, threatened a crisis; and sure enough, down it went, all topsyturvy into a great hollow. A scurvy trick that of the young Oregonians!

May 26th. We quitted early our camp-ground, and soon approached the western and longest branch of the Blue, which seems to fulfil its destiny, in leading the Missourians by its hospitable waters and fuel, in the direct route of their new West; and, having ministered to their necessities, turns them over—the "divide"—to the like friendly offices of the Great Platte.

The muddy and shallow waters and treacherous quicksands of this river, are apt types of the political hacks of a late day, who would make it, under its better Indian name, Nebraska, godfather to an iniquitous new territory; hastening without a shadow of the excuses of "destiny," necessity, &c., to break all the last and most binding pledges of their country's faith, her voluntary and most solemn and plain obligations to the congregated remnants of many defenceless tribes of Indians, who own every acre of its arable land.

We were struck with the beauty of this other Blue; its bold hills are indented deeply with narrow vales of a thousand forms, their soft green pleasantly relieved by oaks. This, by way of introduction—for the road led us hastily away again to a high plain, where we were for hours out of sight of all of earth but its grass. But we *did* overtake a long line of wagons, and a great herd of cattle. Passing as rapidly as we might, we learned that several such companies were still in advance. The cattle were grazing like buffalo on the prairie, and by estimate, I hit upon their real number, of one thousand; and then, by comparison, was assured that I had seen at once a million of buffaloes. We descended at evening into the wide savannas of the Blue to make our night-camp.

A few hours after I had written the last sentence, a hurricane passed over us:—it was midnight, and intensely dark, the rain falling in torrents; there was an unceasing and strange roar of thunder; and the furious wind, rioting with the wet canvass of many tents, sounded a deafening accord. The sublime does not frighten, and I was filled with a joyful excitement. I imagined mammoth and mastodon revived, and rushing to repel the invasion of their ancient haunts,—exciting to madness by their roars attendant multitudes of buffalo and wild horse.

Next morning a warm sun set us to rights by 9 o'clock. We still ascended this western Blue; crossing now and then the feet of the hills protruding into the bottoms;—at times, winding through some great ravine or sand-gully, washed by the rains of ages. The bottoms are sensibly lessening, but still a fourth of a mile wide; the grass is still deficient from drought;—but at evening, turning short down from a high bluff, we found a sweet little valley, of which we seemed the first discoverers; and which, with its grove, was fresh and beautiful from the night's rain.

May 29. To-day—as yesterday—we marched some

twenty-two miles, following the stream, and passed near night an emigrant company. A cool wind has blown from the north; pure and invigorating; such as it is a pleasure to breathe. The hills are diluvial—mere sand—with a soil that scarcely supports their sod. As the hills break off near the river, they are washed into many singular shapes; and being white, stand in bold relief; bright green generally prevailing. Many slopes beyond the stream still show their old growth of grass strongly resembling ripe wheat; adjoining are weed stubbles and dead trees, which together are the picture of corn-fields in new clearings. These surround green meadows and hills, with groves and shrubbery, which we easily imagine conceal tasteful dwellings. Such beauties, to be seen on the stream in a day's ride, must deceive no one; for beyond, all is barren; and the vast territory, from near the rivers to the mountains, has scarce a tree to the square mile; and much of it is little better than a sand desert; even game is seldom found.

Marching rather late next morning, with no expectation of parting from the pleasant guidance of our little river, we found after a few miles, that we were ascending very gradually a high plain; the "divide" of the Blue and the Platte; no water was then to be found for twenty-three miles, unless pools of the late rain. We found such a pool at mid-day—and an emigrant party: this, for a specimen, was ascertained to be composed of thirty-one men, thirty-two women, and sixty-one children; twenty-four wagons, and two hundred and twelve cattle.

We also met, on the ridge, Pawnees with some two hundred horseloads of dried buffalo flesh, which they were conducting to their village, perhaps seventy miles lower, on the Platte. This is a temporary supply. After getting their corn fairly growing, the whole tribe moves off on their summer hunt. On the summit, a rather singular incident happened to me. I fired a pistol at a troublesome dog, which was then chasing some loose mules; it *resented* this attempt on its life in a quiet, but ferocious manner; absolutely fastening its teeth in the ham of the horse I rode; of course he kicked and plunged with great violence, taking me by surprise,—for I did not know at the moment the cause—and very nearly throwing me: I then fired again and killed the brute. It happened that the head of the long column was then about to meet the Pawnees; and a report was just received of their having robbed and maltreated some straggling emigrants; altogether, they had a technical "alarm," of which—with the excitement of my pitched battle with the dog—we, in the rear, were profoundly ignorant; and a little while after, I was astonished at a rebuke for my contribution to it, of the two shots; the Colonel being equally ignorant of my reasonable excuse, and of our private *émeute.*

We arrived, near sundown, on the hills of sand bordering the remarkable valley of the Platte. Between us and the river lay two miles of level green savannas; the wide expanse of the great river was in part concealed by Grand Island, and its woods. It was a beautiful sight!—the squadrons were gliding, two abreast, along gentle curves, over the fresh green grass, which was brilliant in the slant rays of a clear sun. The horses had a gallant bearing;—fifty blacks led; fifty grays followed; then fifty bays; next fifty chestnuts—and fifty more blacks closed the procession: the arms glittered; the horses' shoes shone twinkling on the moving feet. It was a gay picture, set in emeralds. Just then a hare, of the large black-eared species, bounded away from the front, pursued by a swift dog; it was a beautiful chase for a mile over the green-sward, which we insensibly halted to witness.

The broad bottoms of the Platte are nearly level, and but from two to six feet higher than the water; they are composed of sand, through which the river expands to its level from bluff to bluff,—often ten or fifteen miles. There is no rising above the universal flatness; and it resembles the ocean mouths of most great rivers. You have a horizon of green meadows, and sometimes of water.

We encamped on the bank. We had, in twelve days, marched two hundred and fifty miles; and partly as explorers.

May 31. The trumpet sounds of reveille called us forth this morning, as usual, under arms; and we instantly witnessed a scene of beauty and of sublimity, which the wanderer over the earth sees now and then when least expected. Above the river, and the unlimited plain to the west, dotted with white wagon-tops and vast herds grazing, densely black clouds, driven by a strong wind, came thundering on wrathfully; the lightnings crashed from mass to mass; from beneath, the muddy and troubled waves, almost black with shadow, seemed rushing on in league with the Storm-Power, to overwhelm us.

But turn to the east! The sun is calmly rising over a glittering expanse of water, and shedding a rosy glory o'er half the heavens; but the west, from amid intenser shadows, gives but a reflection of baleful hue! It seemed a rebellion of the Powers of Darkness against the Spirit of Light. As if to interpose, three hundred men in arms then rose up in the very midst.

This was a wondrous reality, breaking, all unprepared, on eyes that had been closed the still night long, and minds suddenly aroused from dreams of quiet home-scenes.

How singular, that *now*, as I write on the same spot, we have this scene reversed! The sun is sinking serenely on the western wave; while in the east, a black cloud mutters a menace of its power in the coming night. Sad types of the world's doings, and ever varying but unceasing warfare of good and evil.

CHAPTER VII.

HAVING rested a day, the march was resumed up the bank of the Platte. A strange river and country it is! You may ride all day without encountering an object to break its sameness;—not a tributary—a ravine, a tree. To-day the river formed again a portion of the unbroken horizon;—is this the case with any other inland river in the world?

A south wind—on our left hand—blew so fiercely as to make it difficult for horses to keep the road; nevertheless, we marched twenty-six miles—hoping to find good grass, but in vain; and there is no fuel nearer than a mile from the camp. At this point it is scarcely—strictly speaking —a "bottom," for there is a rise of about four feet in one thousand, from the water's edge: and the soil and grass have the characteristics of hill prairie.

June 1.—The wind continued,—a perfect gale—nearly all night; covering everything with a penetrating dust, which it raised from the prairies, so lately soaked. There is a breeze now from the northeast. Last night, sandbars in the river on our windward side were bare: this morning they are covered with water; while others have appeared on the other side, now the windward: this phenomenon must result from the wind; its forcing the shallow water of the very wide river from one channel to another; they being divided by very extensive islands and bars, which must assist in continuing such an effect. Most provokingly, we found this morning good grass extending for ten miles. After all, this strange river has its beauties; nay, there is all the variety consistent with the prevailing flatness. For miles, this forenoon, it was charming: there was a labyrinth of islands adorned with tree and shrub of every shape; some very long, forming vistas,—others, mere dots of verdure, like emeralds set in silver: from thence, the bright summer day was saluted with songs of birds; the cheerful and chatty blackbird, the whistling curlew, the gay lark, and—queen of songsters—the mocking-bird. Then, I observed a view as strange as beautiful: long narrow islands were fringed with tree-tops, through and above which I could see extensive strips of water; then came the opposite bank with trees just alike, which were relieved against the sky: but water and sky appeared the same!—thus there were *two horizons* of beautiful trees, which the eye could not distinguish! This novel illusion extended for miles.

But the prairie does not always charm the eye or the imagination: often its sameness and the monotony of slow motion, lull us to dreamy thought; then happily, we create of solitude a world of our own; or people it with the loved absent, or the long dead. To-day, by an easy association, I dreamed of the old warrior explorers from Spain—ere her glory died—of De Soto, Cortez, and others. Hernando Cortez! What a name is there!

What hero of antiquity excelled him? None but Cæsar. His military genius resembled Alexander's; but—as in the comparison of our Washington with the world's captains—with an allowance for the scale of action and of means. (*His* passage of the Delaware, and subsequent campaigns, gave indications of what he might have done ?) The master-stroke of the career of Cortez, was his desperate march to Vera Cruz, and his attack and defeat of the braggart Narvaez and his vastly superior numbers. Truly, his were enthusiastic genius, energy, and constancy, beyond all proportion to what Providence implants or requires in man in ordinary times. In the world's story, among all wondrous events, in Mexico alone History and Romance form a unity. And Cortez, like Columbus, was self-made; he forced his way over great obstacles, with which that age heaped the paths of aspirants from the low classes.

About noon we saw a company of some fifty wagons, winding a toilsome way to the high grounds: it was a proceeding as inexplicable as unusual, and gave rise to much conjecture: at last it stopped; we came up abreast—far to their right: then soon we learned the truth: they were burying an infant! It is Sunday; forty-seven wagons and families form a procession, which so slowly and painfullly leaves far its course to reach that grassy hill which poetic affection would choose for a place of sepulture. There they solemnly consign to the unblessed earth,—to the howling wilderness—the father's hope—the mother's love and her pride. Pity her! it is no common loss! Wonderfully must the outward pressure of hardship, severance from the world and its distractions,—the solitudes of wild Nature, the want of kindred sympathies—strengthen the bonds of family love!

Pity the mother! who bears a burdened heart to encounter her rugged and unkind destiny. Honor those hardy woodsmen for their attentions! their hearts are right.

But "march! march!"—shift the panorama! The sandhills approach the river; they are elevated and picturesque; and here is the first prairie-dog village (and, as I expected, their inseparable buffalo-grass): the dogs are in great excitement, and never saw such sights. See that old gossip with eager and important bustle, rushing with the news from door to door! but she is now excusable, and may tell the truth: behold hundreds of horsemen,—a hundred wagons,—hundreds of cattle,—and sheep too! But these marmots are a hackneyed subject. There are beautiful antelopes too, which excite the hunters. It had turned sultry; white clouds shut in the warm atmosphere, and reflect back the heat like an oven lid: ahead of us, for a wonder, is a creek-bed, fringed far into the hills with tree and shrub; we pass on, and turn into a sweet green bay (or bend) of fresh grass, and skirted with trees: they are on islands, to which we must wade for fuel; but are close by. Here we make our camp: the sun shines out brightly, but muttering thunders marshal forth black clouds: instantly the wide greensward is alive with horses, rolling and neighing with the delight of release and welcome food: next rises, as by magic, a canvas city: the men run over the islands for the driest sticks: curling smokes soon give token of supper. We turn and look back; at a little distance is a long line of wagons, attended by lowing herds. Just now an antelope dashes between, pursued by greyhounds; shot after shot are fired; the poor animal is hit,—falters,—is pulled down. What an animated invasion of this primeval solitude: the prairie nymphs must shrink in amaze! Since the world began, this beautiful meadow was never peopled thus.

June 2.—There has been a hard rain in the night; and its quiet was disturbed by yells from an emigrant camp, half a mile off: why they should thus play Indian, is beyond my comprehension. We march early: the bottom widens much, and is very barren; sand-hills, washed into picturesque shapes, and partially green, invariably bound our view to the left; and to the right, the river variegated by islands: they nearly all have groves—not regular, forest masses; but each tree has had room to develop, and reveals against the sky, untrammelled beauties, and in infinite variety.

We touched near midday the river, and found—which is rare—a good watering-place; the banks are only two or three feet high—are generally vertical; and the horses then can scarcely be forced into the opaque water, which, if only an inch deep, looks bottomless. It is surcharged with mud, and millions of odds and ends of all things near, which its great swiftness keeps suspended. Here too, was found clear, cool water in a well only two feet down; just above were the remains of many Indian fires, and buffalo bones, and the willow frames of old wigwams.

We are too early for the backward grass season; but here it has been swept off by ten thousand buffaloes. After a fatiguing march of thirty-two miles in eleven hours, we encamped on a spot which, having escaped the annual fires, the buffalo have neglected. There is no fuel but *bois de vache.*

June 3.—We have rain at camp every night; but it seems to extend little further; and the dust, when there is not a side wind, is so annoying, that we sometimes abandon the road. This morning, at marching, blue-black clouds overhung the sand-hills, to which they imparted their hue; and their irregular sketchy outline presented a singular and beautiful appearance; but it must be a very desert that is not pleasing in early summer morning! And if this flattered us with hope, of even the picturesque, we were this day disappointed. We had once, however, an unbounded water view up the river; and the fast growing signs of buffalo gave some excitement to the dull march.

When it was time to stop, there was great difficulty in finding any grass. We turned at last into a long strip of meadow, between trees and bushes—so very rare on shore—and the river-bank: the buffalo has been before us, but we have found some scant grazing;—it is buffalo-grass,—very backward, and looks like curled gray horse-hair.

Three fine horses were picketed beyond the screen of bushes, out of sight of camp, or any other animals; as usual in such cases, they were uneasy; imagining, perhaps, something fearful in the bushes; or more likely, were excited with the fear of being abandoned in these unwonted solitudes: be this as it may, about sundown they broke loose, and scampered off for the hills: some men were hastily mounted and sent in pursuit; but they have returned late, unsuccessful.

June 4.—Ten men were sent at daylight, on a new search: I feared it would be unavailing, as horses will join and run with buffalo; but fortunately, the trails of their ropes were discovered in the heavy dew, and they were brought back in two hours. Meanwhile, two empty wagons were sent back to Missouri, with a small escort, with broken-down horses: "all flesh is grass," and the grass is very poor.

This proved the great day of such excursions: the day of meeting buffalo. It was toward noon that they appeared in large numbers on the hills at our left. Immediately the fever rose; and as party after party prepared and rode off for the chase, the coolest heads became affected: we knew that even better opportunities would certainly occur; but the first fresh view of the chase became almost irresistible to all but old hands like myself. We see them charging helter skelter, up hill and down, without prudence, skill, or regard for horse-flesh: the perverse wind brings from the rear clouds of dust, which adds confusion to excitement. Let me attempt to describe a fragment of the scene: a horseman is seen dashing at a gang of twenty or thirty; he appears to penetrate their close order, and they are dividing into two parties; he has selected his victim: a puff of smoke appears; the report is heard; then a wounded buffalo rushes forth alone, but followed by the hunter, who is reloading, and loses ground: now he gains again; is very near; we eagerly expect his discharge; but no! they are diverging rapidly! the horse has shied in affright, and the buffalo, too, has dodged: the horseman pulls up and tries again: now he regains his place near the flagging animal; the smoke is seen again, and the report follows more slowly: they have stopped; the bull is tired—enraged and desperate: he is at bay: with a toss of his vast head, he makes a sudden and fierce dash at his enemy! Our hunter stops not to show his skill, but flies with prompt good will: fifty yards is all, and both again have halted: another shot! and now the bleeding and baffled beast turns to fly again; and there! they have disappeared over the top of that far off hill.

An hour or two after, a horseman is seen gradually

nearing us; he approaches very quietly, and puts on an air of business-like coolness. Oh! nothing extraordinary has happened; he even appears unconscious that a tongue is conspicuously dangling to his cantle. It is his trophy! and, when green, to my taste, good for little else.

Meanwhile, the "Forks of the Platte"—the junction of the "North" and "South" branches—has been passed, and few but the guide has known it. Cheated of knowledge and view of a principal point of note! too bad! We have got far out from either river, and can just see the water of one, and a fringe of trees beyond, which, no doubt, mark the course of the other. We are ascending the South Fork, but shall cross over in a day or two to the North. Now we stop to water at a small running branch, the first we have seen; it is without a tree; a buffalo calf approaches, and is evidently trying to join our cattle; but some men turn it off: there is the mother, which a hunter pursues up the steep hills: it is exhausted, but his horse refuses to go near; he has fired—probably ineffectually: we pass on. At 3 o'clock, we encamp at some ponds, in the middle of the bottom. Many horse-loads of meat are brought in: the buffaloes—nearly all cows and calves,—are not yet fat.

We pass continually companies of emigrants; they all have many breeding cattle. The girls must consider us a lively feature of this dull region (or they are not common girls). For our part, it is reported that one of them has been seen actually—that is, evidently, invested with a "tournure;" who would believe the tyrant Fashion held so wide a sway!

June 5.—This morning at daylight the buffalo had approached so nearly among the horses, that the officer of the guard sounded an alarm: they were driven off without accident. We were soon abreast of the point of bluff between the two rivers: it is eighteen miles above the junction; we are 30° west of the meridian of Washington City. We are now fairly on the buffalo grass: its sod is a near approach to wooden pavement. This branch is not half so large as the main river; but the general character is exactly the same; near the bluff, but extensively winding, is a kind of slough; the river water soaking through the sands here, rises perfectly clear: there *is* a new feature—large bare spots, white with salt.

Again to-day—and it was very warm—we had buffalo chasing, chiefly by officers, who killed an abundant number. I now first indulged; mounting my led horse—too spirited and fractious for ordinary use—I passed forward to meet a herd that had just forded the river, and I knew would cross to the hills a little forward of us, *against the wind*, as their instinct invariably leads them: it was given them, it is supposed, for their protection; but they carry it to an extreme, which I have often observed, led to their destruction. But my buffalo are in motion, and will not wait a discussion: as I passed the head of the column, a friend thrust into my hand a six-barrel pistol; taking it almost mechanically, I dashed forward after the herd, which are now at desperate speed: my noble Brown is in his element, and goes joyfully to work; he soon places me alongside a fortunate bull, whose destiny it is to test the value of this patent plaything. With some difficulty, I succeeded in snapping it twice, and then consigned it, indignantly, to the uttermost depths of my off holster: I now draw my old Harper's Ferry "buffalo slayer," and select a barren cow—round behind as a barrel—and at five paces—all at full speed—deliver my fire; the shot soon stops her; she keeps her head toward me, and I fire several times before her quick motions allow me to strike her full through the lights; the blood instantly spirts from her nostrils, and she is soon out of pain—cut up and in a wagon.

We passed this morning an emigrant camp; they were lying by,—had lost oxen, frightened off by buffalo,—several persons were sick,—a poor woman at the point of death. This Oregon should be a paradise!

The hills beyond the river are wilder and more elevated than before—all there looks arid, sandy, desolate; this side, we wade through sand; *all* is strange: prairie-dog villages; antelopes; large gray wolves; buffalo attract but little attention or remark; but of all, how strange seems the eternal wind—the high south wind; to what purpose does it day and night so fiercely blow—blow! A flat muddy river, sand, buffalo, and wind, are the universe! But no; ungrateful; three rose-bushes bloom in my tent, and I have almost ice-water from a hole in the sand close by: and that beautiful hare so gracefully bounding over the plain, was it not made for man's pleasure? or food for wolves?

June 6.—The clear stream on which we encamped last night, is a very singular one; it rises in the flats near the river; but does the river supply it? it is clear and cold, has quite a current, and contains fine large fish, which the river does not.

It was a sultry morning, but soon arose the south wind, which has blown a gale with most unpitying persistence all the day. After travelling a few miles, the guide bore down to the river; on the way, we were diverted by the pursuit of a young hare, by a number of men on foot; it was captured after many laughable tumbles, occasioned by its doubling.

The column marched right through the river; it was about eight hundred yards wide, and from eighteen inches to three feet deep; the quicksand made it laborious and tedious. The regiment then dismounted, and the horses were held to grass wherever it could be found. I passed over alone to a long island near the shore; it was grown up with grass, young willows, and the most delicate and beautiful rose-bushes, in bloom, and very fragrant.

I stood on the point of the island and gazed down the river, from whence shone the morning sun; our wagons were slowly making the winding passage, followed by cattle and sheep; to the right was a vast meadow, which insensibly swelled into green hills; on its bosom, like a string of white beads, were seen extending to dim distance, the tops of Oregon wagons; a few buffalo seemed calmly looking on; the hills gradually melted in perspective, to a faint, blue horizon, terminating in the water view; for the river here, adorned by many green islets, and sparkling in the sunlight, extended below, as far as the eye could wander; on the left was a vast range of sand-hills, on which, for ages, the rains and winds had worked their pleasure; exposing, at places, great masses of white marl in fantastic shapes; in the foreground, armed men and horses lounged or grazed at ease in picturesque groups. The high wind, though monotonous, gave music to the foliage, to the tall grass, and to the rippling waves; these waves, and the unbounded reach of river, reminded me of the ocean; that ocean, whose visible grandeur expands the conception to compass the vast earth,—whose ceaseless motion types the moral unrest—the troublous action of the toiling world.

The music of the wind, which hushed or softened to accord all other sounds—the happily mingled beauty and majesty of the view—my pleasing and isolated position, and the repose,—snatched from that action which now was only pictured to the eye,—had an irresistible charm: I fell into that dreamy state, in which, while the senses, keenly alive, are intoxicated with pleasure, the soul is soothed to happy thought; is winged by beauties to the high and abstract sphere of its nobler elements; or, skimming the fairy arches cast by Memory to the oases of the desert life behind, there meets in rosy bowers the absent loved! then, blissfully oblivious, we soar again with flattering Hope, to fall, with sudden shock, in the darkness of the land ahead. For, alas! while thus we dream, stern Care plucks us by the skirts: we shrink, and struggle, and linger, to drain the cup of happiness; but our earthly element drags heavily; a voice, trumpet-tongued awakes us to the REAL.

Truly, the trumpet had sounded; the men, the horses, had gone from careless rest to labor; all the living elements of the scene had disappeared; the sun himself was veiled; and I was now in a wilderness, as tame and dull as it had been to every careless mind—to every untutored eye. But the fleeting beauty, so faintly described, *was* real! and its enjoyment was mine!

It is wonderful how many go through the world with eyes shut, with minds unawake; but without the keen relish of the beautiful, without souls sensitive of lofty emotion, they have the enjoyments of animals, and are dull to painful reactions.

June 7.—A winding valley, a hundred paces wide, is overhung by a lofty white cliff on one side, and by the thick and most glossy foliage of ash trees on the other; a crystal streamlet murmurs amid the grass, over its gravel bed; a crescent silvers just the top of the precipice; whilst between it and the tree-tops, the stars look down through this pure dry air, with a wondrous lustre: here and there camp-fires, dying out, cast an uncertain and pale light upon white tents; the horses, hungry and grazing in the obscurity, doubtful of this strange spot, make uneasy sounds, always answered by the rest. Since nightfall, an emigrant company, belated like ourselves in the passage over to this Northern Platte, passed at random through our straggling camp—blinded by the lights—in much danger of upsets, at which women and children were plaintive, and to the detriment of picket ropes, and discomfort of our horses and tired men.

I was lying on the grass by a small fire, greatly fatigued, but with face upturned in dreamy enjoyment of all this beauty, so strange to the long wanderer on treeless plains;—a *sentient* beauty!—of the heavens and earth,—which seemed to look down upon me as a long-expected guest! My Friend joined me.

Friend.—Ah! gazing at the stars? The three mortal hours we passed on the verge of the table land, whilst the guide sought a clew to this strange labyrinth of hills, or mountains—

"And found it; much thanks to the buffalo, and to the aid of their paths"—

Friend.—Were enough, with an empty stomach, to evaporate an ocean of romance.

"Considering too, how dry it was; we had not drank for thirteen hours."

Friend.—Considering too, you slipped off alone to the island yesterday, and "fell asleep;" but, as I verily believe, only dreamed; for, in our silent ride to overtake the regiment, you were still rapt, past all observation.

"What on earth was there to observe? there was sand, wind, and ten miles!"

Friend.—And nothing more?

"There were wild hills to our right; and I remember a great ravine, a torrent bed, which I thought would make an excellent ambuscade: nothing more."

Friend.—Then you overlooked something strange, and twenty times repeated, a natural paradox; a miniature and extravagant illustration of the formation of all our Western valleys, where the banks are always the highest ground; namely—little *ridges* of sand and gravel, only four or five feet over, all coming from ravines, and crossing the bottom to the river, and evidently made by water; little aqueducts, with scarce a rim to hold the water! The wind changed, too, and a whirlwind on the river raised the water in a column of steam.

"Ah! I dare say, I was still half asleep; the wind and waves, and monotonous cries of cattle-drivers on the river, were very composing, a regular lullaby. But what a mighty table land was crossed to-day, the very top of the earth! While no sense was cognizant of anything higher, this plain seemed to slope away! The total absence of forest is essential to this grand illusion, and I doubt if Europe present an instance of it."

Friend.—They seem favorite resorts of buffalo; we observed it on the Arkansas. Those were grand chases we had this morning!

"To be so unsuccessful; the buffalo run down a slope at racer speed; their strength is principally before, and 'they let go all holds.'"

Friend.—This oasis is truly beautiful! and with a surrounding wildness and desolation which have a real grandeur; for miles, we seldom see over a gunshot in any direction; it seemed that nothing but water, which had everywhere riven the sides of the steep hills—could have found the outlet, which, in fact, it made; then the thin column, far winding, now disappearing in part, and next seen in the most unexpected positions; the grizzly bear alarm, and the strangely echoed shouts; the clouds of dust bursting through the gorges!—nothing gave promise of the quiet nook which delights the senses, while it ministers to every want.

"Thanks, for the broken wagon which kept us here, whilst the rest went on to the river."

Friend.—This must be a kind of Indian Post-office: we found arrows and lance-poles singularly marked and disposed; and various colored strips of cloth with evident arrangement; a record by symbols, which no doubt is plain to them.

"As I gaze up from this deep vale—now so dark—on that planet so serenely bright, the little opening between rock and leaves seems but the gateway to a path of ether, never so short and inviting! Methinks I see a pitying smile, which reveals the hollow littleness of all our eager struggles."

There are times when the lethargic soul shrinks even from itself; is numb, nothing can excite it; we forget to hope! And with some such answer, or soliloquy, to which I remember no reply, I must have slumbered, and dreamed; but my acts and troubled thoughts were lifelike, and of which the stars were certainly no portion. I would not repeat it, but I was tortured by a dear friend, who seemed to know me not, or to be estranged; and there was a spell as in a nightmare—which always made me powerless to clear up the cause or exact nature of the calamity. This heart-pain half aroused me; but I scarce knew where I was: there was a sense of something wrong; but my apathy, or a kind of *ennui of sleep*, was so profound, that I lay wondering whether or not I still belonged to the world; and so, must have slept again; for then I surely dreamed. A night alarm in an ancient castle led me to the gate. And though all were then dumb with fear, I knew that a flood was coming down far slopes and threatened death; but beyond, I looked and saw, on a plain which was a lofty mountain top, a vast multitude; the earth's habitants, mingled, I thought, with celestial visitants; for their faces shone; they sat motionless on horses, and wore helmets and bright mail; but Terror was on the multitude, and a baleful and uncertain light shone from their midst. Then, there was a rush downward of strange animals, like elephants and horses; which, I thought, would trample down all that stood in their way: next, the mailed warriors charged, with lances set, upon flying men on foot, who were like no others I ever saw; of pale red countenances, and strange garments and mien; they too were armed, and resisted, but many were slain; and, as they drew near, the warriors fought too, with each other; and thus was supernatural war brought with awful reality, to the very door, which I struggled to maintain against them all. Suddenly I was in a hall with several of those who had fled on foot, and asked them in the Spanish tongue, who and whence they were? and was astonished that they knew such language, when they answered, "From Egypt."

Next I was conscious of flickering gleams of light, which seemed reflected from cavernous arches, and of rumbling reverberated sounds. I was half awake with awe, which fancy again was softening, when a glare of light—a crash, as from the crags over head, and a sudden fall of water, recalled me to life, and my aching limbs to motion; and I stood upon my feet in 'Ash Hollow.' "

CHAPTER VIII.

June 8th.—The excessive fatigue of yesterday's interesting march,—the mournful and wild dreams, and the storm of the bivouac, having all passed away with the night, the sun rose with dazzling beauty upon the romantic glen. Nature, as if in the freak of a most smiling mood, has there assembled in the desert the admired features of her favorite regions: the contrast is delightful at meeting; painful at parting.

Thus, wander where we will, man is at best,

> "A pendulum betwixt a smile and tear."

But sometimes our frail mechanism goes all wrong; the tear is a shower; and the smile, but a ray of fleeting light.

Leaving then only too early the most sparkling and rich foliage, the white cliffs and the crystal streamlet of that narrow valley—which some wretch has named Ash Hollow—we were soon monotonously clanking our rusty sabres over the flat sands of the *Northern* Platte,—this twin offspring of mountain and homely plain. But truth to tell, just here, for fourteen miles which we marched today, this bank of the river is broken into hill and ravine; the white sand scarce shaded by weeds, and the bluffs, near by, deeply washed by rains, were wild and desolate; and there were cliffs of marly rock; and one of indurated clay, under which we marched, was honeycombed by thousands of swallows, which gaily circled and twittered over our heads.

We passed also two gravel *beds* of streams, now dry, that were positive *ridges;* and actually, on one side,—marked by a slight margin of grass,—without a bank!

Amid all the arid desolation, as usual, were some beautiful delicate flowers; honeysuckles, and the white and fragrant bloom of mosses. I thought they redeemed and softened it—as sometimes Pity the desolation of heart.

It was the fate of a melancholy buffalo, whether misused and misanthropic,—shunning the vulgar herd,—or exiled as an old and hardened sinner to this solitude, to encounter us here; and it was the unhappy destiny of a very Nimrod amongst us, defiant of scorching sun and sand, oblivious that no centaur, he rode a hapless horse, and taking to his eyes the "scales" of this ancient beast, to give him impetuous chase. The bull truly fled with a lean and hungry speed; but followed, like a manifest destiny, the beaten track careless of all evasion, right on—on! Seduced, perhaps by this facility, my friend, the Nimrod, pursued thus mile after mile, straight on!—disappearing at times, to be marked again by the shining sand he ever scattered to the air; and finally we saw that he had fired, and the chase disappeared. This unerring and deadly shot after so long and pertinacious a pursuit, gave him credit with us all; until at last, we came up; and there surely lay the bull: but, strange to say, no scrutiny could discover a wound!—and soon the marvel was, how he had lived so long; he had only closed a long-standing mortgage to the crows;—the ardent hunter was not there to dispute possession! He had suddenly become interested in some undiscoverable object which happened to lay far from the road.

June 9.—The country is rather less wild in appearance, and the bottom smoother; but there is still much bare sand; limestone rock occurred in the dry bed of a wide water-course.

The pest of a light dust-bearing breeze from behind may be noticed, as giving a color to one's thoughts, as well as linen; although, in truth, both are habitually chequered. Pity it is, that petty annoyances muddy so much the current of our lives.

> "'Tis the vile daily drop on drop that wears
> The soul out (like the stone) with petty cares."

Happy his philosophy, who weighs them as dust in the balance! For my part I manage generally to laugh at material troubles; for those that attack the soul, I commend as a remedy such a chase as another friend of mine took this morning. He was following at the heels of a small herd of buffalo with that reckless rush, to which in glad excitement we then abandon ourselves, when a great bull, just before him, popped into a gully; the horse plunged on him, sending his rider sprawling, but with accuracy between the bull's horns! The first of this interesting group to recover his legs, was the horse, which ran off with alacrity several miles. Next the bull rose, and shook himself, very much with the astonished air, I imagine, of the lassoed Kentuckian, who "liked to know how that was done." Meanwhile my friend is on his back at the bull's feet; "imagine his pheelinks." I once threw a bone at such a beast, who, "smarting with his wounds grown cold," reared up and brought down both hoofs with a precision and force, that mashed it to powder!

This bull, perhaps, took the affair for a practical joke, and giving the gentleman one good look—which he will remember—with great good nature ran off. Had he been wounded, or distressed and enraged by the chase, he had killed him!

We met here a number of boats laden with buffalo robes; and although drawing but eight inches of water, they had been some two months descending the hundred miles from Fort Laramie; the hardy boatmen, who are also the trappers, hunters, &c., of the Fur Company, spending perhaps half the time in the water. Only for a short season in favorable years, is the river navigable at all. This attempt was now abandoned; and wagons and carts had been sent for to transport the packs back to the Fort!

These men, called *Engagés*, are generally French Creoles—and form a small class as distinct in character from any other, as is the sailor from his fellow-bipeds who dwell upon shore. But with, if possible, less of forecast, he somewhat resembles the said sailor—isolated on the prairie desert, as the other on the sea. He has a patient and submissive obedience, with a seeming utter carelessness of privations, such as would drive a seaman to mutiny; with the same reckless abandon to some transient and coarse enjoyments, he is a hardy and light-hearted child of nature —of nature in her wildest simplicity: and in these, her solitudes, he receives a step-mother's care, and battles with a stout heart against her most wintry moods. He resembles the Indian, too, and is generally of kindred blood; he possesses his perseverance, his instinctive sagacity, and his superstition. A very Gascon, he has the French cheerful facility of accommodation to his fated exigencies, and lightens all by an invincible and contagious mirth. He is handsome, athletic, active; dresses chiefly in buckskin; wears a sash and knife; lives precariously, generally on flesh alone; is happy when his pipe is lit; and when he cannot smoke, sings a song. He is armed and vigilant while at his severest labors.

He joyously spends his ten dollars a month in alcohol, tobacco, coffee, and sugar, and in gaudy presents to some half-breed belle; paying the most incredible prices for these extravagant luxuries.

June 10.—The nights are cold; the mornings warm, until about 9 o'clock, when a breeze springs up, ending generally in a very disagreeable gale. We came in sight early this morning of the "Court-house," a hill, or immense mound, which strongly resembles such a building, with wings; it rests imposingly on a bluff; the sides are near a cream color, with apparently, a black roof. The country is much smoother and pleasanter, and we passed to-day a tributary to the Platte, some sixty yards wide, and resembling it in its characteristics. Our camp is on the river, and without wood fuel. The Court-house appears a half mile off; in reality it is four or five. We came in sight to-day, also, of the Chimney Rock, at a distance of thirty miles; it had the appearance of a tall post seen a mile off. These celebrated formations seem the *frames* of lofty hills, which the elements have wasted away; they seem formed of marl, or a conglomerate to which the sand gives the character of mortar. I discovered to-day the most beautiful species of cactus I have ever seen: it is a single sphere resting on the surface of the ground; the inner leaves of the flower have the most delicate shades of pink and flesh color, and the outer a pale lilac. A small and delicate species of ground-squirrel abounds: it is remarkable for cheerful and exquisitely musical notes; resembling, but clearer and pleasanter than any bird's.

Those of us with any anatomical pretensions, are in a regular puzzle over a skeleton head of a small quadruped, which was found here; it seems totally deficient in holes or sockets for eyes: the verdict is, I believe, that it is a nondescript.

Friend.—And how do you like "A Glimmering Light on Mesmerism," which I perceive you have been reading?

"It shows a research quite extraordinary for a soldier —generally exposed to much literary privation; his inquiring and sceptical mind has been excited and puzzled by the strange developments, or pretensions of this *magical* philosophy."

Friend.—In our day the deep searcher of the unknown, the wonderful, the occult in science, or religion, fears not persecution, but rather neglect; he cannot interest the public mind; it is the mechanical age, and the greatest triumphs of science are the most practical: it is the age of steam.

"Only too true! Other works of genius are scarcely recognized: poetry is as dead as astrology: life is exhausted, and the mind overpowered in the attempt to master a vast accumulation of facts."

Friend.—Poets have turned cosmogonists; and the arcana of nature present the only field for speculative science; and there truly is infinite room for observation and study, to form synthetic solutions of these mysteries, still the dreams of "our philosophy."

"But even science is at fault—philosophy at a discount. The public mind is occupied with the theorism of demagogues and infidels, who, abandoning themselves to licentious speculations on human destiny, attract multitudes of fanatical followers, whose minds they bewilder, and whose morals they debase."

Friend.—What you say can scarcely apply beyond those hotbeds of vice and folly—the great cities; their immense command of the press, which taxes all the powers of steam, should not deceive you by its clamor—as it does themselves—as to their real magnitude and importance to the world.

"Has it never occurred to you, Friend, that we ought to be astronomers?—the science came from desert plains."

Friend.—Yes, and botanists too; I think no one *can* be on the prairies without observing much, the motions of the stars.

"I believe that nearly all think only of eating, drinking, and sleeping! But nothing perhaps, *has* been so universal a subject of thought and conjecture, in all ages, as these beautiful mysteries. What food for poetry, they have ever been! What strong imaginations were required to invent the constellations! But, as if our true links to a higher sphere, they have led the human mind to a grander reach,—to a more profound and brilliant success, by far, than in any other science."

Friend.—Do you believe the stars are inhabited?

"Yes! I hold with Dr. Chalmers there; although the Book of Genesis has it, that they were set in the firmament to give light upon the earth; it is not credible that the scheme of creation, with all its wondrous economy,—with its infinity of microscopic life, should include globes far vaster than our earth, and destitute of life."

Friend.—Perhaps microscopic life may be an essential element of the mysteries of life, death, and reproduction. And may not those immense spheres be the balance weights of the machine called the universe? necessary to all the conditions of that wonderful problem of the essential motions of the earth; their creation cost but the word of Omnipotence.

"The thought might have force, in view of our planetary system alone; but how with the innumerable other suns and systems disposed irregularly at a distance that the mind cannot conceive; telescopic stars that give us no light?"

Friend.—What sort of beings then, do you suppose to dwell in these innumerable worlds?

"Men! Are we not told that we are in God's likeness? Human intelligences, emanations from Divinity, and partakers of God's nature, *can* differ in myriad worlds but in degree: there well may be a greater or less perfection and prevalence of nobility and beauty of form; just as is the case of our different races. I imagine that in other spheres, the souls of men have new trials, and also rewards, in other stages of existence; progressing toward the infinite, in intelligence and happiness. Shall we sleep in death many thousand years? Scripture indicates a suspension of our final sentences, until the day of judgment."

Friend.—Some astronomers tell us that no planet is fitted to support life; they are too hot, or cold, or soft.

"Perhaps the reflection escaped them, that the torrid zone would be fatal to an Esquimaux, or a Polar bear! Astronomers would do well to confine themselves to the limits of exact science; their theories are no more reliable than those of other men; they are too prone to clothe their sublime though naked framework of discovery; with a poetical drapery of mere speculation, which—being little more astonishing—is apt to be confounded with fact."

Friend.—Well, yes: stick to facts. Can you not, from

these unknown solitudes, from this virgin soil, contribute your mite to the cause of science ?

"Undoubtedly there is opportunity: but the soldier, like others, to succeed must devote himself (and oftener, is compelled to confine himself) to his profession. But my eyes are open; perhaps I have at times observed something new. But how much knowledge is necessary to decide what *is* new ? For instance, it may have been observed and recorded, for what I know, hundreds of years ago, that the slightest culture—the mere disturbance of the soil—in barren regions, excites new growths. About the gardens of our prairie outposts, spring up weeds, shrubs, bushes, and trees, far away from any the like. But it is my observation, and inference, that the earth everywhere contains the germs of growths suited to the climate; that these germs or principles of vegetable life are a part or property of soils, lying dormant, in some cases for ages, ready for an exciting cause and the proper time to be developed for the use of man, or other animal."

Friend.—I have heard that the plantain and Jamestown-weed have followed the footsteps of the pioneers of our continent,—making their progress from ocean to ocean.

"And it is true, so far as I have had opportunity to observe; and I have heard the same asserted of the partridge and bee, and certainly with a color of truth. But a very great obstacle of science, is an impatient proneness to theory, leading to a hasty assumption of doubtful facts.

"It would now be easy and comfortable to assume, that my guard and sentinels are vigilant; nevertheless, by your leave, I shall, as philosophically as possible, betake myself to its investigation."

Friend.—But a last word—you should fail not to note in your diary, however dryly, all natural phenomena; they may come in play, and serve another if not yourself—*au revoir!*

CHAPTER IX.

JUNE 11th.—We marched ten miles over the smooth level, and turned to the river for water. While there, I sketched on my knee a striking view, including the Chimney Rock, still in front of us. Mounting my horse and riding on at the signals, immediately the scenery which I had admired faded from thought and memory; there had been rain in the night; and the rare atmosphere and the heat of the bright morning, gave rise to a soft and varying mirage, which was thrown, like a gauze veil, with a charming grace and exquisite illusion, upon scenery of strange beauty: truly—

> "At airy distance with majestic motion."

Although as indescribable as the dream structures of uncontrolled fancy, the ever varying and fantastic beauties seen this day, leave a vivid impression; and I attempt faithfully, however feebly, to paint them; for they must surprise, if they give not pleasure.

On the left and front, was the continuous hill range, of infinite variety of shape,—the wild sport of the elements—and of coloring too: the white and yellow marl and sand; the green grass; the dark blue cedars on the tops of mound and cliff; and the moving procession of shadows from the light mist clouds; for the life and grace of motion pervaded every element of the scene. On the left, the square bluffs were like the Hudson Palisades, with here and there a pilaster of silvery white; right in front, stood the lofty white Chimney Rock, like the pharos of a prairie sea; beyond, were white cliffs with green domes; broken in places into cones and pyramids; still further, but towering, was a majestic mound, in the shape of our national Capitol; more to the right, and looming afar over river and plain, was "Scott's Bluff," a Nebraska Gibraltar; surmounted by a colossal fortress and a royal castle, it jutted on the water; thus sharply defining from the pale blue horizon, of the unbounded river beyond, a vast bright bay, reaching fifteen miles, nearly to our feet.

We are moving on: a mile is passed; the pillar seems no nearer; Gibraltar has now its vast sides shaded a beautiful blue; but a low bank of cloud from the right, extends before it like a belt. We move on: the Palisades seem to advance and retire; to rise; to darken, and shine again like silver! Another mile: Gibraltar sinks; the cloud increases and grows black. A mile on,—and this cloud has *suddenly* become a prairie-hill close by! rising on the river flats (as I never saw one before), extending to the water, which it actually overhangs seventy feet! Refraction cannot *now* flatten and obscure it, and show us—as it did—the mirage sea with its lovely shore beyond; and, joining that in front, make it an island, or suspended cloud. Gibraltar is eclipsed; but to the left, now is seen a bright river, flowing amid groves, into a great city: noble buildings are there; turreted cathedrals; colossal ruins: certainly we shall soon be at its gates! A mile on;—the mound is now behind; the mirage river has vanished; the city fades from view; but the mountain fortress looms again, far round the bright waters of the bay; mighty bulwarks now appear; bastions and turrets; all of bright colors: the summits positively swarm with guards and sentinels! Can they *possibly* be cedars? Is it near and real, or very distant? Where are we? The mountains are in masquerade and mazy motion! Cannot the expanded eye detect phantasma? Is it the common earth? What magic is here, to new-fashion the solid hills into fantastic forms! Fairy fingers weave the shining mists into robes of air-born grace and beauty—which the sun illumes, but not elucidates!

It is the simple truth. I know *now*, that the vast bay was not river alone, but not how great a part was mirage; and that strange mound, which, though so close, at first appeared not, and was then mistaken for a cloud!

But we move on; the pillar of Pale Rock is at length passed—a mile to our left—grand, solemn, stern—like a monument to Time—the silent desert record. Still on! Yonder to the left, a vast palace appears; it is no ruin, —the roof and chimney stand; a near hill had hid it. And now, we gradually ascend a smooth plain to a great elevation; and scenery grand and beautiful without illusion opens to view; there is an amphitheatre of five miles extent; a semicircle ends near our left at the "Capitol;" every variety of shape and color too, which the earth contains, seems assembled round: there, is evidently a Titanic brick-kiln, with no particle of verdure; pyramids; white hills, with domes of green; cliffs crowned with funeral cedars: in front, majestic Gibraltar,—far distant still—strangely colored gray, and blue, and white; and above all, the top of Laramie Mountain—ninety miles away! Just then, an antelope was chased, far through the amphitheatre.

We begin to descend toward the river, as dark clouds gather; and we discover beyond it, the white lodges of a great band of the Sioux; the master-spirits and terror of the plains; their horses—a numerous herd—are grazing in the meadows. We hasten to a camp-ground at the water edge; for the wind rises, and thunders reverberate; our tents are raised just as vivid lightning sends the first big drops pattering to the earth. The Indians are now mounted and shouting; and with their robes and long hair streaming in the gale, dash fearlessly into the broad waters of the river, which look black and threatening with the shadows of the storm.

This day, whose light has shed such wondrous beauty on these wild scenes, is nearly done; and the exhilarating thunder-shower over, I cast my looks around, eager to enjoy some glories more; and, lo! a shining pillar, far away among the clouds! All the outer world is lost in misty shadow, save this prairie pharos: of *all* the visible earth, the sun shines *only there!* It stands a pillar of silvery light amid the dark shadows of cloud and rain, and coming night. And now it fades to gray, and appears strange and phantom-like, amid the solemn clouds.

Night.—In the silent camp the friends are lounging in the mouth of a tent looking out upon the starlight.

Friend.—This is a memorable day; and we might pass here, perhaps a hundred times, without being greatly struck with the scenery, which the elements seem to have combined to adorn for our delight; but it must be the most picturesque on the river. I see you have been making copious notes?

"Yes; do you apprehend that any effort of enthusiasm can add embellishment to the subject?"

Friend.—I must confess, not. There are natural beauties; such as the coloring of sky and cloud, which painter or poet scarce dare attempt to express; nevertheless, there may be in the effort, an ill done or apparent straining for effect, which may deceive a reader into the suspicion of exaggeration.

"This 'Scott's Bluff, is a wonderful mountain; we are miles off yet (we saw it at fifty); and to the last moment of light, there was the same chameleon change of coloring; the guards and sentinels still!"

Friend.—One view of it, I am told, resembles strongly some picture of Stirling Castle.

"In the excitement of the visit of the Sioux men and women—did you see the 'Chimney Rock' suddenly reappear?"

Friend.—Admirable! A lofty pillar of fire amid the dark clouds! its base was hidden by distance; but I was as much struck by the sunset, or rather with the strangeness of its apparent renewal after almost darkness—which the clouds must have occasioned; when they broke away—but it was at the north—what a startling but calm beauty and splendor of coloring appeared; and how long it lasted.

"I saw it all; there were still dark clouds at the northwest, where the sun went down."

Friend.—Our friends, the Sioux,—of the Oglollah and Brule bands,—came in with the thunderstorm, with a fine, indeed startling effect; but for the women, I should have imagined they were dashing through the river to attack us. I was delighted with their fearless and hearty bearing; but the contrast of the men and women is painful.

"The Sioux are rather my favorites: their freedom and power have imparted to the warriors—the men—some gentlemanly qualities: they are cleanly, dignified, and graceful in manner; brave, proud, and independent in bearing and deed. Their misfortune, their deep stain—the law of barbarism—is their treatment of women; they apply to them the brute law of the stronger!

"Woman, the martyr! who rises only, and rises ever, as mind feeding upon knowledge, ascends to the throne of humanity! Oh! how powerful is education with its first impressions; how strong the harness of association and habit—despotic *mental* habit, which chains the very soul!"

Friend.—Truly, these squaws bear the mark; bright-eyed as some of them are, a few only seem really to *have* souls. But, do I understand you, that you esteem woman equal, or superior to her mate?

"I have made that ever a question to myself. We say, Nature has given her an inferior part to play; that is, has assigned to her duties, which we choose to call inferior: but there, she actively exhibits beautiful and high qualities, which we seldom possess, and underrate; how magnanimous is their patience, their self-denial and devotion! They are *different from men.* How generally in society, with the audacious but seldom denied claim to civilization, do men (alas! uneducated), like savages look upon them and treat them as drudges,—laborers in their service and ministers to their pleasure. And what ever saves them from this common treatment, and the real degradation which it inevitably entails?"

Friend.—Religion?

"Religion truly, elevates mankind; but, compared to women, how very few men indeed are religious. It is a proof of her naturally superior refinement; and doubtless her recompense for many ills; but it exaggerates her virtues to a humble resignation, of which the obtuse and hard hearts of men only take advantage. No! the remedy is the appreciating refinement of mental culture, delicacy of taste, a high sentiment of the Beautiful—in a word, the spirit of Poetry! How palpably did the Providential romance of an otherwise barbarous age—of chivalry—rescue her from slavery and place her so near her proper level!"

Friend.—All must observe that the noblest, and in general the most eminent men, evince the highest regard for women; that a profound and deferential respect for them is the first characteristic of a perfect gentleman. But would you, like the knights of old, convert love into worship? Do you advocate the blind devotion which led to violence and bloodshed?

"No; you mistake a concomitant for a cause; the redeeming virtue of those ages was this romantic devotion, but tinctured, of course, with prevailing rudeness and crime. Love, always powerful, was ennobled and purified by martial romance; and, thus allied, was successful against barbarism. Worn out by change, romance is gone; but poetry, its vital element, is left; and its refined spirit alone can save love from materialism and degradation, and elevate its objects, so that man can bow with respectful devotion. I view woman as born superior; and often nobly sacrificing herself for our sake; the minister to, and our only hope for happiness. Striving always to make us more worthy of ourselves, and of her. How apt is vain man to undervalue those powers and qualities which he possesses not, or cannot understand: —as rude workmen despise the physical weakness, or the untutored hands of the student, who ennobled by science, pities the lowliness of their mental estate. Woman generally lacks that mathematical element, which in man, makes him often a little superior to some admirable machines; but she possesses instead, intuitively, certain delicate and refined perceptions, which to my mind are the 'impress of divinity.' We admit her mind develops more rapidly than ours, and call it precociousness; we choose to forget that this superiority lasts while she is receiving the education, which we cruelly stint. She is our superior in those qualities of our cultivated nature, which are so high, that the mass not only possess them not, but do not recognize them; but this is only the case when our physical advantage is forgotten in the poetical refinement of a just appreciation;—the homage which makes, if it do not find her worthy.

"Ah! at humble distance, with all my soul, I have sought to study and understand some of these pure and beautiful natures, whose beauty was a subtile essence—a divine revelation through features that charmed not vulgar souls; a beauty that inspired a poetic—a pure and lasting worship at its altar. How earnestly then should woman cultivate and encourage, by every means, this romantic devotion, which is so essential to place and sustain them in their proper sphere. They have to combat in the world the sneers, the vices, the sensuality of fallen natures; but man's loss of their just appreciation, is a sure step towards degradation and crime, which involves poor woman too. All honor, then, to Poetry—the aspiring effort to admire, to develop and to praise, the Beautiful,—the Noble,—the Grand!"

Friend.—There are noble minds, who would pronounce much of that extravagant—too double-refined for any application.

"And there are ingrained conventional prejudices, which warp the views of the highest natures."

Friend.—You believe, then, that human happiness is to be found in some reformed and higher state of civilization? Have I not heard you envy the fate of these red sons of nature—some wild chieftain—with two or three slavish wives!

"I might envy his freedom from factitious laws—the tyranny and fanaticism of society. But as for 'human happiness'—ha! ha!—suffer me to laugh, I pray you (if you will not call *that* happiness). Happiness would be the infraction of an immutable law; that all sin, is certainly not more inevitable, than that all should be unhappy; those who suffer as little as they enjoy, have a calmness which may deceive. I prefer at times to disturb the philosopher's equilibrium, and to brave his fated reactions for the joy which for the moment sublimes both soul and sense.

"Strange! that laughter, man's lowest attribute, is distinctive; while the smile, which seems borrowed from Heaven, and which can confer rapturous joy, if not happiness, is shared, I think, in a slight degree by brutes."

Friend.—Heaven help you of your mood! I give it up.

"My mood? I was never in a more sober mood; I feel as cool and practical as any downtrodden woman."

Friend.—Then your antitheses are rather overpowering!

"Yes, he that follows where truth may lead, will ever startle; I am still at my theme. I attack this semi-civilization, which halts when woman is only no longer like these brutish squaws; and, with the help of the faithful drudge herself, builds up a conventional system which defies the powers of human reason; nay, with an infernal perversity, resists the very light of heaven. But it is a law that we ever *seek* happiness. And it is this free desert air alone, that emboldens me in the search, to question the dogmas which society holds so precious.

> 'But let me quit man's work, again to read
> His Maker's spread around me.' "

Friend.—Nay, I go; luck to your prairie philosophy. It is the hour of rest. May your dreams be rational!

My old friend has been patient to-night; but I trembled lest he should discover the verses, at which his coming surprised me! And with all his prosaic affectation, he had nearly forestalled them by his tribute to the close of this day, which indeed might, altogether, have inspired a buffalo. And if so afraid of his ridicule, how shall I venture to record them? Well, three verses may be overlooked, as it is a first offence.

> The sun set in clouds;—but this glorious day
> Parts not in gloom; the thick veil is riven—
> And river and sky in lovely array,
> Are radiant now with the light of heaven.
>
> Like an aurora, or the flashing trace
> Of an angel's flight, to the utmost north
> The glory shines: unwilling to deface
> The Beautiful, Night hovers o'er the earth.
>
> Gently the chameleon colors fade,—
> Slowly ascending to the zenith's height:
> Till lingering darkness buries all in shade,
> And Light and Beauty bid the world good night.

CHAPTER X.

JUNE 12TH, '45.—It had been determined, rather than cross the river, which deepens as we ascend, without losing its quicksands, to take to the hills and turn Scott's Bluff: accordingly we this morning marched three miles still nearer to that mysterious mountain—and, without being disenchanted of its colossal ruins and phantom occupants, turned toward the left, and ascended the wild sandy hills. I anticipated a dull ride over ground as uninteresting as barren: but a new surprise was in store for us: having ascended about sixty feet, we saw before us a plain, more than a mile wide, but narrowing, winding, and walled in: the ascent was slight, and it was apparently a river-bottom; in fact, it was marked everywhere with drift, cedar-logs, &c.—the thought, "Can this be the Platte bottom?" came intruding on us with its absurdity. Thus we continued, winding round "Gibraltar," ascending insensibly this smooth inclined plain, mile after mile, thirteen, fourteen miles! Then, before we were aware, or we hardly knew how, we found ourselves riding above—looking into—a deep glen, with large trees, cedars, shrubbery, rocks, and crystal waters! And where is its outlet?—nowhere, but high up, too, on the smooth grassy plain, on which, in flood times, it had cast its drift; yes, all over its twenty square miles. We had got very high up, without observing it; but to complete even a faint idea of the remarkable scenery, I must add that this singular flat valley is walled in everywhere by lofty bluffs; their gray sand, and clay, and marly sides, often vertical; their tops crowned by cedar forests. This ravine is very precipitous; our horses could with much difficulty be led down to the water; wild fruits grew luxuriantly amid its rocks and trees. It heads very near the mountain top, at a spring of icy coldness, and without exaggeration.

Thus after winding, as one might have thought, through a strange opening around Scott's Bluffs, the surprise that we were at the top of a mountain gap came with an almost boundless view;—on our right—to which we must now direct our course—far below and twelve miles off, were the grassy meadows of Horse Creek: beyond, its blue hills—then, far away above many a treeless hill and plain, rose to view the famous "Black Hills," and Laramie Mountain, their highest peak, towering at eighty miles.

We turned then to descend another plain, of twelve miles, inclined to the southwest; a puff of air from the west came now and then cool and refreshing; but the reflected sunshine was literally scorching; without sensible perspiration, great blisters were burnt over our faces. It was paying dear for the avoidance of a little quicksand—so thought, doubtless, all the animals. We pitched the camp in the pleasant meadows of Horse Creek, near its mouth; it is sixty yards wide, and resembles the Platte, but has clearer water. We are enjoying the rarity of good fuel, from some dead cedars.

Seeing to-day an antelope with a young fawn, some three hundred yards from the column, I rode to the spot to endeavor to secure the little creature for a pet; they are famous for their fearless attachment to their young, and their skill in concealing them. This noble animal had another enemy afield: an immense dog, greyhound and bull, came rushing to attack her; the coward expected her of course to run; but maternal instinct had conquered fear; she coolly stood her ground, until with one judicious and vigorous spring, she received him with a butt that sent him rolling over and over! And he feared to repeat the attack, but followed her a little, at a respectful distance, as she leisurely moved off. Now, hundreds, perhaps, had seen the fawn there a minute before, in the open prairie; but she had hid it, so that three of us searched it for half an hour, in vain!

These antelopes are second to the buffalo in numbers: of the first, we saw none to-day; they are disappearing like the elks, which are said however to have migrated permanently northward. Fifteen years ago, they were found close to Fort Leavenworth; now we have come over five hundred miles without seeing one. Can we wonder? I have felt on this march, as if still among the settlements; continually amongst emigrants with their herds; meeting one day boatmen, the next, villages of Indians: and this migration, which here, where streams or springs are so rare, must necessarily follow these great water-courses (which seem providentially disposed to lead it on) unfortunately meets on them the great mass of buffalo; for they too must come to the water;—their day is passing.

We are now in advance of the whole emigration; two of their men are with us this evening; they speak of the great discouragement of the women, who even wish to return; and many men have been at times of the same disposition; they have lost many cattle in this first quarter of their journey. They scarcely know where they are going; and these men eagerly question our guide—who has been in Oregon—on the simplest and best known points.

I have read of small animals, marmots perhaps, and of our squirrels, migrating in vast bodies: overcoming with patient energy but great loss, every obstacle which they blindly encounter; moving ever onward, impelled by some inscrutable instinct, or destiny.

This migration severs the ties of home and country; leaves lands of exceeding richness, which may be purchased after years of free occupancy, for a dollar and a quarter the acre, with navigable rivers throughout, and pushes on with women and children, to the dangers and exposures of an immense journey—they hardly know whither—but that it is beyond the advantages and comforts of society. Is it a providential instinct? And was it the same that three hundred years ago impelled its many thousands of victims to the dangers and diseases of the new American world?

It must be so. Should we then admire as praiseworthy the energies and the sacrifices of these first laborers in a great work? Or can we, regardless of prospective results, deny them magnanimous or patriotic motives; attribute all to the wantonness of discontent,—a diseased appetite for excitement and change,—to a restless habit of vagrancy?

I hope I am not uncharitable, if I incline to this last opinion. Are we not taught to recognize in the history of man, that God shapes evil to good results?

There is a comet at the northwest; and a sudden and violent norther threatens the overthrow of our frail habitations; and so, to lightning and thunder, we have a rattling accompaniment of mallets and tent-pins.

June 13th.—Twenty-four miles to-day, over a desert! hills and river valley equally a desert! In this last, we have seen many large cotton-woods, seemingly the wrecks of a blasting tempest, mere limbless or distorted stems of trees; and others, the bleached and desolate drift of a flood.

We came over a lofty bluff almost overhanging the river, which commanded a view over vast and sternly sterile plains, breaking up at last into confused mountain spurs, and dim blue peaks beyond; but to this gloomy grandeur the river, far winding amid white sands and green islands, and the foot of many another precipitous bluff adorned with evergreens, lent an element of softening beauty.

Friend.—What oppresses you? You seem in mournful harmony with these silent wastes!

"Behold those spectral ruins of trees, strangely white and gleaming in the starlight!—they are melancholy. But no—it is a day that ever, since it first gave me unhappy life, leaves its influences upon me."

Friend.—But better resist such a mood. How do you succeed with your diary now? We are passing remarkable scenery; most wildly picturesque; and there is always *some* incident.

"What is written, may always chance to be printed, if not read: how charming then to the busy denizens of the world, whose very brains have received an artificial mould, to read such incident! Now if I could only introduce the word 'dollar,'—good heavens! it was never heard here before! tis enough to disturb the ghosts of the grim old warriors, who, I dare say, have fallen here in defence of this narrow pass: fighting for what? at Ambition's call? not, I hope, of intriguing diplomatist—better for Love, or mere excitement sake.

"Whom then shall I address?—the mock sentimentalist? and begin the day: 'Our slumbers this morning were gently and pleasantly dissolved by the cheerful martins, which sang a sweet reveille with the first blush of Aurora, at our uncurtained couches.' Or the statist?

'Not a sign of buffalo to-day; it were melancholy and easy to calculate how soon the Indians, deprived of this natural resource, and ignorant of agriculture'—but I should soon get too deep."

Friend.—But this soil is devilish shallow.

"Few will follow me pleasantly or patiently through these solitudes, though sometimes 'pleasant places.' I care not at all,—but that I feel I may fail to awaken the sympathy of *any*, while, like an artist retouching with kindled affection his painted thought, I linger to answer the appeal of Wasted Beauty to so rare appreciation."

Friend.—This profoundly silent desert—like a world without life—awes and stills the senses: but the soul is excited to speculations on the origin, the history—if it have one—and the destiny of these boundless wastes.

"Or surrounds itself with the airy creations of fantasy;—or, mournfully wanders back among the dim traces of joys and sorrows gone. I address not, then, the shallow or hurried worldling; but the friendly one, who in the calm intervals from worldly cares, grants me the aid of a quiet and thoughtful,—and if it may be,—a poetic mood!

"*Ay de Mi!* Our life is a sad struggle;—our material nature with its base cravings,—its cares for animal comforts, and all the ills of the flesh, preys upon and tethers the soul, which yearns for the Beautiful, the Noble, the Exalted;—essays to soar in that sphere, whose types are the bright stars of heaven! Or, clings to that electric chain of Love which binds humanity—and in the olden time drew down angels!"

Friend.—A false and self-consuming fire! that sometimes burns to ashes the hearts and hopes of proud men, and leaves but wrecks, mournfully floating upon the dull currents of life.

"And welcome, then, the rapids and the final plunge! Yes: the struggle is ever, and leads us sorrowing to the dark portals which shut out the life beyond. *There* may this holy fire from heaven find more happy sympathy. *Here*, amid ages of pain, it grants us but moments of felicity.

"Methinks, amid those bright stars, studding the blue ether of this moonless summer night, I see a seraphic face, that smiles with more heavenly light to rekindle the wasted torches of Life and Hope!

"Fond traitor! constant friend—blind guide—beautiful Hope! that leadest us wandering ever,—heartless, but living still.

"Yes! Time, the inexorable,—Time, the physician and the conqueror,—Time, the *hopeful*, rolls on, dragging us at his chariot wheels, wounded, suffering, unpitied,—but living still!

"Ah me! We are not only chained to the rock, but galled by all the thousand links,—the petty cares of life! *Therefore*, I love best this desert wandering, where we are free of *all* tyrannies; and our wants are simple and few. Nature, our beautiful mother, enthrones us on her bosom,—and to elevate our thoughts and aims, displays all her wondrous and harmonious ways and works; or, with sublime simplicity, points upward to the stars!

"There is nothing petty here. When we hunger, we go forth to the spirit-stirring chase; when we are weary, its furred trophies give us welcome rest; and our rude beds have a starry canopy, whose beauteous mysteries fix our wandering thoughts, until blessed sleep draw the curtain of oblivion."

CHAPTER XI.

June 15th.—*Near Fort Laramie.*—Ten miles over desolate hill and plain brought us yesterday to the Fort, on the west side, and a mile above, the mouth of the pretty little river of the same name; the water is clear and rapid: the Platte,—here, about one hundred yards wide,—is not much larger, and more resembles it, than itself as found below. Fort Platte, belonging to a rival company, stands near the confluence.

I came on in advance, and spent an hour at Fort Laramie; it is about two hundred feet square, with high walls of adobes, made of the clay and sand soil, just as it is found; the dwellings line the wall,—which is a part of them,—and have flat adobe roofs, and wooden galleries. The Fort swarmed with women and children, whose language—like their complexions—is various and mixed,—Indian, French, English, and Spanish; they live nearly exclusively on dried buffalo meat, for which the hunters go at least fifty miles; but they have domestic cattle.

Here, barbarism and a traditional or half civilization meet on neutral ground; but as a struggle, it is certain that the former has the best of it; although it has the disadvantage of being represented chiefly by females—both softening and impressible: but their credentials are ill-looks, dirty, and revoltingly coarse habits, &c. &c.; while the male representatives of civilization have the orthodox, although questionable aids of alcohol and gunpowder, avarice, lying, and lust.

The struggle is at close quarters; civilization, furnishing house and clothing; barbarism, children and fleas.

The Colonel had sent a staff-officer ahead, to examine the grounds for a camp: but arrived before he had completed his labor. The rival companies, anxious for the reflected importance of the military vicinity, rivalled each other in praise and misrepresentation of the merits of their respective rivers—as to grazing. The result was, that the Fort Platte scale at first preponderated; and up the Platte we marched,—two miles, without discovering the grass; then it struck the beam, and we passed over an immense and very steep bluff into the Laramie scale, —I mean river-bottom; where we did find good grass, and camped three miles above the Fort: but the extra two miles over the lofty dividing-ridge, was terrible work for wagon mules; and it bruised, I fear, fatally, a pet antelope fawn, which I had in a wagon:—it lies now in a neighboring tent, uttering from time to time cries and moans, which are distressingly similar to those of a suffering infant; said its soldier-nurse, with real pathos, "It is thinking of its mother." I purchased another at the Fort; and a goat foster-mother.

We meet the Sioux to-morrow in council; about nine hundred warriors are expected to be present.

The weather is very cold: fires and great-coats are comfortable. The dwellers here—who, however, lie in emulation, give discouraging prospects of grass toward the South Pass: this staple of the country is so scarce, that our three hundred horses, moving daily, can hardly subsist. The trade of this post is principally for buffalo robes; nine thousand were lately sent off by the American Fur Company: and how many by the other company I do not know. They get about two thousand pounds of beaver skins a year.

June 16th.—Colonel Kearney with an escort, and attended by the officers, rode this morning to the plain between the forts, and there met the Sioux in council. There were about twelve hundred, of both sexes: three flags on lofty staffs, first caught the eye; two were our national flags,—the third was said to be of Indian design; it was crossed diagonally by two bands, said to represent the winds; beneath were clasped hands; above, disposed in a regular curve, were nine stars; a little beyond, the people of Fort Platte had prepared chairs and benches, backed by a curtain of elk lodge-skins; and the ground was carpeted with buffalo robes; the Indians, all seated, faced us in a great semicircle, behind which was another, of women and children, who, in fact, also completed the circle in our rear.

The Colonel made a short plain speech, which hinged on the Oregon road, which the Government determined should be kept open.

Bull's Tail, the principal chief (the buffalo, be it remembered,—for this confounded name needs some apology, —carries aloft his tufted tail in combat, like a black flag!) Bull's Tail, then a gentlemanly and mild-looking man, made a short and sensible reply, which promised well that the Colonel's advice would be obeyed; and turning to his warriors, addressed to them some words to increase its impression. Presents, then, were placed in the centre: and the chiefs selected seven Indian "soldiers," who, receiving equal portions of every article, distributed them at their own discretion: their awards being final. I looked back over the screen at the distribution to the women, of strouding, beads, &c., which, of course, was very interesting: the mirrors were given, however, to the young men! Now, this unsophisticated trait will probably be interpreted as a compliment to the women at the expense of the men; or, the reverse: it was, I think, a mere exponent of the relations of the sexes; their women work and drudge; their men are idle, and have more *use* for mirrors in self-adornment: just the reverse of the picture of a certain stage of civilization.

In the midst of these proceedings, a squaw commenced a chant, in which she was soon joined by many women and some men, with a very fine musical effect; it was expressive of satisfaction and thanks. The Sioux,—they call themselves Dahcotahs,—are large, fine-looking men; wear their hair long, and are cleanly and showy in dress; adopting our fashions when they can; a great many wear our fur cap.

Several shots were then fired from a howitzer, to their great satisfaction: and the Colonel told them that at night he would send up stars to the heavens, which should "tell the Great Spirit that they had listened to his words;" meaning that some rockets would be fired. We then returned to camp.

It is still very cold; some snow is said to have fallen: the latitude is 42° 15′; altitude above the Gulf, 4470 feet: but they say that the winters are mild, with very little snow. Fort Pierre, a trading post on the Missouri, three hundred miles distant, is the nearest point of navigation.

The emigrants are overtaking us: but to-morrow we march, leaving one company to await our return. My poor little antelope is out of pain—it is dead: and it is rather singular, the other, at the Fort, was killed to-day by the kick of a horse.

June 17th.—We set out this morning in a cold drizzle; about ten miles from camp, at the Warm Spring, I left the regiment to make a detour of several miles to the Platte, to examine a point which had been spoken of as suitable for a military station; the river there emerges from the most advanced spurs of the Black Hills; a little below muddy and tame, it here gushes a sparkling mountain stream from a pass which it completely occupies, between precipices of bright red sandstone two hundred feet high. Standing a little lower, over the water boiling through a still narrower passage which it has worn through a ledge of rock, I could see through the gap many loftier hills or mountains of red sandstone, all, far and near, crowned, shaded, or dotted with dark cedars; beautiful it was,—and even grand, with its wild confusion.

The squadrons marched thirty-six miles to Horseshoe Creek; so far, because although they repeatedly touched the river, water and grass together could not be found nearer. Wearily I followed them all day over this broken and desolate country; its gray sterility unrelieved by a single and mournful growth of gray artemisias. There were now and then striking views of mountain ridges, covered with cedars, which sometimes dotted them as regularly as hills of corn,—and walled with red rock precipices; and through which it was hard to believe the river passed, so utterly invisible at a little distance was any opening; but the picturesque it seemed had not tempted any unfortunate wild animal into these barren wastes.

Right pleasant then at last it was, to see down a slightly inclined and singularly smooth plain, two miles wide, the camp, and horses grazing, in a horseshoe bend of a creek with green trees.

June 18th.—We had a thunder-shower last evening: and the stream, which we found with a very little clear cold water, soon ran boldly, nearly a blood red. After some half dozen miles winding over high prairie hills, they admitted us to the river meadows; but soon confined us to a narrow pass, which we threaded pleasantly enough, through cotton-woods, willows, and rose bushes; and these now generally mark its locality; and then, rather than again ascend these precipitous bluffs and remain among them for several days, and perhaps without grass, we forded the river at a swift rocky place; and were near losing our beeves,—to say nothing of the drivers.

At four o'clock we discovered a narrow grassy bottom, where we gladly encamped under some fine trees; and have plenty of dry drift for fuel. It seems a settled matter now that we should have two hours of great heat at midday, with the other twenty-two cold and boisterous. We saw to-day a great quantity of cotton-wood sticks, which had been cut about three feet long, completely peeled of bark; no doubt by Indian horses: they might be called Nebraska corn-cobs—and are particularly scarce too.

We saw two deer and some hares in the course of our day's wanderings; the result perhaps of some eccentricity, or misfortune. This last explains, at least, the presence of a famished squaw and two children, whom we surprised hiding from us near our camp ground. Some animals have an instinctive fear of strangers, but not of *their* kind,—this human fear of *their* kind—this natural mental impulse,—mark inferiority of mind to instinct? Or, that mind makes us more fearfully savage than brutes?

But to their story,—which without a word of language in common, we gathered from the language of signs; (perhaps other animals do the same). The children, about eight years old, are the daughter and nephew of the squaw; she is an Arapaho, but married among the Arickaras;

her husband with four lodges of that nation were attacked near the Missouri River by the Dahcotahs; the men were all slain, and their families made prisoners, or slaves; but she, from friendship to her native tribe, was liberated eighteen days ago; and was provided with a small pack of provisions, a dog to carry it, and a fire-steel; (now that is a scale of outfit that would please the most stingy quartermaster, or travelling husband extant!) Her provisions being exhausted, she fell upon a military expedient, of eating the "transportation"—generally oxen and mules with us, but the dog is quite as good; (I once knew a sergeant to starve three days before he could make up his mind to kill a favorite mule which he had ridden a thousand miles: a kind of prejudice or instinct—often the same thing—which I admired). The dog, then, was killed for food; and some of it is still on hand; and since we have fed them to an amount that would be dangerous to a white, they have returned to the dog, which is certainly well singed, but rare to a fault—usually the case with the game course. If they survive such high living, they will be sent to-morrow to Laramie, in the charge of a dragoon.

June 20th.—We marched yesterday but fifteen miles: being greatly impeded by the stout artemisias, and little hillocks of rubbish washed by overflows or flooding rains about their roots and stems. We passed a wonderful place, apparently a great basin, near a mile through, where an adventitious mass of white clay and sand, granitic sandstone, trap-rock and friable conglomerates,—black, yellow, and gray,—had been the sport of rain and flood; there were all shapes, mathematical and fantastical; among ruined towers and pyramids, we passed over hard smooth plains, level and inclined, of a dazzling whiteness; which, with the infernal heat and dust, had quite a dizzy and bewildering effect; there was no token, not a reminiscence there, of animal or vegetable life. If any but a dragoon or an Indian in great straits has ever been there, or shall ever return,—and it shall have the slightest use of a name,—that name I give and patent, "The Devil's Adobe Yard."

Our progress was suddenly arrested by the unfordable river, and a precipitous bluff, which was pronounced utterly impracticable for wagons. It was a nearly cubic mass of iron ore one hundred feet high; but as it was *necessary*, we got over; and enjoyed too, a fine view of the Southern Mountains and their majestic Laramie Peak. The country began there to show a tinge of green, which attracted some straggling buffaloes and antelopes: and there we first saw a bird unknown to us, but called here, we find, "sage-hens;" they are fine game, and probably a species of grouse; but they have a much longer tail, carried differently, and are so large, that we at first mistook them for turkeys.

A poor fellow shot himself in the arm that afternoon, and suffered amputation.

This morning we left our surgeon and a small party to return slowly to the Fort, in care of the wounded dragoon.

We then crossed back to the south side of the river, and have had a long march; enjoying an unusual variety of scenery and incident. We were forced into the hills again, which were smooth, and found ourselves near the forest clad mountains at the south: we came down to a fine stream, with groves (so beautiful for their rarity); and here some buffalo came dashing down a long slope beyond, and to the pleasure of this unlooked-for change of scenery, was added the excitement of lively action,—for many dashed off to the chase; the game took various directions, and ran long and with much incident; and in this vast wild amphitheatre we watched them with intense interest.

There are times thus, on the dullest march,—and in the dullest life elsewhere,—when, as by accident, a general excitement comes as the sudden whirlwind when the sun is reigning with the calmest tyranny; delightfully refreshing, like a shower to drooping flowers, they give our souls new spirit and power to rise from the moral drought of routine and dull material life.

But our creek had little grass; and so we ascended to high hills again, while over the mountains to the south-east rolled dark thunderclouds, which threw a purple, a strange and mysterious light, on the wild scenery; the storm seemed to pursue us; but suddenly, in a bright gleam of sunshine, we looked down upon the welcome river, and struck at last the welcome road. But then we saw another storm, coming from the northwest, and this gave us some dashing rain; but soon all was bright and calm again; and at length we were gladdened with the view of Deer Creek, whose little forests made it doubly inviting. And on entering them we surprised two deer, which were shot as they ran. And fat deer they were, poor fellows!

It is half-past nine at night. The storms, the labors, and the excitements of the day are over; all have enjoyed the food which toil has sweetened; and many the soothing pipe; the horses graze quietly around at the pickets; the camp-fires burn irregularly through the woods; weather-beaten troopers are grouped about them, silently drying their fresh meat on little scaffolds and boughs;

—leafy domes, supported by natural pillars, which art has imitated, are illumed here and there by the fitful firelight;—some sprays of foliage now and then catch and throw back bright gleams from the solemn obscurity;—the broad moon has risen and begins to silver some tree tops, which are gently stirred by the light airs, that waft over the deep azure the fleecy fragments of the shattered storm-clouds; harmonious now is the tree-frog's monotone,—in all this is the spirit of beautiful repose; the *true* harmony and economy of Nature, which at night renovates her creations by universal sleep.

Sleep has its fearful dreams,—Night its storms,—man his passions: God over all, in *all* has wonderfully mingled Good and Evil.

CHAPTER XII.

June 20th, '45.—We marched to-day twenty-seven miles to the crossing-place of the Platte River. In all this distance there was grass but at two spots; and few buffalo were seen.

I was riding near the head of the column, over the bare prairie, when suddenly, within twenty yards, up sprang a grizzly bear! He ran about eighty paces, threw himself about, and stood some moments gazing at us with his head high raised. "Grizzly bear!" was shouted down the column, and gave an impulse to the true hunters, which strongly tested the punctilios of discipline: a half dozen of us spurred to instant pursuit: away we galloped, toward the mountain, at greater than buffalo speed.

That bold hunter, Capt. M., the foremost, headed and turned the bear—round a slight swell—when some of us suddenly met it; whereupon, a dragoon's horse, in great fright, gave its rider a tremendous fall; his danger added new excitement,—several shots were instantly fired, and a ball fortunately striking its shoulder, turned off the furious beast toward the river; near it, he took refuge in a very small hammock, where Capt. M. very rashly followed. The bear then came at him with expanded jaws and a savage roar, which sent the horse about with a desperate leap, which made the saddle pommel tear open the Captain's vest to his chin! The bear then dashed on, into the river, where, at twenty paces, a load of large shot was fired into the back of his head, with no apparent effect; three men followed him there, and might have killed him, as he ascended with difficulty the opposite bank; but he escaped into an almost impenetrable thicket of plum bushes, where, it being very extensive, we sought for him in vain.

It was a singular thing, that the moment the bear sprang up before us, near the same spot a very large and perfectly coiled rattlesnake began so loud and threatening a rattle as to divide the attention of many with his bearship.

A hare shot to-day, although quite poor, weighed seven and a half pounds; the legs were twelve inches long. I supped on a "sage-hen," which I shot with my pistol; its quality and flavor seemed to partake of both the grouse and chicken.

June 22d.—Independence Rock.—Yesterday we forded and left the Platte, to turn confused masses of mountains with picturesque red-rock precipices, which there begin to wall it in; it is called the Red Butes. We passed one spring, with a little grass, about half way of our march of twenty-seven miles to another. The last half was the most desolate and wild region we had seen: high plains where there was nothing but clay or sand, and a few stunted, dusty artemisias, interspersed with great rock-hills of dark volcanic appearance. We had to dispute possession with buffalo, of the small well-cropped oasis where we encamped; and with another grizzly bear, which we routed out at dusk, after it had greatly alarmed the horses.

About five o'clock this morning we were in the saddle, anxious—with the famed Sweet Water for our goal—to finish the remaining twenty-five miles of desert. We passed several springs, with a little grass, bog, and some plum bushes; as we neared the river, the country grew more wildly barren; there was a great plain of white sand, and here and there, of glittering *Epsom Salts!* Amid the mirage and white dust, and the dizzy glow of reflected light and heat, which nearly turned the brain, I have still in my mind's eye a kind of vision of the indomitable hunter, Capt. M., scudding over far black slopes, which seemed themselves in wavy motion, fiercely pursuing flying buffalo: it was a rivalry of all the German extravagance of their favorite legend of the wild huntsman. The facts seem simple, but there was an unnatural strangeness, a suffocating, alarming heat in the dazzling plains, and the black hills, that gave a dreamy confusion and doubt to realities. Did then the strange mirage cheat the senses with apparitions of a desperate hunter, on that wonderful gray horse, pursuing black monsters, far, far, and indistinctly into the glowing haze?

After all, we knew it was Ben. M. or the devil! But it had always been said that he would follow a buffalo to the abode—left to that imagination which here seems realized.

But onward moved our silent procession; each followed the whitened horse before him; nothing more could then be seen; and expiring fancy and distressing fact were shadowing forth together the prospect of numerous equestrian statues of salt—and none of us looked back—which might figure in our unhappy history; when, presto, a puff of good-natured air blew pain, and dust, and doubt away! We were on a verdant sod, laved by a crystal stream. Close at hand was Independence Rock—a little mountain of granite.

Ah! not long, bright Sweet Water! did we refrain thy tempting embrace: thou wert a Lethe to the desert behind; all illusion faded from the delightful realities of thy bath.

The rarity and dryness of this air is proved in an ancient buffalo skull, with the ears an inch thick, hide dried and preserved.

It is near midnight. Silence reigns in the desert; but now and then come the cries of wolves from the mountains. They give an almost supernatural tone to these solemn solitudes. The repose which twenty hours of excitement and toil demand, is banished. Hark! how they howl! Be grandly dreary, and ye will be attuned to the heart! Yes, never better to a sentimental girl the gentlest breathings of an Æolian harp. Ah! how very doleful is that plaint! Never, *never*, the doleful! Give me the placid calm in which the soul may revel with fairy creations, adorned by all the flowers of thought—or proud action, the storm of wild and passionate will. The gilded and painted memory, or fierce oblivion.

Come, O sleep! thou luxury to the happiest; thou matchless blessing to those that may not be comforted. Come deathlike; profound as Adam's first. Fated progenitor! Then from near thy soft heart, sprang its resistless enemy, evermore armed against the peace of thy unhappy sons! Nay, the very angels surrendered Heaven, and trembling, yielded to her arms.

June 25th.—Independence Rock, which we left yesterday morning, is about one hundred and twenty feet high, and a thousand long; it is the first appearance of a strange ridge of granite masses, near a hundred miles long, which stand in the midst of a great plain, in a direction perpendicular to that of the Rocky Mountains. The Sweet Water for nearly half its course, from the South Pass to the Platte, runs near its southern base.

Some of its dome-like elevations are about 1500 feet high; apparently no tree or shrub,—no beast or bird relieves its stern and lifeless gray; its monumental solemnity. For how many ages, since its upheaval by the primitive fires, has it stood—changeless in summer heats and wintry storms—in untrodden solitude; in awful silence!

But the "Rock" is isolated; and I rode ahead several miles over a plain, yesterday morning, hoping to surprise a chamois or "bighorn," at the "Devil's Gate," the actual extremity of the ridge.

So named, perhaps, by some earnest believer in Satanic grandeur, it is in truth the gateway chosen (for its romantic beauty, I should say) by that fair and gentle offspring of mountain dell, the better-named Sweet Water; for, we practical mortals led our martial train with peaceful ease by a much gentler portal to its valley—a smooth gap of prairie hill. Whether thus formed in the cosmical throes of nature—river and sundered rock together—or, whether the waters dammed and falling, wore away the softer trap-rock vein through the granite, less resisting than the hill of stubborn argil and gravel—so it is, the stream here finds an outlet through a profound and narrow chasm in vertical granite.

There are vegetable and mineral attractions and repulsions. The elm-twig distorts itself, turning short back to avoid the contact of the locust: the parasite selects the noblest oak, which trails its tender foliage high over the many self-dependent neighbors, as the tenderest woman oft chooses the most sturdy and rugged mate; and certain it is, this merry little river, whose sparkling waters often demurely purl over golden sands, this very coquette of all the mountain offspring, if it ever approaches the fir-clad mountains of soft, inviting blue, turns suddenly back; leaves, too, the grassy bed of the valley, and cleaves to the stern rocks: nay, as if for love, or strong excitement sake, now and then it enters their very heart, which seems to open to embrace it; and thus, careless of the dry and melancholy plain, goes sporting through their stony bed in fierce or joyous triumph: and then for change again, it comes quietly forth, more deep and staid and with an innocent smile to the bosom of the tame and neglected valley. But I have left the "Gate" to describe the walls and interior.

My first delight being calmed, I secured my horse and slung my rifle—that I might better clamber with both hands, and alone with Nature ascended instinctively to a happily selected niche of this her favorite temple. Alone! O, who among men would choose more than one witness to such an interview!

I was a hundred feet up, and well within the crooked

chasm: all breathless, I cast my eyes first upward to the grand walls, still three hundred feet above, and approaching in dim perspective; for crowning evergreens formed nearly an arch; as if offering a link of beauty to the stern masses, frowning gloomily above the abyss which had sundered them forever.

Below, the waters roared as if to gather courage to dash amongst the shapeless rocks; boiling angrily, they increased by their misty spray the dizzy awe of the downward view. With a slight pause or two, they reflect a gleam of light, which relieves but heightens the majestic solemnity of effect; and then seem to hurry forth from the dread labyrinth, to meet gladly again the light of day.

I have stood on Marshall's Pillar, overhanging New River nine hundred feet; I have studied Harper's Ferry from every point; but Devil's Gate, with its solemn calm profound, enrapts the mind with a spell which no glare of day comes to break; and has so striking a unity in its grandeur, that it must receive the meed of sublimity.

From the granite range, five or six miles to a parallel mountain ridge at the south, is called the "Valley," of the Sweet Water; it is, in fact, chiefly one slope of barren hill, whose sands and gravel are only redeemed from nakedness by melancholy artemisias and absinthia; to the north of the granite, the country is flat and more valley-like; I should say then, that the granite was erupted in the centre of a valley in the very course of the Sweet Water.

This afternoon we stopped in the opening of a romantic pass, where the river was narrowly confined by little mountains of rock, to leave a small party with the weakest horses to await our return. Two hunters, who had been sent after buffalo, joined us there with trophies, but with the uneasy haste of a retreat: they had found a grizzly bear with three cubs, and had managed to kill one and had taken a second alive; but then the furious dam had given them a chase, which they dared not stop to encounter, on ground broken by large sage bushes: so they had gladly brought off, as a compromise, the two cubs;—the live one, exhausted by the chase and the excessive heat, seemed dead, and they laid it in the edge of the water; a crowd of men were gathered closely around, when suddenly the little beast assumed vigorous life with so fierce a growl, as to disperse his spectators like a bombshell.

We had left the road of loose sand, and now attempted more directly to pass the defile: above us, six or eight hundred feet, great shapeless rocks, piled loosely, or suspended on inequalities of the parent mass, threatened to fall, as many had done before; these, scattered about in the sparkling rapids, and among the rosebushes of the narrow bank, nearly barred our passage; but we fortunately accomplished it. Soon after we emerged on a little green level—still between the mountain precipices—we surprised a flock of chamois passing from one to the other: before we were well recovered from our own surprise they had accomplished their object; but immediately several hunters were scaling the granite in pursuit; and a lucky one reached gunshot distance,—when his carbine awoke from silence echoes which had never found a voice. Wounded or not, the goats, which on reaching their native rocks had regained an easy confidence, seemed now winged by terror, and skimming the almost vertical slopes and fearful precipices of smooth naked granite, with a daring velocity which was wonderful, admirable, incredible! I cannot express the thrilling and delightful surprise it gave us.

We ascended then a long, sandy slope, still between granite; the reflection was blinding—the heat scorching; there was no sensible perspiration, owing to the rapidity of evaporation; but clouds brought shadows to our relief, and never too was toil sooner forgotten. At the top we paused insensibly, and all gathered there, first to behold and gaze excitedly at the glittering summits of the Rocky Mountains. Their sharp pyramids of snow seemed to penetrate,—or all sun-lit—were sublimely relieved by the dark clouds. We descended to find a level camp ground on the Sweet Water; and the telescope now reveals faintly many more pinnacles penetrating dim, airy space, beyond the eye's power to catch the bright reflections of their snow mantles. Like phantoms they seem, mysteriously shadowing forth an unknown land,—a new world.

Near the camp, rising from the greensward, stands a solitary rock of granite: it is two hundred feet high. I ascended and sat long musing there—not alone, for I found company in a single shrub which strangely flourished near the very top.

I am little curious in little things, and seldom in any manner "play the devil" (to which *they* often lead so wonderfully); but in this stilted position, I was a daylight Asmodeus: the doings of all the little world below were open to a glance; and owing to the strangely ascending quality of sound, which I had observed before, I could hear all their uttered thoughts; at four hundred yards remarks came distinctly, to which the person addressed at twenty paces, answered "What?" I lingered until the torches of some *ex tempore* fishermen, with spears or gigs, warned me that my descent was becoming perilous.

CHAPTER XIII.

JUNE 27th.

> "Reposing from the noontide sultriness,
> Couched among fallen columns"—

"How pleasant thus to repose at high noon, of the long hot day, on a bearskin in the deep shadow of our willow; and in full view of the eternal snows, which send this crystal tide with its delightful verdure!"

Friend.—This green valley gave us all the pleasure of an unlooked-for discovery—the charm of a surprise.

"Pleasure generally flies a studied plan. I like too to take misfortune at short notice."

Friend.—As the poor buffalo yesterday did theirs; so, their last mouthful of grass was sweet!

"Did you not regret to dispossess them! They seemed to leave with a real reluctance; but so great a herd must soon have finished our forage."

Friend.—I cannot remember when we rested before! but we had all the *trouble* of a march, to come three miles! Well, it gave us a good appetite for breakfast.

"Not very necessary after the frosty night. But our quiet discussion of trout and buffalo steak, was a good introduction to repose and a pipe.

"How beautifully those light clouds float along from the east, wafted by the gentle airs that just give music to the leaves over head. Ye far wanderers! are ye messengers from that busy world? If so, pass on; and those white summits—those representatives of Nature's simplicity, will receive you quite unmoved!

"What is the world to us? Not much more than we to them!

'Let the wide arch of the ranged empire fall!
Here is my space.'"

Friend.—Well, the poet for once is right; so I feel now, at any rate.

"Is it possible, Friend, and he in *love!*—for, listen,—he adds,—

'Now for the love of Love, and her soft hours,
Let's not confound the time with conference harsh:
There's not a minute of our lives should stretch
Without some pleasure now.'"

"I rather think there is nothing worth living for beside Love, Music, and War."

Friend.—And a pipe; for what content, you heathen, does it not now give you! And the beauty of this sparkling but calm morning is something to live for, and gratefully too.

"Beauty! I worship beauty! I enjoy it in the tiny flower—it charms me in the bright spring landscape, where Nature has kindly played the artist, or in the sunset clouds which methinks good angels paint in heaven's own colors; it enchants me in smiling eyes and lips wreathing their divine intelligence into a halo of love!"

Friend.—Bravo!

"Thus love at last, as love at first—all absorbing—feeding upon music,—sporting with war;—love, the link of earth to heaven,—love is all in all!"

(*Friend.*—He must have been reading Saint John!)

"The beauty, then, which now soothes me momentarily, is but a sweet minister to the soul—to which absence is the doomed evil, but space immaterial—and leads it with a melancholy joy, to the imaginative communion of love."

Friend.—You are a monomaniac, by Jove! incapable of argument, or even conversation.

"I detest argument! it is the favorite resort of fools, to convince—themselves.

"I am only in a mood; buoyant and bitter; tameless as the Arab coursing his native desert; free as yonder soaring eagle! it's this wild mountain air! Let us have a fling at tho world,—the poor dollar-dealing sinners, cooped up in their great dens—"

Friend.—But you began by a fling at me—

"Only a *love* tap, Friend; *my* way of argument. Let us with the desert's freedom joyously flout convention and opinion—upstart usurpers!—let us make mocking sport of the prosaic solemnity of ignorant prejudice;—let us shoot popguns, at least, against the solid bulwarks where folly and selfishness sit enthroned!"

Friend.—Then fire away—though hang me if I know what you would be at.

"You are so practical! Well, I mean that fanatics, hypocrites, and malicious gossips generally rule society: sometimes under the cloak of religion, sometimes as envious, presumptuous censors, they intimidate the true and innocent, who resist not, nor despise,—but slavishly cower before their unblushing falsehood: thus, all pure simplicity of manners, all the most private and sacred relations of life are blurred by their foul intrusion. I mean, too, that life is burdened with a thousand artificial cares and anxieties; the growth of envy, jealousy, and folly, the prolific brood of another arch-tyrant, fashion."

Friend.—Well! what care we in this honest wilderness! Care for nothing you cannot help, is the sum of my philosophy.

"But who lives who may not be wounded through another!—Then so be it! let us treat the whole world as it has done us, and—forget it! I dare say, that beyond some family ties, there is not upon the wide earth a heart in sympathy with our good or ill; whose even beat would be as much disturbed, were this wild sod to cover us forever, as at the most ephemeral of the trifling cares which make up their petty lives."

Friend.—At *last* you have struck a chord that answers as to the touch of truth! And as for love, 'tis but the poet's wildest fancy,—or passion's thin disguise: it soon tires; or, lasts so long as *interests* bind.

"Too bad! too bad!—I say it is the divinity within us! warmed indeed by heaven-bestowed beauty, and humanity's other noblest attributes,—but clinging to immortality with earnest hope.

"There is a pure soul love,—a deathless friendship, which all life's trials and worldly baseness cannot soil or sap.

"If *that* were truth, better never to look into her Medusa face; better to cherish illusion: blind credulity would be heroism! ay,—and policy,—like that of the great Cortez, who burnt the proofs of a conspiracy, rather than foster damning doubt."

Evening.—In this day of rest, each has followed his bent; some, headed by Capt M. of course, have wandered to the stony and hot hills, seeking the excitement of hunting;—others fish; (still worse, but *de gustibus;*) others sleep away the day. As for myself, with my pipe and pen, and my plum bush—my occupation appears. Nothing disturbs me, but that a luckless brood of magpies inhabit *my* plum bush. Heavens! how they chatter! How querulously and fiercely they chatter! No girl-school could equal it. I shall assuredly skin, and stuff, at least one of them; or slit its tongue—which might make the matter worse.

This same plum bush is a singular affair: its stems are three feet through,—so closely wound together, that little is wanting to a solid mass: but the half are dead,—and on their dry limbs hangs the wool of buffalo, rubbed off yesterday.

The bright Sweet Water, giving in the morning strong indications of a devious and capricious course, we yesterday reluctantly resigned her cheerful company, and betook ourselves to her companions, the hills; in the hope, however—which was not disappointed—that we should find something new and pleasing in their more serious company.

After a delightful drink of the water of a little green bog, which has masses of ice near its surface (and without accounting for this strange fact, I will merely mention that hot as it is by day, water froze last night in my tent), we gradually ascended what seemed a vast plain;—the granite masses began to disappear;—to the left, the blue mountains became prairie hills; the snow-clad Wind River Peaks were steadily before us. We exchanged loose sand for a gravel soil; for some soil there is, with a scant yellow grass;—but mosses are more common: the universal wild sage is thinner and smaller;—heathcock and hares have nearly disappeared—there is, instead, a brownish rabbit,—and curlews too, whose wild cries are well atone with the scenery. About mid day we were ascending a very dry hard road—as it seemed—when we met a stream of water!—making a deliberate, but very sure progress. It was not much, perhaps, "for a new country," but I thought it remarkable. Then we found buffalo, and had a good old-fashioned and successful chase. We were on very high ground, and the scenery was noble; far away toward the left, to the south of the Pass—that giant gateway to the western continent—the mountains rising again in forbidding grandeur;—great plains in front, which might lead to the new ocean, but in part relieved by towering mountains, glittering with snow down nearly to our level;—while more to the right, a majestic table bluff seemed there to bound the earth.

But suddenly, with a delightful surprise, we looked down into the smiling face and bosom of our little coquette, Sweet Water, all renewed in grace, and blooming in a glittering dress of green: absence gave appreciation and zest to the meeting. She was now in a sweet secluded valley, three miles long, on which high stony hills, everywhere walling it in, frowned in vain. She only smiled the more!

And its attractions had gathered there a vast herd of buffalo, which surprised us as much—so unusual have such become. But here comes my Friend again:—well, rest is evidently not a time for dull narrative.

Friend.—Most industrious of scribblers, I give you good evening! How charming, for a change, is our old friend, Siesta! I hope the beautiful nymphs of this happy valley—if they suffice you—hovered over your dreams. But, in truth, I think you dream all day (when no wild bull is afoot). Hast thou, most favored mortal, tempted an Egeria from her sacred fountain and grove to meet thee, where others groan in very spirit, in the hot and dusty stony barrens!

"You are quite overpowering! *Your* dreams surely were spirituous. But a truce to day-dreams; light as they are, the whole world granteth them not a foundation spot!"

Friend.—(*He has turned the tables.*) Well, the Captain has got back; and has had an interesting excursion. He went a dozen miles over—or down—to the Wind River (or a branch), which he says is a thousand feet lower than this; and that the mountains, to which it gives its name, appear from thence far more lofty and grand.

"I am sorry I did not go! Is it not water of the Yellowstone?"

Friend.—Yes; but first of the Big Horn, which takes its name from your "chamois"—they are all goats—*that* is a fork of the Yellowstone. But is not this a sweet valley! I have bathed in the beautiful little river, where it is five feet deep; the sands seemed of gold,—and on the bank I found ripe strawberries.

"They have a story of Capt. B., whose travels this way were published, that he spent a day or two here, collecting the yellow mica sand, in the belief that it *was* gold. But while you have been indulging in the beautiful, which I hope stirred somewhat the poetical element, —which exists perhaps in all, and is dormant in few elevated minds,—I have found in the rugged hillside food for thought at least;—the impression of a sea-shell in limestone;—this, at the top, or rather at the *base* of the Rock Mountains (for this South Pass, sixty miles wide, has not the characteristics of a mountain,—is merely the highest steppe of the continent), is a fruitful subject for palæontological research, if such be not without the pale of your practical system."

Friend.—Bah! your modern geognosy is a humbug! or, too deep, at least, for a wandering dragoon. Now, would you go about determining the age of the formation from your knowledge of the shell? or give *it* physiological gradation from your profound knowledge of superposition of strata?

"I might do either; for knowledge throws a reflected light. If I know this to be a mollusc of an existing species, could I not infer that it was a comparatively late eruption that threw up this mountain and the incumbent limestone?"

Friend.—I am decidedly non-committal; but it is enough to ruffle one, to have such a long word thrust at him, amid all the charm of a complete *laisser aller* in a glorious wilderness, a thousand miles from all the schools of pedantic, groping, and guessing philosophy.

"But, good heavens! do not condemn a word for its length. Palæontology is an almost poetical triumph, which throws an attractive grace over the sterility of geognostic investigation. As we eagerly decipher the inscriptions and symbols on the human tombs, which throw beams of startling light over the obscurity of fabulous antiquity;—so, when we discover the traces or remains of the extinct life of the old world, *their* natural tombs—the fossil rocks—are monuments by which Time thus records their relative ages."

Friend.—Allow me then a few years of devotion to the study of the analysis of primitive zoology and botany, and I will then, if possible, give you my speculations with all the boldness of *poetical* science upon the formation and age of the continent—all by the light of your chronological, fossiliferous, infernal shell!

"I understand you:—*Ne sutor ultra crepidam.*"

Friend.—You do, indeed; for it is my decided opinion that you have a profound—smattering of the subject.

"Candid! Would you prefer discussing 'sacred fountains and groves?'"

Friend.—That, ingrate, was only to flatter a little, for once, your humor, your "mood,"—which, in all its tenses, I should call the *doubtful.*

"Well, Diogenes, let us meet on middle ground; did you notice yesterday that grand level-topped bluff? others perhaps scarcely looked at it,—to me it was sublime! I cannot tell why,—but even with the snow-peaks in view, it seemed the summit of the earth."

Friend.—Perhaps it was the strong impression of massiveness, which its great extent added to its really grand elevation!

"There may be something in that. To tell the truth, it reminded me of a feature of Niagara; that scene of hackneyed sublimity, of which it is supposed that nothing new can be said or written. But it was the rapids, and not the falls,—whose smooth descent the eye measures by the banks, that impressed me most, and with an effect that I certainly have not heard or read of. Standing on the Canadian side, much below the falls, in full view of the rapids, in all the foaming majesty of their long rocky descent, I could see nothing beyond—nothing between them and the sky, whose glittering light clouds seemed blended with their bright foam and spray. Then came with the strong semblance, the sublime idea that the mighty flood was rolling forth continually from the high heavens!"

CHAPTER XIV.

JUNE 30th, 1845.—Camp in Oregon.—In three days we have come but thirty-seven miles through these lofty, barren solitudes, with no very remarkable features differing from those already described. Too barren to attract many buffalo, we find in the pretty little green valleys of the Sweet Water, where we occasionally touch it, fresh buffalo-grass, on which our horses are sensibly recruiting. The stream rises daily, after noon, about six inches—from melting snow—and falls as much at night, when we generally have a black frost. Every day showers of rain or snow fall on the mountains, the former far down the great slopes.

Willow bushes still abound in the little bends of the Sweet Water; but we have not seen above half a dozen trees since we left the Platte. There are a few antelopes, which are very tame; and heathcocks: several have been killed weighing five pounds.

We make it 281 miles from Fort Laramie, and 850 from Fort Leavenworth: the country from Laramie here I would describe in general terms, as a sandy and very hilly desert, difficult for loaded wagons, and with scant grazing for the teams.

At noon to-day we left the Sweet Water, and came over the South Pass: the ascent is gentle and quite smooth, to a slight gap in the prairie; to the west the descent is rather more rapid, two or three miles to a spring branch, which runs into Green River, a fork of the Coloradò. We are in camp on the edge of a narrow trembling bog, which scarcely bears a horse; but he must venture for food.

There is a lofty bluff rising from the camp, whose level top extends to the actual pass, and slightly commands it: from it, the view west is extensive, and over a decidedly champaign country; it resembles the figuration of drifted snow: more to the north, the white-topped mountains can be seen for at least a hundred miles: they make near us a turn eastward; and just there is the spring of the Sweet Water, which thus rises at the west of some of the highest peaks: to one standing on the spot, its undecided course seems much inclined toward the Pacific.

A kildeer and sparrow are the only living creatures which we have seen in this mountain edge of Oregon.

To-morrow we march to return; thus drinking, two days in succession, both of the Atlantic and Pacific waters. We have now the 5000 emigrants to meet; and worse, their 5000 cattle, which, we fear, have left little for our horses.

Night—on the lofty bluff overlooking the South Pass.

How solemn is the night! Silence and solitude—eldest born of time—reign unquestioned.

Calmly sleeps the moonlight on the gray earth, which no green thing proclaims is not a wreck,—a monument of life extinct. The winds sleep too; their wings are motionless,—there is no whisper in the air: shadow has taken to her embrace the unhappy wanderers that sleep below. Those mountain pyramids of gleaming snow point mutely to the stars, which, radiant in solemn motion, alone speak of Life and Hope!

Oh, Life! thou unsought mystery, that springs from nothingness, to grasp at Eternity.

Eternity! Awful shadow! incomprehensible Dread!

On whose black threshold the spirit shrinks shuddering, —till Hope comes,—like the star in the east.

A continent is spread beneath me: a new world in ocean midst: the great ocean, at whose ever-heaving surge—typing infinity—man trembled and forbore many thousand years: but at the appointed hour, Fate led him by the hand; he came—and truly found all new: the perennial life and death of changeless vegetation; and the new red race. For three hundred years he has labored to subdue the untamed vigor of the primeval curse.

And now, he who of old would scale Heaven with a tower, climbs here with his burden of discontent, vainly seeking rest in timeworn deserts. Yes! now he would scale these venerable heights, which storm and rain have furrowed—fructifying other lands: the continent's hoary head, the mark for battling thunders, since Lightning brooded over the great deep!

How oft, O Moon! has yon snow-shining spire marked its shadows on this lofty dial? How long since erupted from ocean, they were cast upon the face of the waters? And how long since the plains arose,—in whose warm and gaseous slime grew monster forests,—now whelmed and burnt to coal.

Speak! thou pale and silent witness; tell of Earth's throes,—when a continent had birth: tell when the Storm-power chose these solemn mountain-towers, piercing the sky-mists, for his throne? and his sublime laboratory of river-feeding rain; his fire-created and blasted, but icy throne!

Tell when Nature's poor red child came, and with dawning mental light, obscured by superstition, first trembled at the feet of these granite monuments of the new creation!

Calm, and beautiful, and serene! thou floatest on unanswering, with thy bright companions,—the starry hosts which sang together before the face of God, ere Earth-time began; but twin-born with earth, chained thou art to her,—though—like hope—thou soarest with the stars! And, sweet companion, goest thou? Must Earth's chill horizon hide thy heavenly face? must the icy barriers of destiny now break—mayhap forever—the strong spell which bound us? Must my solitude, whence I worshipped thee afar, be so darkened?

Nay, inconstant! how smilingly thou wilt shed thy light on happier ones!

And lo! She kisses the icy mountain; and now, the farewell ray, comes calm—careless—cold. * *

And strong Darkness reigns! How awful her presence, here on the Storm-throne!

Child of clay! descend to the humble valley, and seek with thy kind sleep and forgetfulness.

CHAPTER XV.

July 1st.—Not reluctantly we turned, this morning, our backs upon Oregon, land of promise and fable. "Homeward bound!" "Lives there a wretch"—never so much a vagabond,—whose tongue was taught to lisp that honest, noble Saxon word—Home—whose heart it stirs not with an emotion which distance increases, and time cannot chill.

But to retrace one's steps is dull: dull even to the wilderness wanderer, to whom the face of Nature is all in all;

who seeks, by change and novelty, to charm away the sense of mere routine, fatigue, and privation.

The very trustworthy Mr. Fitz Patrick, our guide, has been much in Oregon; and he asserts that the country we have passed through, and consider uninhabitable, is less forbidding than it: some narrow river-grounds excepted. It seems the rule, that in very barren lands, the exceptions —very striking of course—should really make great amends: how far they lend imagination to general descriptions, depends upon veracity, judgment, and *interest.* The truth will out some day. It is certainly very difficult to return from Oregon: and the tales that are told may be like the blarney of the curtailed fox. It is said they remove thence to California; which would prove not much; for movers they will be to the end of the chapter.

We have collected numerous pets; beasts and birds; horned frogs, or lizards; plants and minerals; heathcocks—one weighing seven pounds—and hares have been skinned and stuffed: unfortunately, we have no arsenical soap; and since we left our surgeon and his stores,—not even corrosive sublimate: there is but one shot-gun—an unlucky one!—and the shot is expended; and we have had little opportunity: the expedition is military, and most rapid; and though less so for a few days past, uncertainty has prevented the gratification of the great desire of some of us to ascend a snow peak.

We came but thirteen miles; and in approaching our pleasant camp-ground on the river, surprised some buffalo, and slew four or five; poor beasts! they are now between two fires.

This upper Sweet Water needs not, I think, the grim hills for a foil, to be pronounced charming: with what gentle music does its swift waters—now o'er glittering sands, now amid rocks—break the dreary silence around! In what graceful curves does it sweep round, here a garden spot of currants and gooseberries, strawberries and clover; there, a little densely shaded thicket of willows. Heaven knows what Naiads may nestle there, in rarely disturbed enjoyment of beauty; but other airy —at least not imaginary—occupants are there, who rejoice in blood! Mosquitos of marvellous size! But fortunate we are in blanket-enduring mornings and evenings, which silence their war-notes and chill their wings.

July 2d.—We have marched twenty-two miles to-day, over the hills of sand, and gravel, and rock, and sleep once more in that sweet valley which had so extraordinary attraction, that we made two camps in its three miles. A west wind, fresh from the snows, was cool; but the dust of many horses' feet, which it bore with it, was a serious annoyance. I caught, at a little stream in the hills where we made a short stop, two half-grown heath-cocks: this was too good fortune to be thrown away; so we set to work immediately, and constructed of willow-twigs a very respectable cage: I shall try hard to get them home.

The Sweet Water enters this valley through a deep, narrow pass of several miles; the scenery very fine: but the "groves of cotton-wood and beech," of which we read, are but a sprinkling of birches and cotton-woods; the river is there inaccessible; but we vary from our old track, and now and then come upon something new, and pretty, too; and some wild horses this morning were the first we have seen.

Our valley is still brighter than before; the mountain showers have visited it: what could resist its attractions!

July 3d.—Almost with reluctance, we turned our backs

this morning upon the smiling meadows, the plums and willows which surrounded the camp; and although our faces were homeward, we were rather dolefully absorbed, as usual, with present littleness—I mean with the twenty-five miles of dreary, hot hills before us—when suddenly we met our friends, the emigrants—the foremost company; they were well and thriving, as the foremost generally are—but had "slept out"—of water; having travelled thirteen hours without reaching it.

I saw a poor woman weeping. The sight of our return! the home! the friends behind! the wilderness before!

We have received a favorable account of our party left with the poorest horses and beef-cattle, which are but eight miles below us this evening. We have been solely dependent upon game since we left them.

July 4th, 1845.—The parole is Independence—countersign, Liberty. Glorious words, and a glorious day! It was glorious in the "Continental Congress" to declare the colonies independent, and sign their names to it: more glorious than some of the after-conduct of the constituent States. There was a great deal of baseness, of intrigue, of money-seeking; a great deal of faltering in the revolutionary war: and the more glorious was it to those who withstood all; and particularly in the South, where they were fewer, and had to resist the Tories and the slaves, added to British power. But to Connecticut, of all the States, is due the fame of preserving from the beginning, her chartered democracy; the others surrendered theirs, and became subject to the will of the base Stuarts.

Our independence achieved was due—first to Washington—be his name and memory freshly embalmed, ever on this glorious day! Secondly, to the infatuation and imbecility of British generals; and thirdly, to French aid. Let those who ignorantly think that we would have succeeded without the assistance of the hereditary fool and despot—our friend Louis—turn to Sparks' Washington for convincing evidence to the contrary, as well as the Great Man's decided opinion.

Independence, Liberty, Equality,—brave words! Most nations now enjoy the first, but not in a commercial or social sense: Paraguay, barbarous and insignificant, under the late Dictator did, and Japan now, alone possesses it without this qualification—necessary to civilization. Other nations,—as England,—possess the first and second; but her liberty trenched upon, not by the monarch, but by the aristocracy, who make and administer the laws. France enjoys the first and third: and this blessing of equality in as high a degree, perhaps, as our boasted Republic; where a love for the distinction of titles is remarkable among all nations. And the Turks, too, have equality;—they are all equally slaves. The Russians are totally deprived of liberty and equality. (Why do not the fanatics of England make an abolition crusade against the white slavery there existing? Their interests do not prompt it;—we must address her fear.)

In China alone the government is ministered—theoretically at least—by an aristocracy of learning and virtue. Portugal and Spain are remarkable for their imperfect enjoyment of independence, while liberty and equality are both wanting.

But the Oregonians, and these emigrants thither,—pure democrats all, and independent as woodsawyers—are preeminent for equality and love of liberty. Last night, they asked the Colonel to fire a "big gun" this morning. He readily assented; they were delighted, and their spokesman exclaimed, "Do, and I will treat you all!" The Colonel replied, he drank nothing but Sweet Water (not even *eau sucré*).

Accordingly it was fired! and awoke echoes from the granite mountains that never had startled before the chamois themselves; and the shell exploding amid the far-off answers of rock to rock, produced a glorious confusion of sounds—more rare, if not more windy than all the orations of the day combined, and the inebriate, but hearty shouts of excited multitudes.

Then we marched, and as usual on this day found it exceedingly hot: the sunshine everywhere reflected by rock and white sand, might have barbecued an ox,—or at least killed a horse,—if exposed long enough.

We found our party where we left them; their horses a little, and the beeves *not* at all improved: but two buffalo had been killed, and two big-horns: one of the former, "the largest that ever was seen," received twenty-one shots; they have cured its scalp for me; no cushion is deeper or denser; it would make a fine winter saddle-cover, were it not too cumbrous. We came eight more miles by meridian; when, finding grass, the heat drove us to encamp.

Speaking of governments, Oregon is now, perhaps, the only pure democracy existing in Christendom (I have heard nothing of late of San Marino), and is practically independent:—may she so continue! The fear is, they cannot do so without us (as well as we without them). Let us only proclaim in their behalf—"Hands off, gentlemen!" in our biggest capitals of diplomacy; and, if needs be, fire the big guns too;—but in heaven's name let us fight on Christian ground; Oregon would be worse than Florida, and our contest with those Swamp Parthians, the

Seminoles. The only—*quasi*—colony we have is Liberia; and that is nearer than Oregon—in time. The Oregon railroad is, and will remain for half a century, a notable humbug: that over the Isthmus of Panama, or the Nicaragua canal, is the great hope, or work of our generation.

I have now visited the regal province of Canada;—the domain of democratic Oregon (three feet deep in the boggy "bowels of the land"); also the problematical regions of Texas (to whose revolutionary war my military "countenance" was willingly lent). I have visited, too, Mexico (horrid compound despotism of priest and soldier). I hope Texas will revisit her "province" of New Mexico, and give us an opening; for I long to have a hand in relieving the Mexican millions of the galling yoke of her grinding oppressors; a crusade worthy the banners of Liberty! (But the poor, ignorant devils, could they understand and keep freedom? Liberty, like manhood, requires education to be worthily worn.)

I have also visited the courts of very many "sovereign nations"—of Indians (where human nature is nearly as sophisticated as at other courts). Thus I am quite an American traveller, and might one day give the public the cream of my adventures; but as a titled and hirsute foreigner is the exclusive pet of us republicans,—so America is a subject that can in no way excite, interest, or tickle us, but through foreign malevolence and ignorance, or the delightful praise of cockney condescension. If the book be European, and larded with sonorous titles, —treat of antiquities (venerable in guide books),—of the stereotyped romance of ruins, converted by a prurient imagination from dens of robbers to seats of chivalry, and abodes of beauty,—then, all success to it!

How stale, flat, and *unprofitable* in comparison, the

primitive grandeur of our native land;—the sternest frowns and sweetest smiles of virgin Nature;—our beautiful prairies,—and sublime as ocean, on which the sun rises and sets in solitary glory;—our own glaciers and avalanches, cataracts and volcanoes—unknown, unnamed! And our independent red men (*gentlemen*, that never work), our Indian chieftains, who rise to power and influence solely by mind and daring;—democrats, but not the less distinguished by knightly bravery in numberless combats. They have genealogies too, *beyond all rooord* (older than William the Conqueror;—how often *was* England conquered?). Truly our never-conquered Indians offer noble subjects; it is a rare mine of romance, not wholly unworked. And the proud, dignified, and eloquent Indian—even surpassing the old knights in the romantic vigils and penal vows of *religion*—seldom falls so far short of romance as his white brother, the tame subject of civilization. But, alas! he *does* lack a vital element—devotion to women! But nature seems at fault, in so generally refusing them beauty; and gives him a poor excuse,—which white millions have not,—for the same beastly conduct.

All this shakes not our mental dependence—our foreign-fashion loving public taste. And then the infernal trash—much of it from the stews of Paris and London—utterly undersells us, to the almost total suppression of native labor; and to the robbery too of the best foreign authors, whose works would command a copyright.

So much for the Fourth of July,—and a dry one!

CHAPTER XVI.

July 5th.—We have paid to-day for our short ride yesterday; twenty-eight miles mostly over sand, ground to impalpable powder by the innumerable emigrants, whom we are meeting.

About four miles from the camp, we took a lingering, farewell look—at eighty miles—at the glittering snow-peaks.

I more particularly examined, this afternoon, the remarkable geology of the vicinity of Devil's Gate. The granite masses erupted for forty miles above, from the very bed of the river—but throwing it always to the south of the principal chain—here turn to approach the forest-covered ridge which bounds the valley on that side; but in thus leaving the river, they had stopped its course, but for the chasm, or "Gate," in some parts not more than forty feet wide. The road leads over a very narrow gap, a hundred feet high, commanded by the lofty granite;—on one side a chaotic pile of boulders, ten and twenty feet in dimensions, through which is a great vertical vein of trap-rock.

Thus liberated, the river enters a vast sunburnt plain; and, as if to take a last farewell of the romantic ridge, runs five or six miles to the foot of the solitary Independence Rock, thrown out like a grim sentinel upon the desert's boundary; then, as if warned of the salt and lava desolation beyond, turns again, and hastens to join the Platte, to aid in the evident struggle before it, with all the rocky powers of chaos and volcano.

Having thus, as from impulse, surrendered name and

identity, and the excited contest over, they emerge from the secret and sublime mountain passes, in dreary unity, upon the boundless flatness of barren plains,—though some fleeting enjoyment of flowery savannas succeeds—before both are lost in Missouri's dark and turbid flood.

Farewell to thee, then, sweet daughter of Mountain! Thou smile upon our mother's melancholy face! Go,—with thy bright and blithe innocence,—like many another victim;—go purling merrily when you may, ignorantly happy, to the dark course of thy destiny. Thus do the Fates spin our warped life-threads,—thus do we weave its chequered or sombre web!

The baggage to-morrow takes the road which we came, through the desert; and we are to explore our way to the most accessible point of the Platte, and thence follow it through the wild, romantic Buttes. We hope to find grass,—almost hopeless on the wagon route.

My poor heath-cocks are dead! They had begun to eat a little, and every care was taken with them; but they were untameable;—they seemed to pine for their native freedom, and to die broken-hearted.

I have got an ancient "big-horn," or chamois skull, with the horns, weighing eighteen pounds; but they are said to be quite small.

The emigrants are unexpectedly thriving. I saw, however, one poor woman, who had within a few days lost her husband, now driving a wagon. But it was somehow understood, that she was particularly desirous of an immediate successor to said husband and driver deceased;—or, for a conveyance back with us;—perhaps *both* boons would have been accepted.

I am told, that by the time our rear passes their companies, toward what they will ever consider their *homes*, the women generally are seen to weep. Heaven help them!

July 6th.—We took a course over a desert plain, and soon after found ourselves ascending a gentle slope; and so we continued for twelve or thirteen miles,—reaching insensibly a great elevation; and then—unexpectedly as suddenly, arrived at a precipice.

Then all press forward to the brink, absorbed or uttering exclamations of astonishment and delight. The nerves are thrilled with the sublimity of depth and space;—sight, without a barrier, seems to lead us over a just-discovered world. Recovered a little from our giddy surprise, the first object beyond the void of a thousand feet, which compels attention, is a rose-red wall of mountain height, to which a profusion of cedars gives a softening shade of beauty: then we begin to observe a circular amphitheatre, twelve miles over, where Nature in pleasant mood, seems to have scattered lavishly as carelessly, objects of beauty and grandeur; mountain and rock are colored as a flower-bed;—evergreens have been showered over them. Silvery gleams attract our sight—there is water—it is the river! In the midst of its secret, fierce course, a sweet glen has tempted it to a gentle pause on its soft bosom.

It is then a river valley! Truly, close to our right, through an unsuspected chasm of wondrous depth, the happy Platte, having been somewhere secretly united to Sweet Water, has come to meet us, as witnesses to its triumph, or sharers in the excitement of a pleasure tour.

Lowly, but bright and joyous in its life of motion and cumulative power, it advances, courting first all sweet and quiet recesses—yet daring all opposition to its wilful course. How we watch it now! Yonder, it sweeps in curves of beauty;—but suddenly lost, we gaze conjecturing where it may next appear; unexpectedly, it has paid a smiling visit to a grim mound, that stands modestly far aside; satisfied, it comes forth to new discoveries;—a determined barrier seems opposed; but carelessly yet, it sports in some little meadows which can scarce be seen. Then it advances more seriously to a green hill, which seems bent in homage. But no! Nothing less than the loftiest mountain of proud rock, must give it passage! and through a narrow—a sublime chasm, it fiercely rushes forth to new labyrinths beyond. That is the Hot Spring Gap; was earthquake then called to its *aid?*

I was charmed,—and lingered;—what time I know not. The guide had sought some possible winding or zigzag descent. The Colonel was at my side. I had heard him exclaim, "Poor Mac ought to have seen this!" When he called me to action, we dismounted and led our horses to follow the guide. I cannot tell how we got down;—there was a rocky chasm of a dry stream, or waterfall,—a ledge of rock now gave us a giddy path—the roots and branches of cedars now lent us support;—there were, momentarily, dangers, surprises—new beauties.

I was thinking why Nature had hid away since creation, as if in a secret storehouse, such treasure for sight and soul. We were discoverers: it is certain that white men had not been here. But then, her favored, untamed children! Ages back, their leading spirits had drunk in here the inspiration of noble thoughts, for eloquent expression or high resolve!

When fairly down,—near the river bank,—I looked back and saw the moving picture of men in long file, leading horses down the bright-colored face of the precipice. Beautiful! Now dapple grays are passing in front of blood-red wall, and blacks are relieved by white, or light gray rock;—parts of the long procession would disappear,—or, be dimly seen amid shrubbery; or would suddenly emerge from the concealment of some nook of clustered evergreens.

We had struck the river too high up;—and had soon to ascend again; and it was at forty-five degrees that we scrambled up one ridge of loose round stones, from the size for street-paving, to two feet in diameter;—then for miles along the face of precipice, by the narrow paths of buffalo. Soon after, forced to cross the river, nearly swimming, we came suddenly to a high steep mountain, sundered to the base, forming a chasm where the torrent forced to break desperately on shapeless rocks, gives ever to the sublime walls the echoes of its torment.

Unwillingly we turn away, to seek a circuitous outlet, guided by buffalo paths over a lower mountain of confused and many-shaped peaks. At the highest part two monstrous buffaloes suddenly met us in the way: the gaunt keepers of the pass paused in astonishment, and seemed to stare the question, "What did we there?" or, "Where *are* we safe?" thought they—if buffaloes think. But they were spared! Our pleased excitement as explorers brooked no interruption, or needed no addition. There we trod our path on beautiful feathery crystals of gypsum in red clay; and white and gray varieties resembling lava. Safely over, we again had to cross the river: it was very deep and muddy; for the sublimity of our passage through these fastnesses, where white man has rarely, if ever trod, was heightened by black clouds, thunder, and rain.

Then we were in another circular opening, or valley, fifteen miles wide, quite surrounded by mountains—the chosen abode of desolation and grim silence!

At the eleventh hour of our toils,—generally leading the horses,—we stopped for the night in a little open space by the river, where we rescued some dry grass from a gang of hungry buffalo; one of which maintained his ground until slain. We have had to-day, five alternations of cloudy coolness and rain, and oppressive heat.

I was joined, after our frugal supper of dried meat, at the watch-fire of the bivouac, by my Friend, who came, I suppose, to while a dull hour; but to give him his due, he brought up some coffee, and we made in tin cups refreshing and strong sleep-dispelling draughts.

"Heaven knows," he said, "why guards should watch in this valley of desolation, with world-forbidding battlements; we might sleep a month, safe from aught save grizzly bears."

We discussed our day's adventures;—disappointed of grass for the poor horses; but delighted with unexpected beauty and magnificence of scenery. We had evidently struck the Platte too high; much above where our only known preceding party had passed.

A busy time, he thought, for journalists; and wondered how I mustered industry or energy to write after great fatigues.

It was a pleasure, I told him:—often it occupied me while the difficult preparations of supper went on; or passed the dull hours of a night-watch; and of bright mornings I sometimes wrote, when others slept perhaps, the hour or two when horses were tended, breakfast got, and baggage packed. But new and beautiful scenery, though never tiring to the eye, I began to think dull to describe, or duller to be read—the pen lacking so much, even the feeble pencil's power.

Friend.—Ah! it is *very* true! Tell me to-night some

story of men—not matter: a military one, I suppose, it must be.

"Men!—they are my aversion. It is an unpleasant animal:—the female, however—"

Friend.—Ah! no more of that, Hal, an thou lovest me.

"I love Nature best;—nature in her virgin wildness. But I have been reminded somehow, of a very pleasant day's service in the Southwest; of scenes, or scenery, in which men took a part; and being in action, were a suitable and picturesque addition."

Friend.—It may do then; let us abstract ourselves from this sad gloom, and cheat the leaden hours.

"It was three years ago;—an episode, or more accurately, a sequel to the Florida War. We were in camp near Fort Gibson; an express came in the night with information that three hundred Seminoles, lately landed south of the Arkansas, had become rebellious, and crossed to the forbidden side. At reveille, while a thunderstorm was bursting, the squadrons received orders to march at eight o'clock. Eight miles down, we ascended with difficulty the Menard Mountain, where it abuts on the Arkansas; then, after a few miles of fine open forest, we found ourselves passing through large prairies fringed and beautifully interlocked with oak groves. There was little sign of man; the rich Cherokee had been careless; in twenty-two miles we saw but one dwelling, and an unfinished house,—which promised, however, far to excel in comfort those of the western whites. We encamped at dusk on the river bank, under the leafy domes of a majestic forest.

"Early next morning, the leader of the Seminoles, who were near, was induced to appear in camp. The colonel, by interpreter, asked him what he had to say for himself. The proud chief wore a sash, which we believed had belonged to some officer slain in the unfortunate Florida War; and in it was thrust a great dirk, which he freely fingered; he had not been asked to sit. He answered, 'In Florida we were promised to be sent to Fort Gibson. This promise is broken: we are now forbidden. We shall go. Our friends Alligator and Coacooche, and their bands are on this side. We shall meet them here in council. In Florida we were treated with more friendship and consideration. I am accustomed to sit, when I have business to transact.'

"The colonel replied, 'If you received this promise, it was unauthorized. You shall *not* go! This day you shall recross the Arkansas, and set out for your lands on the Canadian.'

"The chief, at last, had met his more than match. He endeavored then to temporize; he was astonished, but with skill felt his ground, to be assured if boldness and cunning could fail him now. And so it seemed;—he promised to obey, and was dismissed;—the colonel taking measures to be informed of any unnecessary delay.

"Soon after noon, the trumpet called, 'To horse!' The squadrons were speedily arrayed; the Indians had refused or failed to obey.

"The colonel said to us, in his cool way, 'If we come to blows, put your sabres well in; but on no account strike woman or child;' then we marched. My squadron led. Two miles down on the skirt of the Indian camp, a lad, who was mounted, attempted to pass us; the colonel himself seized his rein, and gave him in charge to two dragoons, but such was his indomitable obstinacy and boldness, that he persisted in efforts to elude this arrest, utterly regardless of the sabres flashing about his head! Until, seeing that but few men remained in the camp, the colonel, rather than that the boy should be sacrificed, commanded his release. We found on the Illinois River, at its mouth, the chief, and about a dozen men and their families. Nothing but their weakness saved them. Their tents were torn down,—they were seized and forced to an Arkansas ferry, close by.

"It soon appeared that the Indians had taken possession of the flat, and had been crossing the Illinois River. An armed party was sent over in a canoe, loaded the boat with their baggage, returned, and took the chief and party over the Arkansas.

"Very near sundown it was ascertained that the band were nearly all beyond the Illinois River—a hundred yards wide, and booming full; and I received rather a singular order to cross it with my squadron;—with discretional powers beyond.

"If I had stopped to reason on it, I should soon have pronounced the order impracticable; for the full banks of the river were vertical; there was only a small canoe; the sun was setting. However, it was to be done; I had faith, and—perhaps the colonel too; and so—in half an hour I was over with above half my horses and three-fourths of my men."

Friend.—Come now, no romance; you must tell how that was done.

"A mounted Cherokee made his appearance at that moment; how it happened, I did not stop to inquire; I learned from him that a mile or two above—through the dark forest—there was a trail and a ford,—in low water. I sent a division of the squadron under an energetic officer who took him as guide—to cross there, if he could risk it. I immediately sent a party to the Arkansas to find and bring round the flat-boat; and meanwhile, crossed over a dozen men in the canoe: just as it was upset on its third trip—losing some arms, and *very* nearly some lives—the flat was brought; I rode into it, followed by as many horses as could find room; filled up the interstices with dismounted men; pushed over, and landed safely.

"I found that a Cherokee lived in the vicinity, and he told me that the woods were full of Indians. There was little daylight left; but ordering him to guide me, I advanced with my few horses, and the dismounted platoon following: for a time we only picked up a straggler or two, and found scattered baggage. Then I met my mounted division; they had swam the Illinois—loaded with arms and equipments—in military array!

"Soon after the guide pointed out a little bushy prairie, where, he said, a large number of Seminoles were concealed: it was nearly dark: I threw out my mounted division as skirmishers, and soon after signalled the 'charge, as foragers:' when the 'rally' was sounded, they with difficulty found their way back to the foot reserve, and not an Indian had been flushed!

"Then, of course, we marched back to the river bank; and lay down in our cloaks, supperless. But this is all introduction; I have tired you before *the* day is begun?"

Friend.—No, it is not *very* late; I was rather amused at your account of those spoiled Seminoles.

Your bivouac was marvellously like this present one! But go on; and—if you do not stop at a dream or two—you will doubtless soon come to the cream of the story.

"Amigo mio, my dreams are—not what they were!—Well, the night passed quietly enough, though I *was* disturbed by the coming in of women and children; and right early I got over my other horses and men, and—a breakfast.

"I sallied forth then, ripe for adventures. I 'scoured,' as was right, the three miles of open forest—we have to borrow this word from the scullery, while the French say, euphoniously, *eclairer*—then emerged upon prairies, and soon reached a lofty hill-top.

"O! how beautiful and fresh was all before me! It was a surprise; not a trace of man blurred the expanded view, where free Nature had tried her genial hand. It was the year's prime; sparkling under the early sun, were meadows and murmuring streamlets; glades, where sported herds of deer; grassy slopes swelling to smooth hillocks; old oaks, here expanded in solitary magnificence,—there, disposed like garlands on the gentle hills; and again, gathered in imposing groves. Strangely beautiful in the midst were two hill-cones, rising like a triumphal gate, from forest bases. Far extended hill and dale and plain, until lost in the blue slopes of a mountain range; and about its airy outline clustered the rosy morning clouds.

"A free and exultant feeling of power—a joyous buoyancy of spirits—a rising romance, was then fast swelling my heart, and sending the blood in happy currents, when I saw my advanced guard galloping over the plain below, and received by the escort of fifteen captured Indians, a report that their main body was in a wood which was pointed out; it was at the foot and on the side of a bluff, which sent an arm—like that of an L—to be merged in the eminence on which I stood; the wood was on the outer slope, and extended round the angle, out of view.

"Ah! then I was transformed to a General, with my

four admirably instructed powerful platoons for regiments, and my trumpet signals for field and staff!

"I immediately sent another platoon swiftly to search the woods of the near slope—approaching always the advance guard—whilst I hastened with a division round the hill-tops to head the Seminoles, and gain a commanding and central point of observation. Excitement and rapid motion only increased my enjoyment of the rare scenery of that secluded district, where every moment new combinations of beauty enchanted the eye. It was thus that my only half warlike operations and slender means, were magnified to a charming effect.

"My detachments were then lost to view—engaged in the forest below: passing slowly round the brink of the precipitous bluff, I faced the more distant and longer side, —and, having waited a proper time, led my men in extended order abruptly down the descent; how steep it would prove we could not see, so dense was the undergrowth; blindly we forced our way; the horses maddened by tangled vine and brier, leaping uncontrollably downward.

"The wood had been abandoned, and a fresh trail led into the prairie beyond; the advance guard had taken it rapidly, and the support had more slowly followed. Soon I saw the first gallop along elevated ground, to disappear in the forest toward the Arkansas, and thither I directed the latter by trumpet signal. When I reached the wood, I found they had charged through a camp, whence every soul fled to a near swamp: while they were entangled there, I ascertained that these fugitives were Seminoles of an earlier migration; and soon drew out my skirmishers—not without some captures.

"Our spirits were all up; and returning to the prairie,

I made other combinations—managed by signals—amidst its hills and groves; we overrun many miles of country, and made numerous prisoners, giving but one sabre wound. But—

———'I will not tire
With long recital of the rest.'

"It was dark again when we returned to the Illinois." My Friend! he was sound asleep.

CHAPTER XVII.

THE desert truly is here—moral and natural wastes. Gray stunted trees in wintry mourning—draped with moss. Chill winds wail,—wild beasts howl,—and my heart echoes, "Far—lone—forgot."

But those rosy hours will be reflected on the gloom of all years. As, in a day of sombre clouds and wintry winds, suddenly the sun sends athwart the earth and sky a dazzling beam,—so comes a smile out of the dreamy Past, like a ray of heavenly light.

Did I dream?—Had I slumbered at my post?—I *did* dream.

And why not tell my dream?—Life is little better; nay, it is little different. We wander at most in the dark—stumbling on temptations,—walking on the thorns of passions; in an awful but obscure light, refracted by the cloudy medium of philosophy.

Sleep on, my Friend! Though I would question you if I could, in this dark hour, if sympathy may ever pass the mysterious boundary of dream-land;—if that deathlike seeming calm were of careless oblivion,—or of some divine despair.

Wondrous contrasts, at times, have dreams to the actual life around. Alone with death in bloody guise, and tossed on ocean in its hour of storm and darkness, with the roar of breakers in my ear,—I have fallen asleep and dreamed of home and happy scenes!

But when our bark glides smoothly to summer airs,—when the rough sea of trouble and of toil is for a moment calmed, and we lap ourselves in hopeful repose,—then mayhap, some demon, born of darkness, harrows our defenceless souls with images of hellish torture!

My watch is lonely and fearfully silent. There is a power in profound silence, especially in the reaction of strong excitement, that is full of awe. *Silence!*—then every sentiment of my soul has ears, in which air-spirits supernaturally utter distracting *sonorous* thoughts! in darkness, with long unrest, it verges madness.

O! ever splendent stars, which float along the sparkling blue and boundless ether, calming with its deep serene the poor desert watcher;—O! immeasurably far, to whom no struggling ray of earth-light can ever reach,—are ye the abodes of happy beings, guarded from ill by flaming swords of seraphim? May soul of man aspire to the beatitude of reunion there, with the last loved of earth? O! spirit ministers, are ye hovering near, radiant with pity divine, on guardian errands, to touch with hope the sinking hearts of myriad men? And can no mortal eye behold thy subtilty supernal?

Are these wild mountains impassable barriers, that must prison all sympathy from *earthly* communion?

In vain, in vain! Dull tyrant space wears its stoniest

frown ;—there is no whisper of life or motion in the air ;—the elements but echo a human sigh; and thus,

> "I live and die unheard
> With a most voiceless thought."

July 7th.—But now, "the morn is up again," and we have marched many miles fasting, and have been attracted over the turbid river by the sight of grass, and have stopped and breakfasted under some cotton-woods; and in their shade my pipe and pencil are struggling for exclusive attention ;—but pipe has it!—for here comes my sympathetic companion of the night, looking as discontented as if he had not been luxuriously talked to sleep.

"What's the matter?"

Friend.—O, confound the bivouac! the dew or frost has got into my joints.

"Delicate, indeed!"

Friend.—I believe this the very Valley of Acheron! in fact I had bad dreams,—of midnight incantations,—infernal revels.

"Pshaw! it was a calm and beautiful night; and never shone the stars through purer air, into the dark mountain vale. Listen to that sweet bird! it is piping now of some dream of love."

Friend.—Nay, *there*, we have agreed to disagree.

"Thou pitiable exempt from love's misery, thou believest in beauty?"

Friend.—Yes, thou unintelligible lover of antithesis, not to say plagiarism.

"Is anything so beautiful as unbounded faith?"

Friend.—Listen! that's "to horse."

"Answer me then!"

Friend.—Pshaw!—Of course it's beautiful; or rather, sublime.

"It is the *very* attribute of human love!"

July 8th.—After remounting yesterday, we threaded the labyrinth before us by aid of the river, and old paths of the buffalo. One would say there had been war there, among what our fathers called the elements. Earth, when nearly defeated by water, as a last effort *detached* at a defile, a little mountain—of red and warlike rock—to throw itself in the "heady *current* of the fight;" the shock must have been great; but River soon recovering, then very coolly had *recourse* to the manœuvre of turning the enemy; and by the ground he had thus so weakened.

As we wound our difficult way—leading for the most part our horses—through this grand outlet to the confused mountain valleys behind, some grizzly bears were seen climbing the rocks of the mountain-side, and stopping frequently to give us a savage gaze:—and that was all we could well do in return.

At last we emerged on a great barren prairie slope, where the mountains,—to keep up the figure—rallied from their confusion and retreated in regular masses toward the east.

Some of the elements, however, made us pay for this invasion of their battle ground: the Colonel and quite a number of others had been seized with excruciating pains in back, limbs, head, and the bones generally, accompanied by fever; and a party was left to prepare a litter for one man who was totally helpless.

A few miles brought us to the old trail at the regular ford; our route from Independence Rock was a little shorter than the road.

We remain to-day in camp: fortunately, perhaps, there is little or no medicine,—nor a physician. Nature, with only rest for a nurse, will do well; she will not be thwarted by pretenders, whose only sure means of relief is the strange faith which they inspire!*

This afternoon Mr. Walker, whom we met at Independence Rock, and who is now on his way to California, visited our camp: he has picked up a small party at Fort Laramie; and wild-looking creatures they are—white and red. This man has abandoned civilization,—married a squaw or squaws, and prefers to pass his life wandering in these deserts; carrying on, perhaps, an almost nominal business of hunting, trapping, and trading—but quite sufficient to the wants of a chief of savages. He is a man of much natural ability, and apparently of prowess and ready resource.

The party left with the sick man arrived at sundown; he was brought in a litter made of two poles suspended over saddles at the sides of two horses, one placed before the other: it is almost incredible that a man could be thus carried, however painfully, over those rocks; in fact, the men had frequently to take the place of the horses.

July 9th.—To-day,—the sick having been much benefited by rest,—we found a shallow ford and crossed the river. We suffered much from heat, which the white sand greatly increased. Some large emigrant companies were met: one had six or seven hundred cattle; they left the road insupportably dusty. We abandoned it—preferring to encounter the sage bushes. At Deer Creek we found our pleasant old camp ground converted into a very cattle-pen; and so, after our long march, had to wind a weary way, a mile or two up the creek, seeking more virgin ground.

* This disease was probably the *dengue;* and as an apposite commentary on the text, I have heard a physician of high standing say, that he did not know what would cure it;—he had *tried* everything!

In crossing the Platte this morning, the grizzly bear-cub came on the scene in his final act.

It will be remembered by the patient and attentive future reader of this dry and methodical narrative, that its first appearance on any stage, was in "high" tragedy —that the first act embraced an unusual amount of sanguinary incident—that an innocent brother (or sister) being ruthlessly slain, and the baffled lady-mother left (unceremoniously) full of towering and demonstrative rage,—the imprisoned hero himself sank overwhelmed,— or in a well-acted counterfeit of death (and was borne off, remember, on a "real" horse). That in the next act (and three acts shall do for the tragedy of my bear,— *originally* they had but *one*,—but that was at the sacrifice of a *goat*), he came to life in a manner that might very well have been criticised as an overdone piece of stage-effect,—but that in fact, the spectators were much *moved*, and gave full credit to the dangerous passion of his howl.

To-day, then,—for I scorn anachronism—was performed the final act. The stage (wagon) was on "real water." Enraged at his wrongs, his losses, and his galling chain, the "robustious beast" acted in a ridiculous and un*bear*able manner; ay, "tore his passion to tatters, to very rags,"—*splinters;* the stage (wagon) could not hold him: and finally, in despair, he "imitated humanity so abominably," as to throw himself headlong, and so drown—or *hang* himself: (the *author* cannot decide which —even after a *post-mortem* examination;—and so leaves the decision of this important point to the commentators.)

My tragedy is all true,—and if not quite serious, has, as is proper, its moral;—but rather, as I have alluded to the primitive tragedy, let that "future reader" here imagine the entry of Chorus, and their song to Freedom! That dumb beasts prefer death to slavery! Liberty lost, *they* can die without the excitement of the world's applause, or hopes of a grateful posterity! (It is not possible, I think, that the cub could have known that I would immortalize him.)

July 10th.—We took our old trail in preference to the road: the weather excessively hot. At a short noon halt, we saw a mile off, five Indians wading the river: they shook a blanket—the sign of friendship; as it was not immediately returned, they ran off; they felt guilty, perhaps, of levying black mail upon the emigrants. 'Tis strange they are so moderate. In this country all parties who feel weak, become unusually circumspect on discovering the vicinity of others:—man being an animal of prey, if without strength for attack or defence, the necessity for concealment is felt.

After coming nineteen miles, we turned into a great horseshoe bend of the river; where, fortunately, we have good grass, and also some fine large shade-trees.

On the sandy shore we find here numerous petrifactions of the thick bark of trees, and also some fine cornelians.

We have had all the formalities of a thunder-shower, but with a mere sprinkle; and now, after the gale, under a tree, with dark clouds before the sun, it is hot: ten or twelve days ago, water froze in our tents!

July 11th.—Last night we were three miles from a Sioux camp of seventy-three lodges: a half-breed came to us; he stated they were going to the mountains for lodge-poles.

We found also, near our camp, petrified logs and

The poor soldier who lost his arm, suffered a second amputation: he is, however, now doing well.

Our Arapaho squaw and the children, we find, are fat and flourishing: the young ones are unusually handsome and intelligent, and are quite petted by the soldiers. She will go with us south to her parent nation.

July 14th.—The wagons are late in returning. Meanwhile the fire progresses toward our little river bend and camp; and it is raging among the ancient cotton-woods—some standing—some dead and leaning—many pitched and piled at the sport of time, the winds, and drifting overflow: black billows of smoke roll forth—now tossed overhead in threatening, cinder-scattering clouds; now rising in palpable columns to the sky;—then a fierce gust or a whirlwind,—as is its wont in this region of lofty irregular hills,—makes all roar again; while the eager flames dart impatiently on, or overtop all the ruin.

It has crossed the stream! A company has rushed from the dreadful circle, tearing away their equipage in desperate haste; all preparations are hurried on; wagons scarce loaded, go lumbering forth: some saddle—some mount in haste:—and now the flame has reached the dry grass of the central camp. The trumpets blare, and we gallop forth to leap the girdling flame, and pass the blackened but still fiery space beyond.

I look back in admiration:—but now, over the moving mass of horsemen, artillery, and baggage, I see the flaming wreck involve some noble old trees, which, cheery in their solitude, had so long made their smiling presence felt amid the gray wilderness around: but greedy flames do their work, whilst the lurid smoke hangs like a pall over their high green heads.

The poor soldier who lost his arm, suffered a second amputation: he is, however, now doing well.

Our Arapaho squaw and the children, we find, are fat and flourishing: the young ones are unusually handsome and intelligent, and are quite petted by the soldiers. She will go with us south to her parent nation.

July 14th.—The wagons are late in returning. Meanwhile the fire progresses toward our little river bend and camp; and it is raging among the ancient cotton-woods—some standing—some dead and leaning—many pitched and piled at the sport of time, the winds, and drifting overflow: black billows of smoke roll forth—now tossed overhead in threatening, cinder-scattering clouds; now rising in palpable columns to the sky;—then a fierce gust or a whirlwind,—as is its wont in this region of lofty irregular hills,—makes all roar again; while the eager flames dart impatiently on, or overtop all the ruin.

It has crossed the stream! A company has rushed from the dreadful circle, tearing away their equipage in desperate haste; all preparations are hurried on; wagons scarce loaded, go lumbering forth: some saddle—some mount in haste:—and now the flame has reached the dry grass of the central camp. The trumpets blare, and we gallop forth to leap the girdling flame, and pass the blackened but still fiery space beyond.

I look back in admiration:—but now, over the moving mass of horsemen, artillery, and baggage, I see the flaming wreck involve some noble old trees, which, cheery in their solitude, had so long made their smiling presence felt amid the gray wilderness around: but greedy flames do their work, whilst the lurid smoke hangs like a pall over their high green heads.

Quoth Fitzpatrick: "Another such expedition, and there will be no wood left in the country."

Six miles are passed: we have come up the Laramie, over high hill and valley; we are in a fresh green meadow; the bright stream seems to pause in welcome; —the horses graze earnestly at their luxuriant repast: quietly goes on preparation for our long march southward; the winds cease; the sun goes down with brilliancy amid the clouds,—which now too, have found repose. The clear river mirrors all; the green banks—the varied camp —the bright sky.

What, on the troublous earth, compares with the summer sunset!

It is the welcome signal to the weary world to cease from toil, and seek the happiness of rest and refreshment: as if in honor of the occasion, the heavens are illumined with a grandeur and beauty, to which the greatest monarch's most glaring fete is a poor mockery.

Slowly the glowing honors fade; the gorgeous red yields to more modest beauty;—now, growing fancy sees airy structures, in which the presence of angel messengers, resting, has shed a beauty not of earth; the hues are more delicate and lovely and heavenly to the last!— they calmly ascend, while reluctant Night draws his curtain of gray.

What heart so earthy, but is calmed and softened to meditation! So perfect loveliness, slowly ascending to the parent skies, seems to draw with it our souls heavenward.

Slowly, solemnly, *surely*, come the shades and darkness of night! Night! that type of death!—but death, as thus, mercifully preceded by the beautiful promise of a happiness beyond.

CHAPTER XVIII.

July 16th.—Yesterday, marching early, we soon left the beautiful Laramie River, and turned more to the south. We next struck the dry bed of the "Chugwater,"—a small tributary which is graced by a few trees: fourteen miles over lowland prairie, brought us to a higher point of it, where there was a little water; after a rest we turned—with the stream—eastward, and encamped ten miles above;—but there was little grass.

To-day, we still ascended the Chugwater; the immense table-lands, or steppes of the piedmont, abut on its narrow valley; the vertical section exhibiting a sandstone conglomerate resting on clay. After marching about seven miles we saw Chian lodges before us on a level meadow of the stream. While the horses grazed, the officers walked over:—it was a neat-looking, merry little encampment; all seemed lively and happy; and their hunters were then approaching with horse-loads of meat. We were struck with their numerous wolf-dogs, which were very large, and looked formidable; but they are not so; but rather the faithful drudges which civilized man finds in graminivorous animals.

Their masters, and mistresses too, though living like gladiators chiefly upon flesh, seemed remarkably mild and amiable, as well as good-looking. We found a bevy of red ladies sitting around a white, well-dressed buffalo-robe, extended on a frame; they had shells containing different dyes, with which they were ornamenting it, in many quaint or regular figures: either from native modesty, or possessing the boasted easy self-possession of civilized refinement, they did not interrupt their embroidery at our approach, or exhibit any of that curiosity or excitement which we might flatter ourselves our sudden and warlike visit had inspired.

We were introduced into the lodge of the interpreter, a young white man; it was neat, and lately pitched on fresh grass; but I must describe a Chian lodge:—a dozen or more slim, white pine or cedar poles, above twenty feet long, are set up, crossed and secured near their upper extremities; fitted around and pinned to the ground, is a weather-proof envelop, constructed of about twenty buffalo-cow robes, dressed without the hair. More than twenty of us sat comfortably within this lofty pavilion; its mistress, who appeared to have no rival—was a remarkably pleasant, comely woman, and well-dressed, as were many others.

How enviable is the Chian! Such is his simple, clean, comfortable house; so cheap, so movable! When his summer carpet—of green velvet—wears out, how easy to move to another; to select some still pleasanter spring or valley, and enjoy the change of scene and air; free of the curses and the cares entailed by civilization.

After refreshments, we found that a large semicircle of robes had been disposed on the green without, and shaded by awnings of skins, stretched on tripod frames.

We met in council: the Colonel addressed them much to the same effect as he had the Sioux, and then distributed liberal presents: this largess was garrulously acknowledged by the patriarch of the band, who, with the shadow of the authority which had descended to a grandson, endeavored to impress the Colonel's advice.

What heart could be so artificially moulded as not to be deeply interested in this happy, secluded community!

They were a family! a patriarchal family numbering two hundred; all descended—save those joined to them by marriage—from this old chief, for whom Nature, in her pleasant mountain valleys and forests, had gently tempered ninety-seven winters: they were truly children of Nature; and her bounteous and beautiful gifts—even in this sterner clime—her balmy breezes, her crystal streams, her gorgeous morning and evening skies, her gently succeeding seasons, her voices of praise or of warning thunders, and mountain storms, had sunk into their hearts as the only and sufficient revelations of a beneficent Great Spirit.

This grandson—the quiet moving spirit—was a remarkably handsome, mild, gentlemanly man; the interpreter said he was "one of the best Indians in the world;" children were very numerous; like the Arabs, they indulge in a plurality of wives. They wear their hair long, and are partial to our caps of fur: happy for them, if they remain far distant from whites, and follow no less innocent fashions than that of a head-dress!

But whilst engaged in the formalities of the council and distribution of presents, we were startled by shouts and laughter so vociferous and continued as to excite great curiosity, and induce some of us to retire to satisfy it: a merry and comical confusion reigned without; very infectious, but difficult to understand: it seems that while the young squaws were so gently engaged at their painting, a certain bachelor captain, whose countenance at home is considered quite mild and engaging, but whose wont is now to give of it but an uncertain view through a vast bunch of reddish hair, had the curiosity to take a closer view—he is near-sighted—of the colored design;—possibly he was artlessly examining a natural model;—a matter of highly-civilized precedent and practicability:—be this as it may, the *belle sauvage* of intent and downcast eyes, suddenly raising them, was startled by this hairy apparition hanging over her shoulder; so much so as to indulge in a shrill succession of those shrieks so successfully practised by unfortunate heroines of the boards, and natural, of course, to very young or pretty ladies: attributing it to his uncouth looks, for, according to his experience, no imaginable offence had been given, the captain's confusion was natural and complete; and so too was the astonishment of many, when this lady-like screaming was repeated by one and another,—all the young girls toward whom the hapless and blushing captain directed his appealing regards. They ran, shouted, hid, laughed; his own puzzled and innocent laughter was the most ridiculous; for an explanation soon began to be whispered about, which did not much abate the merriment. The captain wore spectacles; and we learned that these girls, lamentably ignorant of optics—as of science generally—were full believers in a little theory of their own, upon the subject of the mysterious glasses; and it was no less than that they enabled the fortunate spectator to penetrate opaque bodies; and consequently—although unusually well and completely dressed—they supposed that, to his eyes, their modest garments were no protection!

Two hours and a half had flown by, when the shrill trumpets called us away. We mounted and turned our backs to our new friends and their pleasant valley, perhaps forever.

We were soon on the high steppe again; but clouds and smoke obscured our view; the prairie was on fire in our front; in three hours we came to a small stream; there was no grass. Now, grass, if green, is a very pleasing thing to most people; but many simple souls might consider us hard to please, if we complain of its want; but if "all flesh is grass," so grass is flesh, to us; and flesh, which is muscle, is more intelligibly appreciable. We have but three wants,—so remote is civilization, which counts them by the thousand,—water, grass, and fuel, and wonderfully little and various in kind of the last; and we find the Earth a "*step*-mother," for she seldom grants us more than two of them, and when in an ill-humor, denies us all three.

After an hour's delay, and consultation between the *guiding* and deciding powers—how anxious is power, well possessed!—we marched on. In four or five miles over burned and toward burning prairies, we came to another little stream, and in a thunderstorm; and here, per force, we sleep on uneven sand-bars and gravel-beds (better than the rocks each side); but our faithful steeds are mocked with a scant supper, but a very civilized show of green bushes bearing gooseberries,—as if for dessert. How like to some feasts!—at which I have *fasted!*

July 17.—The morning was very cold; but as usual our promise of rain was broken, and ended in appearances.

We came many miles over a burned district; one would say such hills as these would boast, if they could, of producing grass enough to burn. We passed two bold branches of Horse Creek: a gentleman told me he saw bees hiving their honey in holes in a clay bank; they are rarely seen so far away from plantations, or from trees. After grazing an hour, we mounted and pushed out into the trackless plains: the day became very hot; and we began anxiously to look for water. We ascended many long smooth slopes, to which the descent was less, and steep, until we reached the topmost ridge of all,—the highlands between the two Plattes,—then gently down again, with abrupt ascents;—as if two sets of long sweeping waves had met. After marching ceaselessly eighteen or twenty miles, we became uneasy, as well as exceedingly thirsty; the guide, too, lost confidence and changed his direction to the east; which made us more thirsty still;—we were looking out for Pole Creek: "The next hill, and we shall see it!"—the next and the next, interminably, until some almost despaired. We came at last to a level plain, which was very unpromising; but soon after, we saw hill knobs, and from this I presaged the creek;—and was not mistaken. We passed several dry branches; the sight of them would give strength and spur to the poor suffering horses.

In all such passages in my life I have been reminded of Sterne's pious and happy expression, "God tempers the wind to the shorn lamb;" always there is some redeeming circumstance: thus here, the ground was hard and smooth; also it became cloudy, and the freshening breeze was a great relief; it rained a few drops, and we almost prayed for more. At last, after thirty-four miles, we espied a green flat, which alone greatly revived horses and men. When, at last, we reached the creek, there was no water to be seen! Some went up a mile. With a large tin cup, I dug in the damp sand and gravel two feet down, and then was rewarded. Three hundred yards below, soon after was discovered a very fine spring.

Meanwhile night came on; and four hunters and packmen, who left the camp before us this morning, came not; an elk or two and a solitary badger were the only habitants we had seen in the half million of acres over which our eyes have ached this day. Now, at 10 o'clock, they are setting off several rockets.

July 18th.—The hunters did not come in the night. Pretty early we saw a small party coming down the creek; but they proved to be Arapahoes, from a camp of sixty lodges, ten miles above; they had seen the rockets. These are countrymen of our poor squaw and the two children;—they were three men and a woman; and singular enough, one of them was a young man named Friday, whom Mr. Fitzpatrick, our guide, had discovered when a mere child, lost and almost dead in a wilderness: he saved him and brought him up: the woman was quite comely, and in her fat cheeks the blood showed itself in a blush. The elder of the party embraced Fitzpatrick, and expressed gratitude to him and the whites for their protection and hospitable care of the woman and her children, and alluded too, to Friday and the singular coincidence; they received their countrywoman affectionately. But they were strangers; overwhelmed with misfortune, she had found good friends, with whom she now trembled to part. She wept and went with them.

Two discharges were made from the howitzers for the benefit of the hunters, and then we marched. We soon ascended a level plain, unbroken for twelve miles; we were in view of the Black Hills, far to the right, and, about ten miles to the left, of the prairie mountain, Scott's Bluff. The plain was gravelly, scantily covered with short, crisp, buffalo grass, much like curled gray horsehair; the south wind came over it as from the mouth of an oven: only three buffalo gave an interest to the dull scene, and one antelope, which seemed intent on death; it came running into our midst and was riddled with balls.

Content to-day with sixteen miles progress, we have

encamped on Crow Creek, which is very like the one we left this morning: its name was given from the number of crows which are found on it, lower down where there are some woods; and that reminds me that for forty miles we have seen but one tree—five miles off—and not a bush or shrub; our sole fuel is *bois de vache.* The hunters have arrived safely; they say they struck Pole Creek twenty-five miles higher than we did, descended it until nine at night,—when, unable to see our fires from a hill-top, they bivouacked without suppers; they rode down it this morning for two hours, until they heard the cannon.

A beef has been killed; the first for four weeks: we have now only flour for twelve days, and a few cattle:—we are about seven hundred and fifty miles from settlements: our only other resource is the subsistence stores sent two years ago to Bent's Fort for Captain C.'s command; rumor is rife of its being used, spoiled, &c.,—for rumor penetrates the prairies, delights in trading posts, where its every tongue becomes double.

The atmosphere has been so smoky to-day that only a few saw, among the clouds, the white top of Long's Peak. It is famous among mountains. In its valley recesses are the springs of the Platte, the Arkansas, it is said of the Rio del Norte, and certainly of a main branch, called Grand River, of the great Colorado of California.

July 19th.—Twenty-six miles of Crow Creek! Flat and desolate, with but a few low hills of clay and gravel; where we touched it, if we found a little grass, there was no water; if water there was no grass. We were in view of snow, but the "sweet south" blistered our faces. Long's Peak, which from this view is double, is seen towering above the mountain range, but sometimes was hardly to be distinguished from surrounding clouds.

Here at camp, we have a little grass and a little water, hot and brackish; it just comes to the surface of the sand, as if to be resolved if this crust of earth were worthy of a redeeming struggle; I think the sirocco has settled it,—it is surrendered to the crows. Clouds too, fresh from the mountain summits, have made a hasty visit, as if on the same errand of mercy; but after shedding a few drops—of tears I thought—they passed on muttering. The scene is not wholly bare, but its gray vacuity has a strange relief. There is a grave, and on its little mound has been piled the skeleton of a buffalo; and near by is a little pyramid of twenty horses' skulls;—how long the tireless wind has bleached these grim mementos—who can tell? But they seem to whisper still of a tale of blood.

But even at Crow Creek, the heavens have smiled upon us in beauty! Just as the sun was sinking—apparently in snow—the sky was spanned by a rainbow—a double one—of wonderful brilliancy; for all within was deep blue cloud.

After all, I have had the fortune to see a dozen far more desolate tracts in our boundless territories; and they begin to be estimated, but never will be sold by the acre.

July 20th.—We marched again over flat, barren ground, and in view of the great mountain range, hid to the snow line or above, by the secondary but lofty Black Hills; our course was still down Crow Creek for twelve miles: before we left it we got water by digging; then after ascending, we came in pleasant view of the South Platte; but before us, apparently two or three miles, down a smooth gentle slope, was Cache la Poudre; but it proved to be seven. Very warm and dry we were, when we arrived at the bank of that beautiful crystal stream—as large as Laramie; several elks scampered off at our approach, abandoning some luxuriant grass, the very sight of which was refreshing; but much more so was a bath which a number of us enjoyed, whilst the horses grazed with a most excusable avidity.

Then we rode six more miles over a weary, dusty, level road to the Platte; forded it, and encamped under some pleasant cotton-woods, with more green grass. Long's Peak, though above sixty miles off at the southwest, rises proudly above all the fine view of mountains: its outline as seen here makes an angle at the apex of 120 degrees.

We have had two hunters lost since yesterday morning, and the howitzer was once more discharged this morning.

CHAPTER XIX.

YET unstained, bright and cheerful, gayly splashing 'mong the rocks,—merry river, knowest thou, surely, where thou rushest in such haste?

Art careless now, in thy morning, of these pleasant green trees' shade?

Ah! be happy while thou mayst, round thy mountain parents' feet; smiling thou, and reflecting every hopeful smile of theirs!

Yes, whilst they shelter, dance in sunshine, now thou mayst—

Friend.—Hillo! what are you about? Writing in tune with the merry cotton-wood leaves? You will have to "frankly confess you have invented a new style."

"Upon my word I was becoming as curious as yourself; a first unfortunate line set the jingle agoing, and I could not stop it; my 'feet' got into such a measure that they were running off with me,—and my discretion (somewhat like an extraordinary leg of which I once heard a clown sing). Shall it stand?—to be laughed at one of these days?"

Friend.—You are wonderfully given to personification; particularly of rivers. I suppose you were thinking of the desolate flatness, the choking sands, and the profitless end, the now fair and promising river comes to?

"Exactly—and it led to melancholy thoughts.

"Well, these dreary steppes, where the mountain streams, fresh from springs and snow, are the chief objects of interest, must account for it; they have at least the motion and music of life;—if they are not persons, there are none other, and I believe they answer me about as well."

Friend.—You have reversed the figure;—decidedly. Shall I call it a personality? There is only a subject or two on which we cannot meet, but unfortunately they are your especial favorites; I have been fortunate in escaping them now.

"And that is the reason you did not ridicule my literary pastime! But I shall not answer for myself till the moon sets to-night.

"By-the-bye,—what, my Friend, do you think the moon was 'invented' for?—to assist that other invention of sleep?"

And thus we whiled the hour away.

July 21st.—We marched south, following the river, here rapid and clear,—a mountain stream, running at the foot of the Black Hills. We were on a hard, level road, over prairies, and river-bottom too, of great barrenness; the effect being heightened by ruins of several adobe trading forts: I only wondered that man could be tempted to tarry here, where animals come not even for security.

We have had a true prairie day, with its incessant fierce south wind. As we approached our camp-ground, a black and threatening thunderstorm was gathering unusually far down from the region of snow; they had seldom reached us,—but now the first big drops, mingled with large hail, were falling as the wagons came trotting recklessly down the bluff to the low grounds which had been selected. With haste the well-experienced men got out the tents; and just as the fourth corner-pin of mine was in hand, and I could slip under its shelter, down came the hard rain! and it has continued for two hours: some of my neighbors, I suspect, know more about it.

The Snow Mountains looked grandly to-day; we are so much lower than at the South Pass, and on Sweet Water, that their height, comparatively, is much greater than of the mountains there. Long's Peak, which from this view is sharpened to 60°, is now almost behind us; while Pike's Mountain, which is more lofty, begins to rise; it looks blue, with the distance of ninety miles; it is at the southwest, and we pass near it. It is said that for above four hundred miles we shall not cross a stream!

This is the first good rain we have had since May. Some say this country has a soil, but that the difficulty lies in its dry climate: all effects have some cause; it is certainly a barren, desolate country: we come hundreds of miles, and see scarcely an Indian, or an animal; it is in fact a desert.

The two hunters have come in; they have been lost and without food for three days; they say they have ridden to-day above fifty miles. A fine range for *elephants*, this!

July 23d.—Yesterday we left the Platte and encamped on Cherry Creek. The hottest day we have had; and no bracing nights, as on the Sweet Water. Strange too to us, to pass in view of wintry snows and suffer thus, and just after a hail-storm. The country is the same—desolate and devoid of life: there have not been buffalo here for years. Pike's *Peak*, as it is called, raises its lofty dome of granite as we advance; it is bisected far down by a vertical white stripe. How distance and the familiar word, belittle a vast chasm of frozen, changeless snow!

To-day we still followed up Cherry Creek, or its dry sands; but towards noon, it came running to meet us; and there were the patronymic cherries,—or rather the bushes; and of the sort called choke-cherries. We are again encamped on it; but the highland is before us, and adorned, as the nearer hills, with pines; and with grass too; and the prospect is more homelike than any other, since we left the Little Blue, near the Missouri line.

July 24th.—We marched early, still up Cherry Creek. From Mount Pike a spur of mountains runs out to the east in a vast table,—the highland between two great rivers,—the Arkansas and the Platte. This stream has its spring where the table-land mountain breaks off into promontories, and these are crowned with lofty pines and rare and welcome oaks.

Following it up, at last we were rewarded by discovering the long valley's highest secret chamber, its court of fountains; these gave an emerald verdure to its gentle grassy slopes; and shrubs and rose-bushes were in blossom, majestic firs and oaks gave arches which excluded the sun's heat and glare; all was fresh and pure; man had made no mark, and doves alone were there. Look back! —nought but blue or snow-white mountains meets the eye.

The sudden transition from long, dreary marches to this matchless spot, gave it a heightened, inexpressible charm. I threw myself on the soft sod—apart—and felt like a worshipper of Solitude in a beautiful temple dedicated by Nature. Silence, as of ages, was only broken by natural music,—a wild but matchless harmony of three voices: of the winds, gently breathing through Æolian pine leaves—of the babbling and murmuring fountains—of the cooing doves.

All were melancholy, and one was of love.

How dissonant here the clamor of rude troopers and the clang of arms!

Civilization ever advances sword in hand, with poisons, pestilence, and crime in her train.

Alas, how short and few are these pleasant pauses in life's journey! Then, oh Memory! guard thy scant treasures well!

We were marching over the flat highlands; the novelty of forest trees diversifying the prairie was still delightful: —there was no water; for fifteen miles we marched on; but a cool breeze fanned our faces, and a pleasant screen of clouds befriended us. We came then to the heads of another lovely valley, which could not be greener. The camp is in a pleasant dale; very near it rises a great hill—a knob of the mountain—with grass, and granite rocks, and fir trees: the many springs send their crystal tribute to a little lake, as if to linger here before they wander forth together to the dull plains, and to be lost in the turbid Platte.

July 25th.—Last night I was moody and sleepless, and

so witnessed several sublime and beautiful changes of weather and sky, accompanied by a startling incident.

The labors of the day, the duties of the evening, all over, sleep had followed, as the laborer's luxury: lights had gone out; the little fires had sunk and paled; sounds gradually died away; the tents gleamed strangely in the moonlit solitude. I would have taken refuge from my thoughts in sleep; but sleep often flies us when most invoked.

At last I wandered forth alone, and ascended the mount.

The moon, not yet full, was high in heaven; the deep shadows of the pines slept on the grassy mountain top; the little lake below brightly mirrored the glittering sky; now and then came deep breaths of air,—like sighs from the gentle heart of Night. Long I reclined motionless upon a rock: there was no sight or sound of past, or present life; but I had no thought of loneliness,—it was a luxurious oblivion! I seemed to grow a portion of the pure and beautiful elements around.

At last,—so strangely then and there!—there came stealing on the night, a strain of soft music!

I sighed, as this heaven-bestowed key to all hearts, and to all moods, aroused within me some of that life, which silence and solitude so profound had absorbed. It was like an exquisite dream, closely following the last weary and oblivious sense.

But soon the music changed to a joyous air; then Memory awoke to make it an echo of the Past, and ever vigilant Hope stole forth trembling, like the moonbeam on the little lake.

O, seductive combination of the graces, the brilliancy, the joys of loveliest life!—that givest grace to loveliness, poetry to motion, and gala gloss to all surroundings—that charmest by music, that expandest all hearts, and exaltest all souls to the power of love—the thronged, the gay, the glittering ball!

O, soft viol, and tinkling guitar—last echo of old romance!—to this solitude you can bring bright memories!

Methinks I see a "high hall," whose lights might shame the day; the many white-robed fair,—the far-reaching couples, floating in that fairy dance,—revolving, like the moon around the sun, in circling circles.

The rosy summer dawn is lovely, and sweetly the birds sing in its praise;—but lo! the sun appears, and gives a magic brilliancy to all,—scattering diamonds and pearls upon the dewy green;—so, always to such pleasant scene, the smile of *one*, must give the light of enchantment!

If it be not there,—or if it be clouded, no winter twilight more dismal then, than that glaring ball-room mockery.

My unconscious voice had brought the cynic to my side, who had wandered forth like myself: but just then, too, from the cold north, and from a dark cloud, which had glided there unseen—like a brooding secret evil—came the hoarse breath of a storm, and its far-echoing solemn voice.

My Friend smiled. It was a smile that seemed a part of the faint flash which revealed the now gloomy night.

"You are answered," he said.

"Why ever look behind, and cherish the unhappy, profitless past? Why hug delusion and disappointment to the soul?"

"Ask the pale plant," I replied, "why it stretches forth in darkness, toward the ray of light."

We watched the storm amid the mountains, somewhile

in silence;. but I had not escaped so; my Friend said solemnly: "The present only is ours; but we should turn from sad experience to the future, there to lay hopeful plans, with good resolves."

"Labor and care and depravity are our curse: but blessings too are the faculties by which we struggle above the Sensual;—perceptions of the Beautiful, and the Sublime,—all the elements of the Ideal realm, where, Fancy-borne, we draw the materials of highest art; they elevate poor grovelling man, and

'Make his heart a spirit——'

Thus to poetry, and much-abused romance, we owe the cherished oblivion of our animal natures.

"Thus Music, whose source and power are in these faculties, is the divine art. If art it be, since the first words spoken by woman upon earth,—as often now,—were rapturous music!"

But the storm which had followed the higher range, now came sweeping on, sporting as with fierce joy amid the mountain tops; and here, and there, and far, the spectral peaks seemed rising to the capricious gleams, and many-voiced Echo swelled the glorious diapason. Sport and music of the Gods!—O! it was joy unspeakable, to stand thus on the very throne of the storm, whilst its fierce wings hurtled the mountains around,—and the wanton thunderbolts made the elements to tremble!

But suddenly, with a direful crash amid the Titanic rocks, there came a wondrous glare, that revealed through a vista of the black array of clouds, Mount Pike, splendent, sublime, serene, amid the chaotic war!—like a *Fata Morgana*, turned to stone. I was speechless. I heard my companion uttering,

——"Oh night,
And storm, and darkness, ye are wondrous strong,
Yet lovely in your strength."

Awed and chilled, we descended the mountain in silence.

CHAPTER XX.

July 25th.—For about three miles we passed an open pine forest on the top of the highlands between the Platte and Arkansas; and seven miles from camp we drank at a small stream flowing to the latter. When we emerged from the woods, a very extensive view opened to the east and south: no more forest was to be seen; the prairies had a shade of decided green, which was a pleasing novelty; but this great slope has a southern exposure, and is high enough to share the mountain showers. Be this as it may, it is the most promising country we have seen since we first came to the Platte near its mouth.

We have actually passed Pike's Peak to-day,—within ten or fifteen miles.

My Friend and I rode together, and had much wonder and admiration to express upon our night adventure,—our happy fortune to witness so much beauty and sublimity. I remembered then, his omission of "the light of a dark eye in woman," in the only quotation of poetry I had ever heard him make. He said it was introduced with beautiful expression, but all the poet's audacity, to illustrate an Alpine storm. "Does it please you?" I love storms, I said, but not those that gather in woman's eyes; they are fearful, and so must have strength, if not loveliness; if, by dark, he mean black, their light is seldom pleasing to me; their brilliancy seems to extinguish expressions,—or, their color to veil it.

Friend.—Well, that's a novel theory; what do you like?

"Blue!—in man or woman. But there is a rare kind —the loveliest and most expressive of all—which are changeable, from gray to blue, as intellect or love for the time prevails—the beaming mirrors of a lovely soul!"

Friend.—Let me once more astonish you, and quote from the authorities you acknowledge.

> "Oh Love! no habitant of earth thou art!
> An unseen seraph, we believe in thee;
> A faith, whose martyrs are the broken heart."

"That, skeptic, convinces me now, that you, at least, have loved!"

Friend.—Let us talk no more of woman. Angel she is thought, but oft a devil known—a pendulum that trembles betwixt heaven and hell.

Just then, I thought there ran a shudder through the air! the sun was veiled, and there came a fierce shower of hail, and rain, and snow. We were under Mount Pike, and within the sphere of its elementary laboratory.

We have been all day on the verges of these perennial showers, which the cold cloud-attracting and condensing mountain-tops send forth from their bases, as ceaseless streams through the far plains. Thus Nature, as with a high-pressure engine, carries on its vast scheme; the surplus steam from the hot valleys giving motion to its rivers. The lofty mountain, which, far as it was, seemed almost above us, was enveloped in snow-clouds the most of the day.

Our camp is on the stream of the "Fontain qui Bouille." We should have much liked to visit the spring, which was but fifteen miles from our course; but "March! march!" and thirty-one miles we have marched to-day. The stream is fringed with groves; and the horses fare well upon luxuriant rushes and blue grass.

July 26th.—We followed the Fontain qui Bouille seventeen miles, and then left it for a more direct course, over the hills to the Arkansas. We found it a weary sixteen miles, without water; broken and barren, and not at all green, was all the prospect there; cactus and Spanish bayonet had claimed it as their own; but there was animal life,—creatures which must be assimilated to these desolation-loving vegetables; there were very extensive villages of those queer "prairie-dogs," and they seemed to have formed an unusual association, and with little nearer approach to the most accepted standards of taste, than their well-known one with rattlesnakes and burrowing owls: it was now ants; and there were thousands of their hills,—some two feet in height.

But the most singular things were hundreds of smooth sugar-loaf mounds, varying in height from five to twenty feet; but these stand near the foot of the hills, on the alluvial plain. We had no time for any satisfactory examination.

The morning was distressingly warm; and as usual, the thunderclouds gathered about the mountains,—Pike's Peak behind us, and a range to our right beyond the Arkansas; and, as usual, they sent forth, as if for battle, their cloudy squadrons, thundering over the plains between. O, beautiful were they, in constant motion, with ever varying combination, as if in glorious sport! But at times they seemed to unite, and threaten us with fire and flood; then, from the dark array would issue thunderbolts and fiery gleams;—but our silent ranks moved steadily on;—and suddenly the sun would brightly interpose; the baffled clouds would break off muttering, with pelting discharges upon all around.

Across the river,—but we cannot see it for trees and bushes,—is Mexico, or Texas perhaps; and sixty miles within the disputed ground are the Spanish Peaks, which we have seen. It seems strange that Spain should have left memorials so far inland;—so far north. How rapidly did she degenerate! So must think at least all believers in militia, and call hers cowardly; for they ran away from every battle which they should have fought,—and in defence of their native land; except for harassing the enemy's escort, "the Duke" accounted them as so many sheep. I attribute all that to want of capable officers and discipline.

And what news are we to hear when we reach "the States?" (when we complete this march, which in some respects, may be unparalled in history.) When it began, there was every prospect of war with Mexico, and even with England. But we consider a war with Mexico so inevitable, that our distant march at this time has been criticised in camp; and we have some idea of meeting orders, to keep our course south to Santa Fe.

Sixty-four miles in two days! Wonderful in the last quarter of 2400 miles, on poor grass; *dragoons*—with carbine, sabre, pistols, cartridges, two blankets, a great coat, picket rope, and iron pin, &c. But it must break down anything but a cast iron horse to march thus incessantly for a hundred days!

There is no game. We have not seen a herd of buffalo for sixteen days, and shall not probably for five days to come: and yet this has been considered the buffalo country. And the Indian country too!—and where are *they?* The very road we have followed answers. It connects a chain of trading posts, where whiskey and gunpowder are bartered for robes and tongues; it destroys soul and body,—man and beast together. Verily the golden calf of civilization has been raised far in the wilderness!

July 27th.—We have had the pleasure of marching today twenty-two miles over a baked white clay surface, accompanied under the broiling sun by a breeze which very gently enveloped us,—as in a secondary atmosphere—with dust, which gave to all a semblance, not strictly defined, whether of millers or hodmen. This charming promenade was adorned solely by a dry and repulsive sort of bush, which served to remind us that any comfortable vegetation could by no possibility there exist.

We crossed early a nameless stream,—supposed to be generally dry—which was absolutely a torrent of mud, twenty paces wide, and near three feet deep; it was almost dangerous to ford. The river for some miles lower was almost as muddy. Here, it is unusually clear: the current is very great, frequently over stones and gravel: its immediate valley is generally several miles wide: the bluffs with little grass have frequently abrupt geometrical shapes.

Again we have thunderstorms around us, but escape with a sprinkle. It is said to be forty miles to Bent's Fort. Our provisions are nearly gone.

July 28th.—After coming an hour or two this morning due east, as yesterday—and over the same white clay, facing a blistering sun,—suddenly a charming north wind came to breathe a new life into us, and drive off our dusty infliction. The valley is here very wide, the river clear and very swift; it is about three hundred feet wide, and deeper than it is far below. It is, too, continuously adorned by groves on the banks and islands. The soil is still very poor,—of sand and gravel; but we crossed one fine meadow of six or seven hundred acres. The river once forced us for several miles to pass over the hills; but nothing like mountains were visible on either side.

A singular animal has been caught here; in fact, it made no effort to escape. A naturalist, who joined us at Fort Laramie, pronounces it a "gopher rat;" but it seems unknown to the dwellers of this wilderness.

Having marched twenty-one miles, we encamped rather early, at half-past two o'clock. Now,—at six,—a dark thunderstorm is bursting over us.

July 29th.—A pleasant day, with a cool breeze, which made all comfortable. As we passed on this morning, we saw, a half mile to our right near the river bank, a small party with a wagon moving westward;—whereupon it was visited, some barrels of alcohol destroyed—men and wagon seized and brought with us.

Over a smooth, gravelly, second bank prairie, we caught sight, at several miles distance, of the national flag, floating amid picturesque foliage and river scenery, over a low dark wall, which had a very military semblance. Very gradually and tediously we approached; and then were we more surprised, at the fine appearance and strength of the trading fort. An extensive square, with high adobe walls, and two large towers at opposite angles; and all properly loopholed. Our near approach was saluted by three discharges from a swivel gun; the walls being well "manned." The Colonel and suite were most hospitably greeted at the sally-port, by Messrs. St. Vrain and C. Bent. The regiment marched on, and encamped at the first grassy meadow, a mile or two lower down. A number of officers partook of a good dinner at the fort.

Amongst a few luxuries which we here attain, are several newspapers, of later date by some weeks than we have seen. The commissary reports the provisions in perfect preservation—especially the hard bread; 'tis a pity there is no flour. We arrived with rations for a single day.

This afternoon a party of a dozen Mexicans passed our camp,—being questioned and allowed to proceed; they have a trading venture for the Chians. The majority of the hands at the fort are Mexicans; and the Spanish the prevailing language; but with English, French, and Indian additions and combinations, there is no slight confusion of tongues.

We have been visited, too, by a kind of double animal, not exactly a centaur, but a form of Mexican humanity, appearing to grow from the caudal extremity of a donkey; furnishing the concern however with an extra pair of legs. The head wore a white cotton cap, and one arm flourished a stick or wand, which seemed a cause of dread and perplexity to the foreparts, which were without appendage or ornament. Between was a bag of wheat of Taos.

There has been quite a lively exchange of broken-down horses for ponies and mules; and very much "unsight, unseen;" a horse was a horse, if he could stand up; a pony was only expected to *go*. Two young antelopes were presented to an officer, who then purchased a mule and cart for their conveyance.

Here we lose sight of Pike Mountain, after journeying rapidly in view for nine days. It is said to be visible from some river bluff, eighty or ninety miles further on. We have found it about four hundred miles from Fort Laramie, and the route we have followed is the best natural road we have yet seen. There is nothing to prevent a light carriage from passing it, twelve miles to the hour; and this so near the mountains, and in view of perpetual snow.

August 3d, 1845.—Our march was continued from Bent's Fort, July 30th:—following the river eastward with our wonted pertinacity of progression; next day we passed by what is called the Big Timbers. It is a narrow forest on islands and low bottoms, extending fifteen or twenty miles: it is known and important as a wintering place, and refuge from storms. Here, beside fuel, those who can have no better, find shelter from the wintry winds which sweep with a furious swing over these vast plains, which themselves shrink beneath the dismal protection of an unbroken sheet of snow. As my once anticipated wintry refuge, it possessed for me an unusual interest.

That day too we encountered a large party of New Mexican Indians, the Apaches,—with some Kiawas in company. They were large, handsome men, of a frank and pleasant bearing. The faces of some of them resembled rather the Caucasian than the Indian caste. Their hair was long, occasionally clubbed behind, in our delectable female fashion. All were mounted, and their equipage had the profuse silver and steel adornments, of which many a rich Mexican would gladly have confessed to more than the style. They embrace in the graceful and pleasant Spanish and Mexican manner; and they fail not to reveal eloquently the true Indian trait of "mucho ambre."

In what tongue, unknown, did ever Indian conceal his remarkable hunger?

They had with them a Mexican youth, who had probably been captured many years before: a very slender, singular being—with yellowish hair, pendent from the temples like two long queues. He spoke Spanish but poorly,—as did our interpreter—but we thought we made out two points, viz.: that he liked the Indians, and that the Mexicans were afraid of them.

These fellows gave us to understand that they had been on an expedition against the Pawnees; and this indicated some contempt—possibly ignorance—of the small matter of boundaries; but no doubt, it was in retaliation; for the hand of the Pawnees is raised against all men.

This day we first came in sight of the drifting white sand-hills, which border the southern side of the river for one or two hundred miles; of fantastic changing shapes, often dazzling white, and supporting a few stunted cedars and plum bushes: their air of desolation does not at all prevent them from pleasing the eye, whilst a certain wildness in their appearance excites the imagination. Indeed, I know them as the refuge and ambush of beasts of prey, and of wilder and fiercer men.

A few hundred paces below this camp were the framework remains of an Indian "medicine lodge," looking like a dismantled circus. We found in it four buffalo skulls, with the eye-holes stopped with dry grass; tied overhead were a bundle of rods, a bow, pipe and stem, and some wild pumpkins. "Medicine man" is the literal meaning of the Indian designation of the individual who always unites the professions of physician and priest; he deals in vegetable medicines, in relics, charms, and incantations. On solemn occasions, many superstitious ceremonies are performed, and mysteries which at least remind us of those of ancient Greece and Rome. Sometimes superstition becomes so extravagant that many horrors of physical suffering are eagerly submitted to. I will mention a single one, repeatedly witnessed by a friend: the fanatic, having a sufficient band of skin divided from the back, and a rope tied to it, drags thereby a buffalo skull, until, from natural decay, the rope tears loose!

The braves, the aspirants to renown, before undertaking some martial exploit, each imposes on himself the most extraordinary fasts and vigils; sometimes on a rock or lofty hill, in unchanged posture—like the brahmin—for days together chanting songs or hymns; their natures thus etherealized by fasting,—their imaginations unnaturally excited,—witnessing in their solitudes, solemn or sublime natural phenomena,—these poor savages then reach a spiritual exaltation or ecstasy, in which the Great Spirit favors them, they assert, with direct communications,—of approval, of promise, or of warning.

A few miles lower is Chouteau's Island,—an old crossing of the Santa Fe road; and known also as the scene of several Indian engagements, first with traders, afterward with our troops; (and on this day sixteen years ago.)

CHAPTER XXI.

August 4th.—We marched at half-past 6 o'clock. That means that two hours earlier a trumpet had called us all from sleep to sudden labors; first, arms in hand, —there is an inspection;—then a "stable call," which the poor horses know well, although they have perhaps forgotten what a stable is, or have despaired ever to see one again; possibly they retain a vague memory of the grain, which, on a time, was served to them at that signal. Now, they whinny a morning greeting to their masters, and seem grateful for a little rubbing of their stiffened limbs, and removal to fresh grass. Meanwhile, the cook of each mess (of six or seven men) has been preparing hot coffee; and offers it with the unleavened cakes which were baked over night against a spade or board, and some boiled or fried buffalo meat for breakfast: as a rarity, he gives them a morsel of fried pork. Then,—at the signal for the new guard to saddle,—baggage is prepared and packed in the wagons; the ceremonies of guard mounting over, the assembled trumpeters sound "boots and saddles," when,—in a quarter of an hour—all bridle, saddle, and arm, and the last preparations are completed; then, "to horse," and the regiment is almost instantly in "order of battle;" and at the "advance!" each squadron in turn ahead, we all ride forth to "battle" with space, with fatigue, perhaps with great heats and dust—with saddening wastes,—with thirsts and fears of finding no haven of refreshment and rest.

In the heat of the day, if there be water, we wait wearily, generally unshaded, about three-fourths of an hour, for horses to rest and take a luncheon of grass, and for the baggage to come up. After eight or ten hours, happily finding water and grass, at the climax of fatigue, with the energy of necessity, we commence the settlement of a canvas village in the wilderness. The horses are first to be attended to; but generally with a skirmishing accompaniment,—a slight scramble for that scarce article, fuel; this is sometimes amusing—sometimes leads to unpleasant excitement. The baggage is then unpacked—if fortunately it have arrived—and fires are lit, perhaps in a rain,—water is brought—generally as far as it happens to be from the best grazing: issue of provisions is made, —and this may depend upon still absent hunters, or the slaughter of a beef; and the cattle, although trained for several months with unfailing exercise, are not always "up to time;" cooking then goes on. We eat with an appetite; but of the coarsest and simplest food. The guard then commences the labors of the night; but the many enjoy with rest—the single luxury of a pipe! (Its apology, is it not written?) The few also, a fine sunset or moonlight, and scenery, which may be tame, may be desolate,—but is generally new,—sometimes beautiful, or grand.

Well!—I have long been a wanderer, and—I rather like it.

Yes! it has its pleasures.

It is easy to turn aside to perfect solitude, when

> "—— the twilight soft comes stealing on,
> With its one star,—the star of Memory,
> Pale,—pale,—but *very* beautiful!"

A gentle air rustles the grass or leaves; the running waters too, give music: and then, they seem the voices of gentle spirits, which may, in this hour of calm and loveliness, awake to Eden memories. As sometimes suddenly, the innocent prattle of children falls as music on the mother's ear,—banishing happily, vexing care,—so, nature now seems soothed, and harmony reigns.

And as the mother, first musing in loving mood, then timidly questions her happiness,—so too, to the eloquence of this sweet hour, my heart first beats a pleased response; and then, in reverie, my soul wanders over space and time, until all sense is wrapt in a thought,—a memory.

Then ever I awake with a convulsive sigh, which comes unbidden—like an echo. 'Tis the answer to the summons of the REAL.

The mortal sound has banished the happy whispering spirits; I am recalled mayhap to find the tone, the coloring, the vitality of the scene all gone: 'tis a dismal prairie now. It is dark; the winds are hoarse.

And so we wear on—like all the world. But often in the broad field of labor and care, which in prospect, was all barren,—we find that heaven has provided for us little flowery valleys of rest, where our souls are strengthened and our hearts refreshed.

Here Friend came in.

"I saw you wandering off, at sundown; have you been attempting a photograph of the calm scene?"

"Ah! no bantering to-night; there is a dreamy art of more pretension still;—that would paint the heart;—that would fix the wandering thought;—that would delve for discoveries in the deep mine of man's nature!

"But I have been writing, my Friend, something for your especial approval; I have been setting forth grim realities,—and most philosophically. I *did* strike at last, but most naturally and truly, a little vein of—"

Friend.—Poetry, perhaps? by the merest accident in the world.

"Nature is poetry! For what are sunsets often gorgeously beautiful, or delicately lovely, beyond all representation? For what, the endless variety, the exquisite combination of resplendent colors, of tints and hues of beauty, in flowers and birds? Not for utility, my Friend;

but to soften our hearts—to refine and elevate our thoughts. Poetry is Worship!"

Friend.—Well, let me hear your specimen of "grim reality." That you could only realize the charm of *simplicity!* For poetry I generally go to Job, David, or Isaiah.

I read to him my day's experiences. He listened impatiently; and at last broke out—

"You are incorrigible! Do you call that abstraction the *real?*"

"Surely it has a mournfully same, and daily reality!"

Friend.—And how easily by a mere turn of expression, you could have given it the interest of a simple narrative!

"Well, I'm too indolent; for, if commenced, I might imagine myself bound to keep it up; and I scribble by no rule, and with no object but pastime; and, to compare in some future day the old with the new tone of mind."

Friend.—And a rather singular acquaintance will the *old gentleman* make! Pray, why then did you trouble yourself with this dry abstract of our daily doings?

"Thank-ye for having solved—in your *complimentary* way—a question of my own! I will tell you: I am convinced that written descriptions, not only from carelessness or design, but from inherent imperfection, invariably paint very feebly; and from consciousness of this, are dashed with discolored exaggerations; they deceive more than they enlighten the imaginations of those who are unable to apply the *conventions* and the tests of some experience; you perceive, then, that I was experimenting?"

Friend.—I should say, and without dropping the figure, that the difficulty lay in the impossibility of all coloring; it tires a reader too much, to attempt more than outlines:

and all action—even military—is so essentially irregular, and depends so much upon individuality, as not to be described.

I find *you* guilty of "carelessness" certainly; and, by-the-by, you have not a word of our detour over the beautiful plain of Chouteau's Island! Then, indeed, your everlasting "Memories" seemed strong enough; and what was better, almost tangibly real; I could almost see the five hundred painted and yelling Camanches charging at full speed to surprise your camp. And then an inexperienced youth of twenty years—

"Nonsense!—a mere instinct—"

Friend.—Led by a military and saving instinct then, —went forth with thirty men to meet them half way—

"Well, well,—I wrote what pleased myself; and,—another object I have, which I did not mention: with scarce a book to read, if one did not write, I fancy the beef and pork and beans would in time form a coating round his brain;—turn it all perhaps to thick and solid skull! How is it with you, my Friend? Does yours retain a slight softness?"

Friend.—Don't you think a slight quarrel would help your case? There is excitement in it at least.

"Never say that! I remember once I was told the same,—threatened, I thought, in jest; but there soon followed a storm of pain to *me!*"

Friend.—And did you suspect that what was death to you, was fun for another,—as in the fable?

"No; I could not."

Friend.—But the healing of the wound was an equal happiness.

"Inexpressible!—but—"

Friend.—Left a slight scar, perhaps.—Those are beautiful flowers. I would not have believed that the prairie could now furnish such a bunch.

"Their modest beauty is scarcely noticed when seen; but if you are interested enough to assemble them thus, you are rewarded by a charming surprise. And how pleasant a study is each! I have an untiring love for flowers. How perfect and refined a delicacy they possess! Examine these blossoms; how pure and delicate a white! See the different stages of their mysterious vitality: some of the corollas are like fine pearls, and are set in an emerald green; some are just expanding and reveal the beautiful life within; others with full-blown petals, which, like fairy shells, still gracefully guard and adorn the stamens now crowned with golden pollen; and their fragrance! what other sense is capable of so refined an enjoyment as it yields!"

Friend:—With what strange complacency does the mass of even the "educated," ignore the charming mysteries of botany! They may be surprised into admiration of a fine flower; but it is a mere sensation;

> —"the smallest part
> Exceeds the narrow visions of their minds."

"And they lose half the beauty, which, such is their perfection, they reveal only to minute examination.

"Did you ever reflect how enthusiastic an admiration for them, is expressed in the language, 'Solomon in all his glory was not arrayed like one of these!'"

Friend.—The lily!—the queen of flowers! And yet, all the world admire them. Are they not generally personified?—credited with a language?

"The language of flowers!—The language of admiration and of love, rather. Charming symbols indeed!—most eloquent offerings!"

Friend.—What myriads there are here—

> "born to blush unseen,
> And waste their fragrance on the desert air."

It is strange. What earthly purpose do they serve?

"What know we of the attributes of their wondrous and miraculous life? But how admirably do they fulfil their divine appointments in the unfathomable scheme of Nature! More beautiful, more fruitful,—even less ephemeral, than myriads of animal existences! Truly they may have a language;—and are at least an eloquent incense to the Creator—by them, 'the hills are joyful together before the Lord, and all green things upon the earth praise Him.'"

August 13.—We have come on regularly, above two hundred miles, since the 4th, and with no very extraordinary incident; we have had some grand thunderstorms at night, and yesterday—the first time for months—rode several hours in rain. We have passed many buffalo; but none for several days, and had despaired of seeing more. Several merchant trains for Santa Fe have been met, and, which was something new, one of them was accompanied by a few emigrants—women and children. Are the Anglo-Saxons breaking out in a new place?

Two marches back, our eyes were first gladdened by the view of green prairies; the regular Missouri grasses; beautiful, indeed,—but not so nutritious as some dryer sorts farther West.

After marching about five miles this morning through the savannas of Walnut Creek, where we had encamped, and of the Arkansas, which we are about to leave, we saw to our surprise a large gang—perhaps a thousand—buffalo on the hills to our left.

Soon about a dozen of us might have been seen very deliberately diverging from the road, whilst the column moved on; what would stop it! After riding a mile or two, we gained a slight hollow, quite near, and to the leeward, of course, of the unsuspicious herd; then we allowed two still-hunters to creep on for deliberate shots, while we inspected our appointments, and made our plans; —never had I been so deliberate! and it was bad luck to me as will be seen.

Now, mount and away! The long hill on which the chase began, ranged directly in the course of the march, and there we expected to drive the game; the wind was from that quarter; and they almost always run against it; the attack of course was towards the desired direction; and carbine men, who fire best to the left, dashed for their right flank, and those with pistols for their left. All would not do: whether to return to their more usual haunts,—or for their advantage in running down hill (arising from their great strength of shoulder), they turned right on us, charged and broke our centre, and went rushing down the long slope whence we came,—about twenty abreast;—the dense column reaching about a quarter of a mile, and like a great black serpent! And thus I found myself on their right flank, where I could not so well use my pistols: down we all went recklessly hugging their flanks; and I penetrated their column, and gained the other side: for this manœuvre they assist, by diverging from behind you—by which at first you are enclosed; they were so thick, that one or two falling, it was only by a powerful effort—very discomposing to his rider —that my horse was able to avoid tumbling over them. There was now a rattling fire, and a slight whistling of balls; and the fun "grew fast and furious." I shot a fat cow while in the jam, and I only know I did not see her fall, and immediately lost sight of her; then I bore down upon another very large one, and whatever the cause, my down-hill shot was a bad one, too high; then reloading, I got in pursuit—with another officer—of a detachment of about thirty, determined this time to powder-burn my game. My noble horse soon bringing me alongside, I perceived on lowering my pistol to the aim, that the cap was gone! I replaced it—losing ground: again I was close alongside, when, with indescribable disappointment, the same thing occurred! Just then my companion, by hard spurring, got near enough *behind* the buffalo to cripple one by his fire. In my over-care, I had on the hill unnecessarily replenished my cap-pouch, from a friend's, with caps which were slightly too large. And thus little advantage did I take of having the best horse in the field, which was still infinitely eager for the chase.

Thus, unexpectedly, we got about eight hundred pounds of the very best meat we have had. But what a weary ride this hot afternoon, following the regiment about twenty miles!

Aug. 24th.—Twenty-two hundred miles in ninety-nine days!

We left the Kansas River this morning, with a blundering Shawnee guide, who called it eighteen miles to Fort Leavenworth. Passing first deep dales and very broken hills, well clothed with forest, we then emerged upon prairies. We found Stranger River eleven miles (it had been called six)—still we marched on through rank grass, and weed, and bush, hopefully; as home was the busy thought that engrossed us. After eighteen miles we were forced to halt at a branch for rest for the animals;

the heat had become excessive; but just before stopping, we had seen, we thought, afar off, Pilot Knob,—a landmark, four miles below the post.

At one o'clock, we moved on again;—forcing our way wearily, through the rank grass of a wet season; rising and descending continually, hill after hill of rolling prairie; like a stately ship which has weathered with narrow escape a mighty tempest, and strained every joint laboring heavily on the swell, which seems endlessly to defer the eager hopes of a haven almost in sight.

But now the Knob, familiar to many a chase,—on horses which the curb and strong arm with effort checked, —rose in full view; the eye was pleased; but the known distance realized the certainty of a killing march to attain the goal. When we struck the military road, ten miles from home, our poor steeds were a moment animated by pleasant memories, and tossed their heads, and champed the bit.

But, good heaven, what clouds of dust then rose from our feet, enveloped us, and followed us like a destiny! And how scorching was the sun in this artificial calm. We dismounted, and some horses then staggered as they were led: we walked an hour, the perspiration raining from my brow, and my brain throbbing; we walked right through streams, dashing the water to the face with our hands. Still on: the endless last mile of disappointment and fatigue:—the sun went down;—but now the houses and stables, white and beautiful amid the green trees, animated us to press on. At dusk we entered the portal, and staggering to the usual parade, renewed the line, which ninety-nine days before we formed in the pride of prancing horses: how many a gap was now! but the half stood there!

And there was, perforce, a silent but eager suspense; then came words of commendation from the Colonel. I can only remember some sounds breaking monotonously a dead silence—like the vague impressions of a dream. And then the ranks dissolved,—the spell was broken, and —we were home!

THE END.

www.ingramcontent.com/pod-product-compliance
Lightning Source LLC
LaVergne TN
LVHW021145110826
845150LV00005B/1126

* 9 7 8 1 4 2 5 5 4 8 1 3 1 *